TERRORISM AND DEMOCRACY

To Captain George Zenick —

From one

mariner to another

[signature]

Books by Stansfield Turner

SECRECY AND DEMOCRACY

TERRORISM AND DEMOCRACY

TERRORISM
AND
DEMOCRACY

ADMIRAL STANSFIELD TURNER

U.S. Navy (retired) and Former Director
of Central Intelligence

Houghton Mifflin Company

BOSTON

1991

Library of Congress Cataloging-in-Publication Data

Turner, Stansfield, date.
Terrorism and democracy / Stansfield Turner.
p.   cm.
Includes bibliographical references and index.
ISBN 0-395-43086-0
1. Iran Hostage Crisis, 1979–1981.   2. Terrorism—Political
aspects—United States.   3. United States—Politics and
government—1977–1981.   4. United States—Politics and
government—1981–1989.   I. Title.
E183.8.155T87   1991
955.05′4—dc20   91-6647
CIP

Printed in the United States of America

MP 10 9 8 7 6 5 4 3 2 1

TO KARIN

whose advice, support, and love have permeated every
phase of this book — and my life

CONTENTS

MAPS

PREFACE

IN JULY 1985 Bill Adler, my friend and literary agent, phoned after watching my commentaries on TV about the TWA Flight 847 hostage problem. Realizing that the problem of terrorism is going to be with us for a long time, he suggested that I undertake a book on terrorism and how we can deal with it. The challenge appealed to me. I had suffered for 444 days as a participant in President Carter's struggle with Iranian terrorism.

I began by reviewing the literature. Although there was a lot of it, surprisingly few of the books were by a single author; most were compendia of articles, but lacked a consistent point of view.

Many of the works dealt with the definition of terrorism — one indeed covered nothing else — but there was no agreement, among academicians, governments, and the United Nations, on a single definition. Other books addressed the history of terrorism, going back to the first century, when the Jewish Zealots sought to drive the Romans from Palestine by acts of violence; to the Assassins of the eleventh to thirteenth centuries who forayed down from mountaintop fortresses in the Middle East to murder infidels; to the anarchists of the late nineteenth century who tried bombs as a form of political persuasion; to the hijackers and kidnapers of today.

A number of articles addressed the psychological causes of terrorism, noting that it is seized on by those who do not believe that their ethnic, religious, or nationalist grievances can be rectified by existing political systems. Discussions of the means of terrorism focused on historical practices, the manipulation of modern technologies like commercial aircraft and lethal munitions, and predictions of frightening possibilities.

Writings on the terrorists themselves described fanatics — individuals, small groups, weak national entities — operating from the Middle East, Central and South America, Europe, and Asia. And suggestions for countering terrorism differed from author to author.

I was uneasy when I completed the survey: I did not have what I needed to offer reasoned and constructive responses when asked whether I agreed with such propositions as (1) we should not make deals with terrorists; (2) we must make them pay a price by employing force in response to their acts; (3) we may, on occasion, have to sacrifice some hostages for the greater good.

The reason, I perceived, was a lack of discussion of how our democracy affects and is affected by what we do to deter terrorism. Talk of options is meaningless unless we consider the constraints imposed by our political system. I decided that was the contribution I should like to make: an appreciation of the ways in which our societal values determine our response to terrorism.

Having seen how those values influenced President Carter's decisions in 1979 and 1980, I decided to review the actions and reasoning of those of our Presidents who have confronted the menace. What were the limitations imposed on them by our democratic system, limitations that may have prevented their resorting to solutions thought useful by others? What were the pressures on them to attempt those actions?

I have built this book around actual presidential responses to terrorism. Naturally I concentrate on the Carter experience, but I also look at five earlier Presidents who confronted one or more instances of Americans being held hostage, and at Ronald Reagan, who faced both hostage problems and a rash of bombings. I have searched for common threads, which, it turns out, go all the way back to the founding of our government. I was not surprised to find that much of the common wisdom about dealing with terrorism does not accord with what Presidents have actually done.

This book, then, is intended as a discussion of how we can deal with the current wave of terrorism from an American perspective, though basically from the perspective of all democracies. The potential for terrorism to increase is there, but terrorists are not invincible; the Zealots, Assassins, and others were suppressed in time. Today many countervailing strengths come from the very fact that we have a democratic system. But that means we need public understanding of our options for curtailing the current wave of terror and the wisdom to avoid actions that might undermine the democratic process we are defending.

TERRORISM AND DEMOCRACY

bunch of good ole boys, run around playing grabass for a few weeks, and claim we had an antiterrorist unit, ready for action."[2] Beckwith made it clear he would need to select his own men, develop unorthodox equipment and techniques, and train for at least two years to bring Delta Force into readiness.

Just four months later, West Germany's GSG-9 brilliantly rescued eighty-six hostages from a Lufthansa airliner that had been hijacked to Mogadishu, the capital of Somalia. President Carter asked whether our military could perform comparably. That put the top levels of the Department of Defense squarely behind Beckwith as he mercilessly drove his small force toward perfection. By the summer of 1979, shortly before Beckwith's two years were up, a group of us went to Fort Bragg, North Carolina, to watch Delta Force in action. Beckwith's team was impressive in responding to a simulated hijacking of a commercial airliner to a Caribbean island. The discussions that followed, however, raised troublesome questions.

When I asked Charlie how he would move his people to the scene of this hypothetical hijacking without being detected, he said the troops would infiltrate individually as tourists, assemble at night, and then assault the aircraft. I questioned whether twenty to thirty impressively fit young men with weapons would be able to infiltrate a small island airport. Charlie felt sure it could be done. As chief of the CIA, I suggested that he take advantage of the Agency's experience along these lines — for instance, with disguises and forged documentation, which were CIA specialties. Charlie had not thought of contacting us.

I came away that day with great respect for the way Charlie Beckwith had developed and tailored Delta's military skills for the moment of contact in fighting terrorists. But I wondered who would be likely to send Delta on a mission and how it would get to the necessary location. Such decisions were clearly beyond Charlie's writ, but I was worried that he might not acknowledge his need for tapping skills in the Air Force, the CIA, and elsewhere. Beckwith and his team were big on muscle and macho, but the problems ahead were laced with subtlety and ambiguity.

That was the summer of 1979. In October the Army decided that Charlie Beckwith had completed his job and ordered him to a new assignment in Europe. His family was already packing to move when Delta Force was scheduled for a final evaluation under his command. For three days and three nights, Army inspectors tested Beckwith's group in exercises that ran across several states. They observed the men's marksmanship under pressure, tested their physical and mental stamina, and made them storm an aircraft and a building, both supposedly being held by terrorists. Delta passed with flying colors. After the graduation exercises, just before midnight, Charlie and some buddies went to a bar to celebrate, and then to an all-night diner for some breakfast.

A little after 4:00 A.M., while they were still basking in their considerable accomplishment, telephones began ringing across Washington, including the direct line from the CIA to the table beside my bed. The CIA duty officer told me our embassy in Tehran had been stormed. After locking themselves in a vault while destroying some of the secret documents, the CIA people had been forced to capitulate. It was Sunday, November 4, 1979, Day 1 of the Iranian hostage crisis. Charlie Beckwith never made it to his assignment in Europe. He was summoned to the Pentagon to plan the use of Delta Force in rescuing the American hostages.

Five and a half months later, after completing the planning and training for the rescue operation, Charlie and his team were engulfed in the swirling sand at Desert One, the first way station en route to Tehran. Once fueled, the helicopters would fly Delta Force to the outskirts of the city. The minimum margin for success had been carefully calculated as six helicopters, but only five were ready. Major General James B. Vaught, U.S. Army, the mission commander, talking to Jim Kyle by radio from Egypt, asked Charlie to consider going with five.[3] Charlie had to decide quickly. If the rescue force did not soon move ahead or turn back, there would not be sufficient fuel to go either way. They were already so far behind schedule that there was a risk they would not arrive at their hiding place outside Tehran until after dawn.

Colonel Charles Beckwith had had the vision to see that Delta Force would be needed at a time like this. He had trained it and brought it this far. Delta stood poised and ready as Chargin' Charlie made his decision.

THE HOSTAGE-TAKING HABIT

This subject [the holding of hostages] . . . has constantly commanded my best exertions . . . Nothing shall be left undone.

— George Washington[1]

JIMMY CARTER was not the first President to send a rescue force after Americans being held hostage. In 1805 President Thomas Jefferson dispatched a ragtag expedition of mercenaries across the desert of Egypt into the Barbary State of Tripoli to rescue 307 Americans.

The commander, William Eaton, an American soldier and former consul of the United States in Tunis, was a different type from Charlie Beckwith, an Army colonel and veteran of Korea and Vietnam. The troops, some four hundred Greek, Bedouin, and Arab mercenaries, eight American Marines and one midshipman, were different from the finely honed and highly motivated Delta Force. The support, three U.S. Navy frigates that followed along the Mediterranean coastline providing bombardment and bearing supplies, was different from the fleet of helicopters loaded with advanced equipment.

Ironically, Jefferson himself had created the very problem that impelled him to let Eaton conduct this mission. During the previous twenty years, in his roles as minister to France, Secretary of State, Vice President, and first-term President of the United States, he was bedeviled by the Barbary pirates, who repeatedly humiliated the new United States of America. The Barbary States of Tripoli, Tunis, Algiers, and Morocco, stretching two thousand miles across the southern shore of the Mediterranean Sea from Egypt around to the Atlantic Ocean, were well positioned for their ships to dart out and capture passing vessels, whose cargoes they sold and whose crews they held for ransom.

In severing their ties to Great Britain in July 1776, the American colonists gave up the protection of the Royal Navy for their rapidly growing fleet of merchant ships. It was not until 1785, though, that the Barbary pirates first struck, capturing two American ships with twenty-one American sailors. When George Washington assumed office four years later, he inherited this problem, which the Continental Congress had been unable to solve.

Despite considerable effort, Washington made no progress on obtaining the release of the men during his first term in office. Then, six months into his second, the pirates struck again, capturing eleven ships and ninety-eight sailors. Washington decided that his only option was an out-and-out deal, but it took another three years to negotiate and have the Senate ratify a treaty with the Algerians whereby the United States agreed to pay almost $1 million for the release of the hostages (about $6.5 million in today's dollars) and another $21,600 annually in naval stores as tribute or "protection" against more pirating of our ships.* In exchange he obtained the release of those sailors who were still alive, fourteen of whom had been held for ten years.

Washington also agreed to build and sell to the Algerians two new "cruizers . . . built of live oak and cedar, and coppered, with guns and all other equipments."[2] This latter provision was nothing less than an outright sale of arms for hostages, long before Ronald Reagan engaged in similar deals with Iran in 1985–1986. Besides being humiliating, Washington's agreement left the country vulnerable to the Barbary pirates' use of the "cruizer" (only one was actually supplied) to capture more American ships and crews and demand more ransom.

In Washington's later days and in the early ones of John Adams, the United States not only continued paying annual tribute, but extended it to the other three Barbary States. Then, just before Adams left office, it all began to fall apart. In September of 1800, the warship *George Washington,* one of the nation's first naval vessels, delivered our annual tribute of twenty-seven barrels of naval stores to Algiers. The Dey of Algiers demanded that *George Washington* be pressed into his service to deliver his annual tribute to the Sultan of the Ottoman Empire at Constantinople. The ship's captain, Lieutenant William Bainbridge, initially refused, but with his ship anchored directly under the guns of Algiers, he had no alternative.

---

*Naval stores were timber, cordage, canvas, gunpowder, and other materials necessary for the upkeep and operation of a navy. Timber of good quality was particularly important in the relatively unforested regions of the Barbary States.

Ignominiously flying the Algerian flag and carrying "an ambassador, one hundred males, one hundred black women, four horses, twenty-five cattle, four lions, four tigers, four antelopes and twelve parrots,"[3] Bainbridge and his ship did the Dey's bidding.

When the Bashaw of Tripoli heard of this, he concluded that his neighbor was getting more from the United States than he, and soon demanded an increase in the tribute he received, including a "cruizer" of his own. The United States refused. Then, just after Thomas Jefferson became President in 1801, the Bashaw had the flagpole at our consulate in Tripoli cut down, a virtual declaration of war.

Jefferson acted. By 1801 he had a small navy, and although philosophically he was opposed to war, he immediately sent it to the Mediterranean in what was our country's first use of force against terrorism.

It took the Navy more than two years to become aggressive. When it finally did, it created a problem. In 1803 the same Lieutenant Bainbridge who had transported the Algerians' tribute sailed the frigate *Philadelphia* into Tripoli harbor in pursuit of a Tripolitan ship. Unfortunately, he ran *Philadelphia* aground, and he and his crew of 306 were taken prisoner.

By March 1805 William Eaton had organized his expedition, and Jefferson was convinced that this was his best recourse for obtaining the release of Bainbridge and his crew. Eaton managed to lead his quasi-army, sometimes without water, sometimes without food, and in the face of several attempts at mutiny, across almost six hundred miles of desert to the city of Derne in eastern Tripoli. With help from the guns of the fleet, he managed to invest and conquer Derne.

Eaton threatened to march on to the capital city of Tripoli and install in power a disaffected brother of the Bashaw's. The Bashaw countered with a threat to kill Bainbridge and his men. The Bashaw was sufficiently worried, though, to lower dramatically his demand for ransom. Jefferson was squeezed. On the one hand he faced the Bashaw's threat to the sailors and the possibility that Eaton's force would bog down either on the additional six-hundred-mile desert march to Tripoli or before the defenses there. On the other hand, he would have to accept the humiliation of paying further ransom. He settled by signing a treaty with the Bashaw for $60,000 in ransom and an agreement that there would be no more annual tribute.

History shows, then, that our first three Presidents made outright deals with hostage takers, even codifying their arrangements in treaties. As a result of the growing military power of the United States, however, Jefferson was at least able to drive a bargain with the pirates. His successor, James Madison, had a larger Navy and by 1815 was able to quell the pirates once and for all by capturing several Algerian ships and blockading Algiers, Tunis, and Tripoli successively.

By the early twentieth century the United States had become much more powerful than any of the Barbary States. Still, when President Theodore Roosevelt confronted a hostage problem with one of the descendants of the pirates, his military power was of little use. He, too, made a deal.

In May 1904, a Berber chief named Raisuli kidnaped an American resident of Tangier, Morocco, Ion Perdicaris, and his stepson, Oliver Varley, a British citizen. Yet Raisuli's complaint was not with the United States or Britain. Employing a logic often utilized by terrorists, he believed that his seizing nationals of those countries would persuade them to intercede with the Sultan on his behalf.

Following in the footsteps of Jefferson and Madison, Teddy Roosevelt immediately dispatched first one and then a second unit of the Navy to Tangier. These dramatic moves on behalf of a single American, plus Roosevelt's rhetoric about protecting Americans anywhere, electrified the nation.

Neither Roosevelt's bombast nor the Navy's arrival on the scene did much for Perdicaris, however. The fleet could do little in Tangier, since Raisuli was holding his hostages in the Atlas Mountains behind the city and probably would have killed his captives rather than surrender them. Nor could Roosevelt count on the Sultan. As the American consul general in Tangier put it, "The Government [of Morocco] has no authority, for the present at least, over these mountaineers."[4]

The President was out on a limb — and at a time when he was coming up for election for the first time as President (having been elevated from the vice presidency following the assassination of President William McKinley). He decided, along with the French, to press the Sultan into granting every demand Raisuli had made, including supplementary ones after the negotiations had begun. It was a deal, just as much as Washington's and Jefferson's, but Roosevelt did not have to own up to it. The Sultan's name was on it.

That we had joined in coercing the Sultan into his actions was cleverly disguised, and Roosevelt is still frequently lauded in the halls of Congress and elsewhere as the President who was tough on terrorists. For instance, immediately after another hostage incident, with U.S.S.

Pueblo, in 1968, both a senator and a representative entered references to the Raisuli affair in the *Congressional Record:* "Let the Commander-in-Chief now and on this day act with Teddy Roosevelt firmness . . . Please recall that it was on June 22, 1904, after a similar international situation, that his Secretary of State, John Hay, cabled the U.S. consul in Morocco, 'We want Perdicaris alive or Raisuli dead.' History records immediate results."[5]

Roosevelt did get the "immediate results" of Perdicaris's release, but not by being firm with Raisuli. What is more, John Hay's statement about "Perdicaris alive or Raisuli dead" was incomplete when it was released to the Republican National Convention that June 22. The other half of the message turned down the consul general's request that he be empowered to threaten to land Marines if Perdicaris were not released soon.

The incident that stirred Senator Hugh Scott and Representative Durwood G. Hall to recall Teddy Roosevelt was the seizure of U.S.S. *Pueblo,* a noncombatant, intelligence-gathering ship, by the North Korean Navy on January 23, 1968. Once the North Koreans had captured the lightly armed *Pueblo* and taken it into the port of Wonsan, they had eighty-three American sailors as hostages (see Map 1). It was President Lyndon B. Johnson's turn at bat.

The day after the capture, the North Koreans laid out their demands: a confession by the United States that *Pueblo* had intruded into their territorial waters for purposes of spying, an apology for the action, and a promise never to intrude again. President Johnson refused and instead proceeded on two fronts.

The first was to apply or consider every conceivable pressure on North Korea. He began by exploring diplomatic contacts, but none had any success. He next weighed economic pressure, but it was deemed ineffectual on the isolated and primitive North Korean economy. He then called up 14,787 Air Force and Navy reservists, along with 372 aircraft, moved B-52 heavy bombers to the Far East, positioned several aircraft carriers off North Korea, and moved fighter bombers into South Korea. The North Koreans did not blink. They kept insisting on a confession, an apology, and a promise.

Johnson's second course was to carry on direct discussions with the North Koreans through the Military Armistice Commission for Korea at Panmunjom. The issue boiled down to how the United States could word a confession that would satisfy North Korea but not mar our

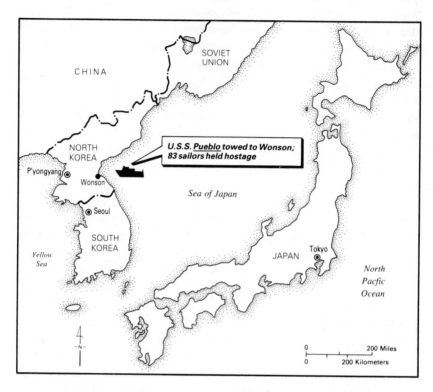

CHINA

SOVIET UNION

NORTH KOREA

P'yongyang

U.S.S. Pueblo towed to Wonson; 83 sailors held hostage

Wonson

Sea of Japan

Seoul

SOUTH KOREA

Yellow Sea

JAPAN Tokyo

North Pacfic Ocean

-N-

| 0 | | 200 Miles |
| 0 | | 200 Kilometers |

MAP I. THE TAKING OF U.S.S. *Pueblo*, JANUARY 1968

national honor. At one point we proposed having our negotiating general write an acknowledgment of receipt of the prisoners across a confession the North Koreans would have drafted, thus giving them a "signed" confession. The North Koreans never even responded to this idea. But a week before Christmas 1968, after almost eleven months, they agreed to an even more unusual proposal: the United States could issue a disclaimer even as it signed a confession.

On December 23, Korean time, Major General Gilbert H. Woodward, U.S. Army, senior representative of the United States to the Military Armistice Commission, repudiated what he was about to sign by stating:

> The position of the United States government . . . [has] been that the ship was not engaged in illegal activity . . . [The] document which I am going to sign was prepared by the North Koreans and is at variance with the above position, but my signature will not and cannot alter the facts. I will sign the document to free the crew and only to free the crew.[6]

After Woodward signed, eighty-two hostages and the body of one sailor who had died were returned.

What value to the North Koreans was this bizarre simultaneous confession and repudiation? Again, the United States had agreed to a deal; again, the hostage takers had obtained almost everything they demanded. The day after the hostages were released, the *New York Times* editorialized:

> The shameful circumstances that surrounded last night's release of the Pueblo crew make it clear that President Johnson was confronted with the most painful of Hobson's choices . . . It is both delusive and dishonest to pretend that world respect for America's integrity will not be injured.

Our next President faced a new form of hostage taking, one that was growing in popularity: the hijacking of aircraft. On September 6, 1970, the Popular Front for the Liberation of Palestine (PFLP), a radical faction of the Palestine Liberation Organization (PLO), set a record by attempting to hijack four aircraft in one day. All were international flights originating in Western Europe. All had Americans on board. President Richard M. Nixon had a problem.

Hijackers need an airfield where the local authorities will be either friendly or, at least, not too hostile. Dawson Field, an unused former

British training airstrip at Zarqa, in the desert twelve miles northeast of Amman, the capital of Jordan, fitted the needs of these hijackers because it was reasonably remote and unguarded (see Map 2). In addition, the PLO was on the verge of challenging King Hussein in what was to become a brief, bloody war for control of the country.

Only two of the four aircraft made it to Dawson Field. On one of the others, an El Al 707, the hijackers were overwhelmed by sky marshals, crew, and passengers. One hijacker was killed, and the other, an attractive 24-year-old woman named Leila Khaled, was arrested. She was jailed in London when the flight was diverted there. The hijackers might not have been subdued so easily had all four who attempted to board the aircraft been allowed to do so. The El Al reservation manager in Amsterdam, suspicious of two of them, men with Senegalese passports, had canceled their first-class reservations. Those two were not to be thwarted, though. They turned around and boarded a Pan American flight and successfully hijacked it the same day. Only when they directed it toward Dawson Field did they realize that they had inadvertently shifted from a 707 to a 747, which was too heavy to land on the desert strip. They forced the pilot to stop in Beirut, where, without difficulty, they obtained explosives. They placed these throughout the aircraft and, with due recklessness, set the fuses moments before the aircraft touched down in Cairo. Fortunately, the 177 people on board were able to evacuate just in time; then the aircraft went up in a fireball.

The initial demands of the hijackers were for the release of an indeterminate number of prisoners from Israeli jails, three convicted Palestinian terrorists from a Swiss jail, and another three from a West German jail. Four days later, they upped the ante to include Leila Khaled from London. That day, they hijacked a fifth aircraft, a British Overseas Airways VC-10, to ensure that they had British hostages to trade for Khaled.

For a brief time an erroneous report circulated that the hijackers also wanted Sirhan Sirhan, the assassin of Robert F. Kennedy, to be released from his California jail. When queried about this, Governor Ronald W. Reagan, the only person with authority to release Sirhan, said, "You can't go down the road of paying blackmail . . . The first payment only leads to many others."[7]

The demand for the release of terrorists from jail caused the greatest problem in Tel Aviv. Two years earlier, when the PFLP first resorted to hijacking, it extracted prisoners from Israel in exchange for Israeli

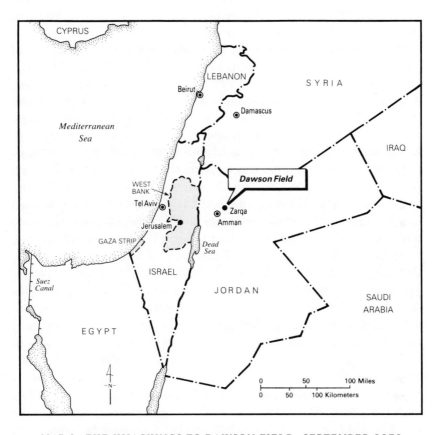

MAP 2. THE HIJACKINGS TO DAWSON FIELD, SEPTEMBER 1970

hostages. A year later Israel swapped several Syrian military prisoners for a number of Israelis who had been hijacked to Damascus by none other than Leila Khaled. The Israeli government was having second thoughts about its vulnerability to hijackers. It announced a policy of no deals with terrorists.[8]

In contrast, it took suasion by the United States to deter the Swiss and West Germans from making immediate deals for their nationals. Fortunately, as the negotiations proceeded, the Palestinians' position weakened when King Hussein's military forces prevailed over those of the PLO. The PFLP relaxed its demands, and all of the hostages were released between September 25 and 29. Then, on September 30, a Royal Air Force plane with Leila Khaled aboard left England, stopped in Germany and Switzerland to pick up the six other terrorists, and delivered the seven to Cairo and freedom. The Israelis released Algerian and Libyan prisoners but refused to give up any of the Palestinians the hijackers wanted. For Leila Khaled it was the second time within a year that she had been traded after involvement in terrorism.

Another deal had been made. The leaders of Switzerland and West Germany had few qualms about swapping jailed terrorists for hostages. The British hesitated, but gave up Leila Khaled readily and pressed the Israelis to release at least some of their prisoners. The Israelis claimed they did this on "humanitarian" grounds, not under pressure for ransom. While the United States was not party to this deal, President Nixon encouraged it, just as Teddy Roosevelt had agreed to the deal with the Sultan of Morocco.

Two and a half years later, Richard Nixon appeared to take a much more resolute stand against deals with hostage takers. Black September, a radical Palestinian faction born out of the struggle between King Hussein and the PLO in September 1970, held six diplomats hostage in Khartoum, the capital of the Sudan. Among them were the American ambassador, Cleo A. Noel, Jr., and George C. Moore, the departing chargé d'affaires.

The demands of the terrorists narrowed to the release of a number of prisoners from Jordan and, this time, of Sirhan Sirhan. President Nixon's reply was "As far as the United States as a government giving in to blackmail demands, we cannot do so and will not do so."[9] Ultimately, though, the fate of the hostages rested with King Hussein, who refused to release the prisoners he held. The terrorists killed both Americans and one other hostage.

Would Nixon have held firm had the fate of his two diplomats been in his hands rather than those of King Hussein? Would he have done so on the grounds that as diplomats they accepted such risks, whereas the passengers on the planes hijacked to Dawson Field were innocent bystanders? Or had he changed his mind about making deals?

Gerald R. Ford was the only President between Lyndon Johnson and Ronald Reagan who was not involved in a deal with terrorists. His encounter with them began as a carbon copy of the *Pueblo* incident. On May 12, 1975, a Cambodian gunboat seized an unarmed U.S. merchant ship, the S.S. *Mayaguez,* near the island of Koh Tang off the coast of Cambodia (see Map 3). There were thirty-nine American seamen on board.

The President's initial response to this affront was to avoid another protracted crisis. He recalled:

> Back in 1968, I remember, the North Koreans had captured the US intelligence ship U.S.S. *Pueblo* in international waters and forced her and her crew into the port of Wonsan. The United States had not been able to respond fast enough to prevent the transfer, and as a result, *Pueblo*'s crew had languished in a North Korean prison for nearly a year. I was determined not to allow a repetition of that incident, so I told [Secretary of Defense James] Schlesinger to make sure that no Cambodian vessel moved between Koh Tang and the mainland.[10]

The only military forces that could reach the scene immediately were land-based, long-range bombers and reconnaissance aircraft from the Philippines. The aircraft carrier *Coral Sea* was diverted from a trip to Australia and was sent speeding to the scene; and Marines were being flown from their bases at Okinawa and the Philippines to neighboring Thailand.

On the morning of the second day at a meeting with the President, the Chairman of the Joint Chiefs of Staff reported that some of our reconnaissance planes had been hit by gunfire from Koh Tang and that several small boats leaving the island had been turned back and several more sunk. A messenger from the White House communications center then brought the President a report that posed a dilemma. The pilot of an Air Force A-7 attack plane was about to sink a Cambodian boat bound from Koh Tang to the mainland when he thought he saw Americans aboard. He had held his fire and radioed for further instructions.

If the hostages were taken to the mainland, as the crew of *Pueblo*

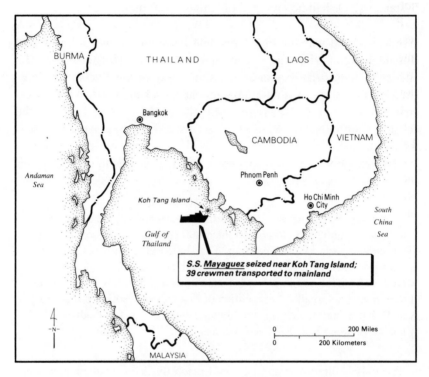

MAP 3. THE CAPTURE OF S.S. *Mayaguez*, MAY 1975

had been, a rescue operation would be almost impossible. Yet if the President authorized the sinking of the boat, he might kill the men he was trying to rescue. He ordered the pilot to shoot across the bow but not to sink the boat.

By the morning of the third day, May 14, it was clear that diplomacy was a total failure. Neither the United Nations nor any of the other intermediaries the President had approached had received a response from the Cambodians. Gerald Ford was left with only a military option.

Coral Sea was now close enough for her aircraft to be well within range. In addition, one U.S. Navy destroyer was approaching Koh Tang, and the Marines had arrived in Thailand. The President began issuing orders: the Marines were to land on Koh Tang and search for the hostages; the destroyer was to send a force to board and seize the *Mayaguez;* and the carrier was to conduct "surgical" strikes on the mainland.

The Marines assaulted Koh Tang by helicopter but took eighteen casualties, a high price, especially when the effort was in vain. The A-7 pilot had been correct and intelligence bad; the crew had been moved to the mainland in the boat the pilot had spotted. Other Marines boarded the anchored *Mayaguez* from the destroyer, but there was no one on board. About this time the Cambodians broadcast an offer to release the ship. It was not clear whether this included the crew, but within a few hours another U.S. destroyer picked all the crew members off a Cambodian boat that was carrying them from the mainland toward the *Mayaguez*.

Almost simultaneously the punitive air strikes were launched from *Coral Sea*. Critics have debated the propriety of this action. Some argue that it should have been canceled once the hostages were safe. Others contend that a society as humane as ours should not conduct punitive attacks on innocent people, even if their government is involved in terrorism.

The American public supported the President. A Gallup Poll conducted soon after showed that President Ford's popularity rating had risen a dramatic 11 percent, one of the sharpest gains ever recorded in such surveys, going back to the middle 1930s. Although the rescue mission was based on faulty intelligence and had cost the lives of eighteen Marines in the process of rescuing thirty-nine merchant seamen,*

---

*Another twenty-three Marines were killed in a helicopter accident in Thailand while preparing for the assault on Koh Tang.

and although the bombing had not effected the release of the hostages — who had already been freed — nothing succeeds like success.

Most politicians also supported President Ford, even liberals who had recently sponsored the War Powers Resolution, an effort to curb Presidents from becoming involved in such military adventures without the participation of Congress. Presidential candidate Jimmy Carter said he thought President Ford's forceful action may have prevented a much more serious problem later.[11]

Jimmy Carter did not then know he would be a President with a hostage problem and would have to decide whether to send Charlie Beckwith on a rescue mission, attempt diplomatic and economic pressures, or order bombing attacks. No President, though, should be surprised at having to deal with the problem of Americans being held hostage by terrorists. The record goes back to the beginning of our country.

WARNING UNHEEDED

I told Brzezinski to permit the Shah to go to New York for medical treatment and just inform our embassy in Teheran that this would occur.

> — Diary of Jimmy Carter,
> October 20, 1979 [1]

THE CARTER ADMINISTRATION had by no means been oblivious of the problems of terrorism. In the late 1960s it seemed airliners were hijacked almost daily. In the early 1970s the Baader Meinhof gang in West Germany and the Red Brigades in Italy had their governments on the run. We sympathized with our allies. We also realized that we would not be exempt forever and must prepare. Early in the administration, the President established a terrorism working group under the National Security Council. It made little progress; it did not even discuss a strategy for dealing with hostage taking.

But in July 1978, at an economic summit of the Big Seven economic powers,* Jimmy Carter proposed that these nations work together to deter terrorism. Specifically, the group agreed to suspend air traffic to or from countries that failed to turn over hijackers and hijacked aircraft. Little did these leaders appreciate how pusillanimous they would be when it came to applying this rule. In 1979, when the Iranian government supported the jailers holding American hostages in Tehran, there could not have been a clearer case of a government abetting terrorists. Still, no other country joined us in cutting off air traffic to Iran. In 1985, terrorists seized a U.S. airliner and took it to Beirut. There, fellow terrorists openly controlled the airfield and supported the hijackers. Only the United States stopped flights into Beirut.

---

*The United States, United Kingdom, Italy, France, West Germany, Canada, and Japan.

The Carter administration expected too much help from our friends; it also failed to read clear signals from the Iranians about their readiness to employ terrorism. Even a "dress rehearsal" failed to warn us. On February 14, 1979, Valentine's Day, I was awakened in the night by a call from the CIA duty officer telling me that our embassy had been stormed by a mob. It was midmorning in Tehran. The U.S. Marine guards had been ordered not to shoot. The CIA staff had retreated into its special vault to destroy classified materials. Then communications had stopped abruptly.

My first thought whenever the CIA phone rang in the middle of the night was that one of the nightmares of intelligence officers had come true: a foreign agent working for us, or one of our own officers, had been caught; or one of our people had defected. What I never expected was that our sovereign territory, a United States embassy, would be forcibly invaded. Although U.S. Marines guard our embassies, it was never intended that they would be called on to defend the property and people against more than individual intruders. All nations depend on the host country for protection against more serious intrusions. It was only two weeks since the Ayatollah Ruhollah Khomeini had returned from fourteen years of exile. The Iranian government was operating under confused and chaotic conditions. Still, I was convinced that the government would intercede and restore the embassy to our control. By not doing so, the Iranians might make their own embassies around the world vulnerable to mob lawlessness.

When the Shah left Iran the previous month, there had been much internal jockeying for power. The Iranian factions that had banded together against him had little in common except their hatred for him and the Peacock Throne. The Ayatollah Khomeini's appeal to the poor and disenfranchised, however, and the popularity of his call to religious fundamentalism forged a cohesive following within days of his return. Even while the Shah's last Prime Minister, Shahpur Bakhtiar, was still in office, Khomeini named Mehdi Bazargan as provisional Prime Minister. Bakhtiar threatened to arrest the provisional Prime Minister and his shadow government. But within six days those Iranian military still loyal to Bakhtiar had crumbled before pro-Khomeini military elements, and Bakhtiar and the Iranian Parliament — the Majlis — resigned.

Still, it was soon evident that the new Prime Minister, Bazargan, had limited power. The country was simply out of control. In some provinces ethnic groups fought with one another; in other areas local groups defied governmental authority. A strike by government workers erupted. In Tehran armed gangs looted homes, stores, military bases, and government buildings. Nonetheless, it seemed reasonable that Bazargan could and would use what resources he had to prevent the lawlessness from spilling over to the international community, especially because that could undermine the credibility of the government he was trying to establish.

When I reached my office at the CIA's headquarters just outside Washington, in Langley, Virginia, there were a few amplifying press reports coming out of Tehran. These described the group in the embassy as Fedayeen, members of the People's Sacrifice Guerrillas, a coalition of leftist factions not allied to Khomeini. However, since most of the reports were from the Iranian government's news agency, we questioned their validity. The latest one alleged that at least one Iranian employee of the embassy was dead and that several other Iranians, plus two U.S. Marines, were wounded. One story on the wire was that our ambassador, William H. Sullivan, had "surrendered" and had been taken away. When our own communications channels with the embassy opened again, we learned that the Iranian government had intervened after about two hours. The Fedayeen had been thrown out and the embassy was back under our control. Some, but not all, of the classified material had been destroyed. One of the two Marines who had been wounded, Sergeant Kenneth G. Kraus, had been sent to a local hospital.* At the end of the day, the crisis seemed to be over.

Because it had subsided so quickly and because it seemed that the Iranians had taken the proper steps to solve the problem, the President had not called together his crisis management team. It was not all over, however. The next morning we began to appreciate just how confused the situation was. On the top of the thick stack of messages on my desk I found one reporting that Sergeant Kraus, while still in the Iranian government's custody just before his discharge from the hospital, had been kidnaped by a renegade group. The crisis management team was called to the White House for the first of many meetings.

Ambassador Sullivan soon reported that he had rushed to the Ministry of Foreign Affairs to protest the kidnaping of Kraus, only to be told that no one there knew where the sergeant was. They too were

---

*According to Sullivan, Sergeant Kraus was wounded by the accidental firing of his own weapon. William H. Sullivan, *Mission to Iran* (New York: W. W. Norton, 1981), p. 266.

trying to find him, they professed. All they knew was that the same Fedayeen who had attacked the embassy were now holding him. On each of the next four days Bill Sullivan sent a message describing his continued protests to the government and the government's repeated assertions that it was unable to find Sergeant Kraus. When President Carter asked at one of my regular intelligence briefings what I thought was going on, I had no hard intelligence to offer. Our Iranian sources were lying low, and we were purposely not trying to contact them to reduce the risk of their being compromised. So, for the time being, we could only assume that if the government was willing to force the Fedayeen to relinquish our embassy, it was not in league with Kraus's kidnapers.

Given all the uncertainty, John N. McMahon, head of the CIA's clandestine branch, and I talked about the risks of maintaining a CIA presence in the country. Khomeini was calling the United States "the Great Satan" and stirring up a virulent anti-American fervor among the street crowds. John felt the situation would get worse. Resentment of the CIA ran very deep in some Iranian circles because of the Agency's role in 1953 in overthrowing Prime Minister Mossadegh in favor of the Shah.

Although we certainly needed human intelligence to help gain a sense of what was happening in the government — who was in or out of favor, and where the power really lay — it was becoming difficult to protect our people. Even before this latest incident, we had closed one of our two special stations for listening to electronic signals from the Soviet Union. John and I decided at this point to recall the top man, the CIA's Chief of Station. His previous visibility through official contacts with the Shah's government now put him in danger.

On February 19, the Chief of Station arrived in Washington, and the following day I took him to a meeting at the White House on the Kraus situation. He emphasized that even though we still had friends in the Iranian government, they dared not reveal their association with us. He said our best course would be to lower our profile in the country and let matters take their course. He recommended that we not badger the new Bazargan government, because the more we were seen associating with it, the more difficulty it would have in establishing its credibility.

The Chief of Station said that we could not fathom the tension under which Americans were living in Iran. Almost all of us at the meeting had been to Tehran during the Shah's reign and remembered a cosmopolitan city where law and order prevailed and foreigners were welcomed. It was difficult now, despite present events, to accept that all Americans in Tehran were in imminent danger, but it was obvious that the Chief of Station was relieved to be out.

A few days later, a small CIA group at the second listening post in eastern Iran was threatened by the Iranian police who were ostensibly protecting them. As this post was especially important to our ability to verify the SALT II nuclear arms treaty, which we were still negotiating, it was not easy to convince the crisis management team in the White House that these people had to be evacuated. Within three days, though, conditions had deteriorated so much that I was authorized to get them out. I was much relieved when they reached safety.

Our concern for the security of Americans was compounded by newspaper reports that on February 15, the Texas millionaire H. Ross Perot had engineered the escape from Iran of two of his American employees who had been jailed on flimsy charges the previous December. Perot sent in a rescue team that helped foment a riot at the central prison, thus enabling the two employees to escape. The team then boldly spirited these men across western Iran by automobile to the Turkish border. There they bribed the Iranian guards to let them leave the country.[2] We were delighted at Perot's success, but feared this highly publicized escape would further jeopardize the lives of our people, especially Sergeant Kraus's. But on February 20, Bill Sullivan cabled that Khomeini's headquarters had issued a public order that Kraus should be freed. Nonetheless, skepticism at anything coming out of Iran was growing. Would the Fedayeen comply?

Shortly after 11:00 A.M. the next day, I was briefing the President in the Oval Office when the receptionist, Nell Yates, interrupted to tell him there was a phone call he would want to take. He picked up the phone and as he listened I could see a wave of relief soften his face. With his hand over the mouthpiece he said that Sergeant Kraus had been released and was back in the embassy, unharmed. The President stayed on the telephone and asked to be put through to Sergeant Kraus's mother in Pennsylvania. He gave her the good news and talked with her for several minutes. He was visibly moved. When he hung up, he turned to us and said that his strongest fear about our problems with Iran was that the Iranians might single out an American like Kraus and execute him. Clearly he was genuinely concerned for Kraus as a human being. At the same time, he was worried about the broader implications for our relations with Iran of any act to harm Kraus. These dual concerns for the human and international dimensions later permeated our discussions on whether to send Charlie Beckwith and Delta Force to Tehran when our embassy was seized the second time.

As much as I admired President Carter's keen sense of personal responsibility for Americans in trouble abroad, I wondered whether any President could afford to be as concerned over the fate of one American as Teddy Roosevelt had been some seventy-five years earlier.

The immediate crisis now appeared to be over. Conditions in Tehran settled down, with no more outbursts against Americans. The State Department substantially reduced the number of people at the embassy. Our crisis management team stopped meeting, and Iran became less important as other problems moved up on the administration's foreign policy agenda. For instance, there was a flap over the "discovery" of a Soviet Army combat brigade in Cuba, and we were hard at work on SALT II. The number of people stationed at the embassy in Tehran started to creep back up.

When I opened my paper at breakfast on the morning of October 23, I was shocked to read that the Shah, who had been living in Mexico since the previous June, had come to New York to enter the Cornell Medical Center. I knew of no negotiations with the Shah and was caught unawares. Since one of my responsibilities as Director of Central Intelligence was to advise the President on the probable consequences of such a move, I was exasperated at having been left out of the decision. Except for a short discussion back in March, when the crisis management team had agreed that it would be extremely dangerous for Americans in Tehran if the Shah came to the United States, I knew of no meeting by the National Security Council or the crisis management team on the subject.

Although the President certainly must have consulted quietly with at least an inner circle of advisers, the expertise of the professionals at the State Department, the Defense Department, and the CIA had not been tapped. Such consultation probably would not have made any difference to the final outcome; we were in a no-win situation. My mind was already pretty well made up; just a few days earlier I had discussed the matter with David Rockefeller at a conference we were attending. David was the principal force behind the plan to let the Shah come to New York, and I had agreed with him that the United States had a moral obligation to the Shah. If the Shah needed medical attention that could best be found here, we had to let him in. In addition, I felt that admitting him would show unambiguously that the United States does not turn its back on friends.

President Carter was well aware of the risks to our people in Tehran if the Shah came to the United States. But when the State Department's medical director, who had flown to Mexico to examine the Shah, confirmed an urgent need for medical treatment in the United States, this consideration must have tipped the scales for the President.

A meeting of all of his advisers, however, might have made a difference in the way we dealt with the embassy and its personnel after admitting the Shah. It sometimes takes the laying-out of all the pros and cons before a bureaucracy will grapple with an unpleasant problem. There was certainly no one who wanted to pull our embassy out of Tehran, despite the Valentine's Day incident and the anti-American rhetoric emanating from Khomeini's camp. We were not ready to write off the possibility of doing business with Khomeini's government. Reducing our embassy further, or closing it, would have been an affront to the Iranian government. Also, the last thing we wanted to do was to cede the territory to the Soviets.

A thorough discussion on admitting the Shah might have made an even bigger difference in encouraging precautionary moves that could be taken without sending a signal to the Iranians. For instance, one point I overlooked was whether our people in Tehran had carried out their instructions to destroy all but the most essential secret documents. They had not, and when the Iranians took control of the embassy, there was still a large amount of classified material and insufficient time for destroying it. In the name of privacy and secrecy in presidential decision making, we may have paid a steep price for not making best use of the expertise within our government. It was an issue we were to face over and over again during this crisis, as would the Reagan administration in the Iran-contra affair.

Another error was our failure in the CIA to give sufficient credence to reports of the Shah's illness. In all fairness, there weren't many people, even in the Shah's family, who had an idea how ill he really was. He had been consulting two French doctors, who visited him in Tehran over six years, but their treatments did not involve trips by the Shah to a hospital, which might have attracted attention. CIA analysts acknowledged they had not pursued the reports of the illness diligently enough. We should have known; we had not done our job well.

That should have warned me that our intelligence network in Iran was seriously flawed.

· 4 ·

OUR EMBASSY IS TAKEN

Recently the Shah went to the United States. They have accepted
him there under the pretext that he is suffering from cancer. I
hope, God willing, it is true . . . It is all right if he dies, but what
will happen to our money?

> — The Ayatollah Ruhollah
> Khomeini [1]

IT WAS Sunday, November 4, 1979. The phone rang. I noted that my
bedside clock read 5:30 A.M., but I wasn't sure whether I was awake
or dreaming, because the CIA duty officer's report was so close to a
repeat of the previous Valentine's Day. "Admiral, a mob has seized
our embassy in Tehran. Our people were in the vault destroying classified papers when communications were severed." I was fully awake
before he finished, and more alarmed than I had been eight and a half
months earlier. I could better understand this incident. We had held
worried discussions about the possible reaction in Iran to the arrival of
the Shah in New York.

Shortly after I arrived at my office, three officers from the CIA's
clandestine branch joined me. "How many of our people were in the
embassy and who were they?" I asked. The officers gave me names
and positions, but had no information about the staff's welfare. We
discussed how this situation compared with the embassy seizure of
February 14, but had too little information to know whether this was
the same Fedayeen group or a different one. I told them to be sure to
keep the families of our people informed.

Throughout that Sunday, the duty officer relayed reports from Tehran. Again we were embarrassingly dependent on press stories, almost
all based on communiqués released by the gang that had seized the
embassy. The Iranian media were calling them "students." The students justified their action on the grounds that we had admitted the

Shah to the United States. I kept thinking back to the Valentine's Day incident, when, in a time of near chaos in Tehran, the Iranian government had nonetheless moved with reasonable promptness after the embassy was seized to regain control. Conditions were less chaotic now. Surely, I thought, it won't be long before the government will step in again. Apparently the President and Zbigniew (Zbig) Brzezinski, Assistant to the President for National Security Affairs, felt the same way; they did not call for a crisis management team meeting.

By the time I went to bed, it was already Monday morning in Tehran and the end of Day 1 of the hostage crisis. A student spokesman inside the embassy claimed Khomeini had telephoned his consent to the takeover. Still, I hoped for another call in the middle of the night with news that the Iranian government had restored our embassy to us. But this was not to be.

The next morning there was no change. When I arrived at the office, I was told that the crisis management team, called the Special Coordinating Committee (SCC), would meet in the White House at ten-thirty. While the President's senior advisers, like the Vice President, Cabinet secretaries, Assistant for National Security Affairs, Director of Central Intelligence (DCI), and the Presidential Counsel have direct access to the President, every President organizes his advisers in a different way for their collective advice. Most problems cross jurisdictions. For instance, if as DCI I wanted to undertake a high-risk spying operation, I would have consulted the Secretaries of State and Defense, both of whom would have been involved. While I alone was responsible for those activities, if they failed or were exposed, the Secretary of State might have had to patch up damaged diplomatic relations, and the Secretary of Defense might have had to worry about the military consequences. It is important to have a forum in which to review high-risk intelligence operations ahead of time. Presidents also need a way to balance both the special interests of their advisers' organizations and the inevitable biases of human beings. Thus, Presidents, at least formally, organize their counselors to ensure that the advice they receive represents several points of view and takes advantage of all available expertise. Too often zealots — and there are some in every administration — see such coordination among bureaucracies as an impediment to decisive action. Actually, it is a sensible way to make certain that everyone exercises good judgment. Whether Presidents are consistent in utilizing such arrangements is a matter of personal style.

President Carter organized several action groups, each for a different problem area. The SCC was the forum for problems in which no single department or agency had the predominant interest, those in which almost every element of the foreign policy establishment was involved. The members of the SCC were the Secretaries of State and Defense, the Chairman of the Joint Chiefs of Staff, the Assistant to the President for National Security Affairs, and the Director of Central Intelligence. The Vice President attended when his schedule and interests permitted. For particular topics, other participants would be added, such as the President's Chief of Staff, or the Secretaries of Treasury or Energy. Meetings of the SCC were always chaired by Zbig Brzezinski. Following the meetings Zbig would write a memo to the President, outlining his view of what had been discussed. He would leave wide margins where the President could write notes. There might also be boxes the President could check to indicate agreement or disagreement. At the next SCC meeting Zbig would tell us the President's responses, but we were never given copies of the memos or allowed to read them.

These procedures were established early in the Carter administration. Since I was not appointed Director of Central Intelligence until seven weeks after President Carter's inauguration, I was not part of the organizing process. I assumed the President's principal advisers on foreign policy, Secretary of State Cyrus R. (Cy) Vance, Secretary of Defense Harold Brown, and Zbig Brzezinski, agreed on it, but I was never comfortable with it because so much depended on the skill, objectivity, and personal agenda of the scribe. Some Assistants for National Security Affairs have seen their role primarily as that of coordinating the views of the President's advisers so that the President could grasp the differences readily and make a well-considered decision. Others have heard the advisers out and then offered the President their own best advice. Zbig obviously did the latter. I was never confident that views contrary to his were adequately presented to the President. Consequently, if I felt strongly about an issue, I took it up directly with the President. However, I was reluctant to use his time this way, as I was keenly sensitive to the infinite demands on him.

The SCC met in the White House Situation Room in the basement of the White House. It was a windowless, wood-paneled room, fifteen by twenty feet, that looked more like a do-it-yourself cellar conversion than the nerve center of the United States government. The wooden conference table with seats for ten nearly filled the room. Additional chairs were squeezed along the two longer walls. There was not enough space for decent visual aids or even simple maps. Communications and display facilities were outdated, and one had to leave the room to use a telephone. If anyone smoked, the air became miserably stale and hot. I was amused to think of what the public must imagine the White House Situation Room to be like — computers, flashing displays, and video screens. Maybe in the movies.

At this first meeting on the Iranian hostage problem, the item at the top of the agenda was a report from me on what the CIA knew. I felt frustrated that I had very few hard facts to offer. The embassy was the focus and conduit for all our intelligence from Iran, and it had been knocked out. Usually my problem was finding the important kernels in too much data. Now, we were not even sure who had taken over the embassy. If the students' claim to Khomeini's support was true, they were a different group from the leftist Fedayeen of the previous February; and with government support, their seizure of the embassy was a state-supported act of terrorism. State involvement made a big difference. We had been dependent on the Iranian government to obtain the release of Sergeant Kraus from an amorphous group like the Fedayeen. There are many more devices for pressuring a government that itself is supporting terrorists; they range from diplomatic and economic pressures to military action.

We discussed our options. Everyone assumed the Iranians would come to their senses, as they had in February, and step in to free the hostages. Most thought it would be a matter of hours or, at most, a few days. No one mentioned it, but we had been so glad to put the Valentine's Day problem behind us that we had never discussed what we would do if the embassy were taken again. We had no contingency plans.

Cy Vance told us the President wanted to send an emissary to Iran to ensure that the government understood we had no demands other than the release of the Americans and the return of the embassy. I sensed it was more Cy's idea than the President's and that what he wanted was direct personal contact with the Iranians rather than communication via impersonal telegrams or intermediaries. Cy suggested three candidates: former Attorney General Ramsey Clark; Chief Counsel for the Senate Select Committee on Intelligence, William G. Miller; and an Iranian expert, Professor Richard Cottam of the University of Pittsburgh.

I alone favored Professor Cottam, who I thought would have the best understanding of the Iranians. My second choice was Bill Miller, whose work with the intelligence committee I respected. He had served in Iran for five years with the State Department, and might well have friends left in the government there who could help. But I felt strongly that Ramsey Clark was not the man to send on this sensitive mission. Cy was correct that Clark did have the qualification of long and vocal opposition to the Shah and of having paid a call on Khomeini in Paris the previous January. Cy felt he might get a hearing. I believed Clark had demonstrated such poor judgment on several occasions since leaving the government that he would not be representative of public attitudes in the United States. I was joined in that sentiment by a congressman from Ohio who later commented on the floor of the House, "My God, Mr. Speaker, we might just as well send Jane Fonda."[2]

Clark, like Jane Fonda, had gone to Hanoi during the Vietnam War as a private citizen. He visited the prison camp where one of my best Navy friends, Vice Admiral James B. Stockdale, was imprisoned for seven and a half years. Clark's visit made life even more difficult for Jim, who had once deliberately injured his face to avoid being photographed with a visitor like Clark lest the photos be used as propaganda about how well the prisoners were being treated. When Clark returned from Vietnam, he made statements like "They [the prisoners] get all the food they want to eat," which seemed naïve at the time and which we now know from the testimony of Jim and others to have been outrageous.[3] Clark later admitted that he had never been allowed to talk alone with any U.S. prisoner in the camp — evidence of his gullibility in making statements that helped Hanoi, not us. I felt it unconscionable to send such a man on any mission for our government. Cy's was a much more practical viewpoint: we should do what we could to get the hostages back. Lyndon Johnson had signed a false confession to achieve just that. We in the Carter administration would have more debates about principle versus pragmatism before this incident was closed.

With Cy and his deputy, Warren Christopher, supporting Clark, and Zbig and his deputy, David Aaron, favoring Miller, the result was a typical bureaucratic compromise: both Miller and Clark were sent. It was worked out so quickly that I suspected it had all been decided upstairs with the President ahead of time and that Zbig's bringing it up for consideration by the SCC was merely pro forma. Clark and Miller left the next day, Day 3, November 6, for Iran.

On Day 3 there was still no sign that the Iranian government was doing anything to solve the problem. The SCC met and discussed what steps the United States could take to force it to move more quickly. Cy suggested encouraging the Shah to leave the United States, in the hope that this might defuse the situation. The students, and by now Khomeini, were demanding that the Shah be returned to Iran to stand trial. If he were no longer in the United States, Cy argued, we could not be expected to meet that demand. Cy's second option was to negotiate with Khomeini and the students. Zbig raised a third option, using military force to pressure the Iranians, and a fourth, conducting a military rescue operation, as the Israelis had at Entebbe, Uganda, in 1977.

Zbig strongly opposed our urging the Shah to leave the United States lest we appear to be pressuring a long-time friend into doing something not in his best interests. Zbig never minced words, but also never raised his voice or otherwise displayed emotion. He simply took it as a given that his argument would be recognized as sound. When Zbig finished, he turned to Cy, who told us that he had been in contact with both the Shah's staff and David Rockefeller. It had only been two weeks since the Shah's surgery for the removal of gallstones and an enlarged lymph node. Moving the Shah was out of the question for several more weeks. But Cy argued that once he was able to move, the United States had to pay the price of encouraging him to do so. In his view, as long as the Shah was in the United States, there was little chance the Iranians would discuss the hostages.

Although Cy was always polite and left room for discussion, he was clear in expressing his views. This was not the first time we had witnessed a strong disagreement between him and Zbig. Usually it was muted, but today the strain was evident, and neither compromised. The Brzezinski-Vance schism that, in my view, had badly hurt the President's foreign policy already could not be set aside even in this instance, when American lives were at stake.

We moved on to the second option: negotiating the release of the hostages. There were no new ideas. Clark and Miller were still in Istanbul, awaiting permission from the Iranians to proceed to Tehran. I suggested we encourage Yasir Arafat of the PLO to talk with the Ayatollah on our behalf. CIA analysts believed Arafat had good access to Khomeini and might be willing to use it to improve his standing with the United States. Cy opposed the idea because of concern that Arafat would not be satisfied just to receive credit in the United States. He would try to make us recognize or, at the least, meet with the PLO.

That would, of course, have complicated the delicate Middle East peace process worked out at Camp David. Conflicts like this, between immediate efforts to obtain the release of the hostages and the broader issues of foreign relations, would continue to bedevil us.

A few days later Arafat grabbed the ball and went to Tehran. We heard rumors that he was on the verge of obtaining the release of the hostages, but within a week it became obvious this was either PLO propaganda or wishful thinking. He may, though, have played a role in the release, on Days 15 and 16, of thirteen of our hostages who were black or female. Apparently the Iranians thought this move would create divisiveness in the United States. The release brought the number of hostages in the embassy down to fifty, with an additional three in the Foreign Ministry, where they had been when the students seized the embassy.

The SCC moved to a discussion of the use of military force. I told the group that those holding the embassy were threatening to kill the hostages if we moved against Iran militarily. Secretary of Defense Harold Brown then presented the military options: use a small amphibious force to capture Kharg Island (see Map 4), the terminal from which most Iranian oil is shipped; bomb the principal Iranian oil refinery at Abadan; bomb Iran's American-made, highly sophisticated F-14 fighter aircraft. Because no one expected the crisis to last long, there was almost no interest in these options.

Harold mentioned that the aircraft carrier U.S.S. *Midway* happened to be in the Indian Ocean. I thought it should be ordered to move immediately at full speed toward the Persian Gulf and take up position off the Iranian coast. It would be in place to launch an attack on short notice should the President decide that was necessary. Despite the students' threat, I believed we had to be prepared for military action, just in case. No one else thought that having *Midway* near Iran was worth the risk of stirring up the hostage holders, so the SCC's recommendation to the President was to keep *Midway* away from Iran.

The fourth option, a rescue mission, was discussed only briefly. Air Force General David C. Jones, Chairman of the Joint Chiefs of Staff, was pessimistic about whether our military could mount a rescue operation that far from the United States or any U.S. base.* That was the

---

*Dave Jones was uniquely experienced in this area, having participated as Chief of Staff of the Air Force and Acting Chairman of the Joint Chiefs of Staff in carrying out the rescue attempt in 1975 for the crew of the S.S. *Mayaguez*.

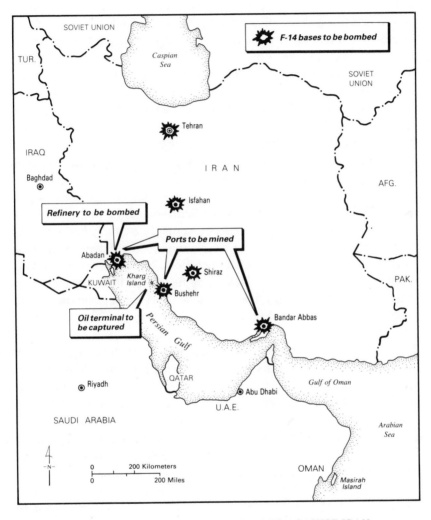

SOVIET UNION

TUR.

Caspian Sea

SOVIET UNION

F-14 bases to be bombed

Tehran

IRAQ

I R A N

AFG.

Baghdad

Isfahan

Refinery to be bombed

Ports to be mined

Abadan

KUWAIT   *Kharg Island*   Bushehr   Shiraz

PAK.

Oil terminal to be captured

Bandar Abbas

Persian Gulf

Riyadh   QATAR   Abu Dhabi

Gulf of Oman

SAUDI ARABIA   U.A.E.

Arabian Sea

N

| 0 | 200 Kilometers |
| 0 | 200 Miles |

OMAN   *Masirah Island*

MAP 4. PROPOSED MILITARY OPTIONS AGAINST IRAN

end of it. Just before the meeting broke up we were told that the President wanted to meet with us at four-thirty that afternoon in the Cabinet Room.

The Cabinet Room is a large, airy, high-ceilinged room on the main floor of the West Wing of the White House, separated from the Oval Office by a small waiting room. It is bright and cheerful, with french doors opening onto the Rose Garden. The large table seats sixteen, with plenty of elbow room. Aside from being pleased to get out of the bunkerlike Situation Room and into a pleasant atmosphere, which I felt encouraged more positive thinking, I looked forward to hearing precisely what the President would be told about our SCC meeting and what his reaction would be.

The SCC with the President attending is, in effect, the National Security Council.* By gathering the NSC, the President can get advice directly from his key foreign policy advisers. Differences can be thrashed out on the spot. That is not to say participants did not pull punches in front of the President. That tendency certainly existed. I often wondered whether it was President Carter's style to avoid confrontation or whether the underlying differences between Zbig and Cy were so deep that the President wouldn't risk exposing them even in this small group. Perhaps, though, the aura that surrounds any President inhibits some people from speaking their mind.

The meeting opened with the President and Cy both saying they did not want to resort to military force to solve the problem. Jimmy Carter had come into office pledged to reducing the size of the military and dedicated to working out arms control agreements with the Soviet Union. I believe that he also hoped to avoid any military personnel losses during his term of office. When Zbig reported the conversation about U.S.S. *Midway* from the earlier meeting, the President reminded us of an incident in late 1978. When it had become clear that the Shah was in serious trouble, the President placed an aircraft carrier on alert to proceed into the Indian Ocean from the Pacific. The order immediately

---

*Created by the National Security Act of 1947, the National Security Council comprises the President, the Vice President, and the Secretaries of State and Defense. In practice, Presidents have generally included the Director of Central Intelligence and the Chairman of the Joint Chiefs of Staff and, from time to time, others who either have the President's particular confidence or whose areas of expertise are relevant to particular discussions.

leaked, making it clear to the world we thought the Shah was in so much trouble that the United States was bringing up force. That only exacerbated the Shah's problems. Now the President obviously did not want to risk a similar misfire. When he decided to let *Midway* continue on a planned port visit to Mombasa, Kenya, I wanted to speak up, but I was silenced by two conflicting principles.

On the one hand, I thought it a militarily poor plan. Mombasa is over two thousand miles — almost four days' steaming time for a carrier — from the entrance to the Persian Gulf. Even there the carrier would be over a thousand miles from Tehran, more than twice the maximum effective range of its aircraft. We had United States citizens to protect, and moving military force into the area seemed to me entirely appropriate. Even if the order to *Midway* leaked, the students could not see her to confirm the move, nor would there be any immediate action against Iran. I thought the chances of harm to the hostages were slight. As a professional military officer, I wanted the President to have this advice.

On the other hand, it was inappropriate for me as DCI to raise such a matter. My responsibility to the President was to provide the information he needed to make decisions, not to be an advocate for any specific course. A DCI's major contribution is his unbiased and disinterested stance in the President's councils. Without that, he brings only one more opinion to the table. Further, as a military officer I understood that this issue was in the domain of the Secretary of Defense and the Chairman of the Joint Chiefs, not the DCI. They have more than enough armchair strategists second-guessing them; I was resolved not to be one of them. Despite my strongly held professional view, I did not speak up.

The meeting closed with no other decisions having been made. The sending of Clark and Miller to the Middle East seemed to strike the desired balance between inaction and provocation, since the assumption was that the problem would not last long, and short-term responses were all we needed to consider. It was clear, though, that whether the Iranian government had planned the capture of the embassy, it was now fully supporting it. Khomeini's son had visited the students the day before, endorsed the takeover, and supported the demand that both the Shah and his wealth be returned to Iran before the hostages could be released. When Prime Minister Bazargan took the opposite position, he was forced to resign. The hostages had quickly become a political litmus test in Tehran. Khomeini then dispensed with the office of Prime Minister and placed the government in the hands of a new, shadowy body of unnamed clerics, known as the Revolutionary Council. He had been telling the world he wanted a theocracy and now was moving decisively in that direction.

When I returned to Langley from the NSC meeting, I began a practice that became routine as the crisis continued. I gathered the key experts on Iran from both the clandestine and analytic branches of the CIA in my conference room and briefed them on what had been discussed in the White House so that they would know what intelligence support was needed.

In this instance, most of them supported the decision not to move *Midway* forward; they felt it might provoke the students to carry out their threat. But their arguments failed to persuade me. I continued to believe the students might kill hostages for other reasons, and if they did, the President would have to do more than just protest. Military action might be his only option. He should therefore have forces more immediately available than in Mombasa. I feared that letting the students intimidate us with their threat put us in an essentially reactive position, which might very well dictate all of our future responses. That ultimately is what happened.

As a naval officer, I was also concerned that we had not discussed the mining of Iran's harbors. I had not raised the point because I was not certain how vulnerable Iran's harbors were, so when I returned to my office, I called Leonard Gollobin, a friend who is a civilian expert on mine warfare. We had worked together on mine issues over many years. I asked him to bring nautical charts of the Persian Gulf to my house that evening without telling anyone. Our inspection confirmed that Iran's harbors had narrow and shallow entrances, making them especially susceptible to mining. Having been involved in mine warfare in the Navy, I had long advocated mining when the adversary was dependent on a flow of merchant shipping. In a situation like the present one, mining had the advantage of not being a lethal act. We could lay the mines, announce we had done so, and let the Iranians decide whether to run the minefield at the risk of ships and lives.

I intended to raise the matter of mining at the meeting of the SCC on Day 4, but Zbig steered all discussion away from military options. That troubled me. Khomeini had just announced that Clark and Miller would not be allowed to meet with any Iranian authorities if they went on to Tehran. With the negotiations dead for the time being, I thought we should study our military choices. Instead, we started to cast about almost aimlessly for other, nonmilitary means of pressuring Iran.

We were back to Lyndon Johnson's futile efforts to use diplomacy for the release of the crew of *Pueblo*. He had called on nations and organizations to intercede on our behalf: the Soviet Union; the United Nations; those countries supervising the armistice between North and South Korea — Sweden, Switzerland, Poland, and Czechoslovakia; and some of the few that had consular ties with North Korea — Yugoslavia, Ceylon, India, and Romania. He had approached the South Koreans, hoping to arrange an exchange of *Pueblo*'s crew for North Korean military prisoners held in South Korea. He had sought adjudication by the International Court of Justice and mediation by several third parties. Nothing had worked.

Like President Johnson, we in the Carter administration were willing to try almost anything rather than look impotent. By Day 5, Thursday, November 8, all we could manage to agree on was the placing of an embargo on military spare parts previously ordered by Iran, with the proviso that the parts would be shipped once all of the hostages were released.

At that time we began to realize that the crisis might not be short. SCC meetings every morning became standard; they lasted longer and longer and sometimes were continued in the afternoon. The hostages had moved to number one on the President's agenda. Despite the capabilities of modern communications, which permit a President to handle almost any problem from almost anywhere, Hamilton Jordan, the President's Chief of Staff and close personal adviser, told us on Day 6 that he was recommending the President cancel a long-scheduled trip to Canada the next day. The President clearly wanted to work on the problem himself rather than just react to advisers' recommendations. Later that afternoon, when the White House press secretary, Jody Powell, announced the cancelation, he said that the cause was the hostage issue.

Lyndon Johnson had played the *Pueblo* crisis as quietly as possible and deliberately avoided raising the public's expectations. Richard Nixon worked to stay out of the limelight during the problem at Dawson Field. But Jimmy Carter, like Teddy Roosevelt in the Moroccan affair, became a symbol to the public of how deeply committed we were to solving a hostage problem.

OUR MILITARY
FOUND WANTING

A good plan violently executed now is better than a perfect plan
next week.

— George Patton[1]

WHEN the sixth successive meeting of the SCC concluded on Day 7,
Zbig was still avoiding any discussion of military options. Then, just
as we were leaving the Situation Room, his secretary came in and said,
"Mr. Brzezinski, the President is waiting." The Vice President, Harold
Brown, and Dave Jones started toward the stairway to the Oval Office,
but when I asked Zbig whether I should come along he replied no,
with a strained expression clearly indicating that something was going
on which he was reluctant to tell me about.

As soon as I got back to my office I phoned Zbig's secretary and
asked that he call me on the secure (coded) phone on his return from
the meeting with the President. When he did, I told him I did not
appreciate being excluded from what I suspected was a series of meetings on military options. What were they going to use for the intelligence for such operations if I was not involved, I asked. Zbig replied
that the Defense Intelligence Agency (DIA) was providing the intelligence.

I was livid. In 1947 the Congress created the post of Director of
Central Intelligence (DCI) largely to avoid a repetition of our failure
to predict the Japanese attack on Pearl Harbor. Back then, the Departments of the Army, Navy, and State had not fully shared their intelligence with one another. The DCI's charter is to ensure that all information available within the various intelligence agencies is put to best

use.* "You are making it impossible for me to fulfill my responsibilities," I told Zbig, and it was agreed that I would participate in future discussions of military options.

Like almost every administration after a year or two in office, the Carter administration had developed a near paranoia about leaks. We certainly had had our share. The usual reaction is to create "compartments" of information and sharply limit the number of people allowed to have compartmented data. While, in my view, excluding the chief of intelligence from a compartment on military options was going much too far, there were good reasons to avoid letting it be known that military planning was going on. If the threats of the so-called students in Tehran were to be believed, any indication that we were preparing for a military rescue operation could endanger the lives of the hostages. At the very least, the captors could disperse the hostages to different locations and make a rescue effort almost impossible. Zbig was also reflecting a tendency of some Assistants to the President for National Security — referred to as National Security Advisers — to keep departments and agencies in the dark.

The National Security Adviser and his staff often are frustrated because they have no direct authority to carry out the President's decisions. That's the task of the bureaucracy, which frequently resists outside direction, even from the President. Bureaucrats are even more likely to resist what they suspect are directives from the National Security Council staff. A result of these tensions is that the staff of the NSC often attempts to sidestep the bureaucracy and do as much as possible on its own.

Zbig's excluding me from the meetings on military options was this kind of maneuver. One of the drawbacks is that people may work at cross-purposes. In this instance, I had unexpectedly become involved in the rescue planning by a complete outsider. The day before my call to Zbig, I had received a phone call from Ross Perot, who had rescued

---

*The Director of Central Intelligence (DCI) is responsible for coordinating all U.S. intelligence agencies, referred to as the Intelligence Community of the United States. He is also the head of the Central Intelligence Agency (CIA), one of these agencies. The two responsibilities require an uneasy and rarely entirely successful balancing act. The more he is seen as the community leader by his own agency, the CIA, the less its members see him as their champion when their interests must be protected. The more he is seen as head of the CIA, the more the community is suspicious of his ability to arbitrate fairly among the intelligence agencies, especially when the foreign intelligence budget is being allocated.

his two employees from Iran the previous February. Suspecting that the CIA may have been cut off from its normal sources of intelligence, Ross offered to use his contacts in Iran to collect information for us. He also suggested the CIA might be able to pull off a rescue effort similar to his, and offered to come to Washington to brief us on how he had done it. I told Zbig I had accepted Ross's offer to collect information but had been noncommittal on any briefing about rescue operations, because I did not want to give any hint we were even thinking about such a mission.

Zbig's reaction was that I should put Ross in touch with Colonel William E. Odom of his staff. I recognized the instinct to take over and keep something unusual, like Perot's offer, under control of the NSC. I also knew that bringing an outsider into intelligence operations could be tricky. There was the possibility of his agents tripping over CIA agents inside Iran. With all respect to Odom, a very competent colonel, dealing with Perot was well above his level, and directing agents beyond his experience. Moreover, the NSC staff is too thin in numbers and experience to be the action agency for anything as complicated as this, as we were to see in the Iran-contra affair.

I explained to Zbig that we could not ask a man of Ross Perot's stature to come all the way to Washington from Dallas to talk to a colonel. I also told him that I had a personal relationship with Ross — something of an exaggeration. We were both Naval Academy graduates and had a number of mutual friends. A few months earlier, when we met at a dinner party, I had told him I admired his accomplishments in the business world. I said that I would enjoy an opportunity to visit with him at greater length, emphasizing that I did not have anything in mind other than getting better acquainted. It wasn't many weeks later that he came to my office at Langley.

At that time, we had a wide-ranging talk about world affairs, and somewhat impulsively I broached an idea that had occurred to me only a few days before. It involved building an intelligence listening post under the guise of a commercial oil-drilling platform in the sea. I was searching for a way to make it appear to be a truly commercial operation, that is, to provide cover for the intelligence activity. Ross immediately offered to form a company, spend his own money to build the platform, and put us in business. I had not been looking for money, but if Ross did provide it, it would make the cover even better than I had hoped. Unfortunately, for many reasons it never came to pass, but I was certainly impressed by Ross's generosity for the sake of his country.

It would not be the last time he offered to finance a governmental activity, as we will see with hostage problems in Lebanon during the Reagan administration.

After the discussion with Zbig, I called Ross back and arranged for him to come to Washington the next day, Sunday. Now that the SCC realized that the hostage problem would not be solved easily, we were working around the clock. Ross was more than willing to accommodate us. On Day 8, then, he and nine members of his staff met with me and a group of CIA operations experts in the Director's conference room at the CIA. All of the people Ross brought with him had in one way or another been involved in the release of his two employees. They stressed that it would be easy to get a rescue team into Iran without its being detected; the men would pose as businessmen and go in through the airport, or would come in by land over remote routes. Of course, when Ross's people had gone through the airport in February, American passports were still acceptable in Iran. It would be more complicated now, as those same passports would ring alarm bells.

Ross and his people thought that if we infiltrated a military team into Tehran, it could canvass the territory, purchase its weapons, and then wait for the right moment to storm the embassy and release the hostages. They had few suggestions, however, on how to move the hostages and a rescue team — a total of more than a hundred people — safely out of Tehran. They had smuggled their two hostages and five rescuers out over land, but a much larger group posed quite different problems. A convoy of cars or trucks was almost bound to be stopped before it got out of Tehran. And it was highly unlikely that so many Westerners could work their way four hundred miles across Iran to Turkey unnoticed, either individually or in small groups.

The meeting with Perot's people forced us at the CIA to consider the advantages of inserting the rescue force clandestinely. By coincidence, just as our meeting was winding down, Harold Brown and Dave Jones came on the phone together to tell me they were working on a rescue plan that required assistance from the CIA in infiltrating an assault force of forty to sixty men into Tehran and then hiding it. I told them that Ross Perot was in my office describing just such a rescue mission, and suggested that they take the opportunity to talk with him.

At his Pentagon office Dave was receptive to Perot's idea of a clandestine operation, though Ross still could not help solve the problem of getting the hostages out of Tehran. He and his team left town that evening, offering to be available whenever we needed their help.

The next morning, November 12, Day 9, I went to my first meeting on rescue planning. Just as I had suspected, when the daily meeting of the SCC concluded, Zbig and his assistant David Aaron, Dave Jones and his military assistant Lieutenant General John Pustay, Harold Brown, and Warren Christopher from the State Department proceeded from the Situation Room in the basement to Zbig's office on the first floor of the White House. This was a large, square office in a corner of the West Wing, with tall windows that reached down to the floor and a view across the White House lawn to Pennsylvania Avenue. A round table in one corner accommodated most of us.

Zbig asked Dave Jones to give us a status report on the rescue planning. To my dismay, I heard that the Joint Chiefs of Staff were still considering several plans, and none was in workable form. They were looking at two options for moving a rescue force to the vicinity of the embassy. One was Ross Perot's approach of infiltrating the men individually into Tehran through the airport, and then having the CIA hide them until they were ready to assault the embassy. The other was to parachute them well beyond the outskirts of Tehran and let them work their way in to the embassy.

Neither approach would do much good, however, unless we could find a way to get everyone out of Iran afterward. The military planners had progressed toward a solution by locating a little-used Iranian airfield at Manzariyeh, some fifty miles south of Tehran, which could easily be captured. Once the hostages were freed, we would "somehow" get them to Manzariyeh and then fly them out of the country. That "somehow" loomed large. The only conceivable solution was to use helicopters to lift the hostages and the rescue force out of the embassy compound and then to Manzariyeh.

Dave Jones pointed out that there were not many places from which we could launch our helos, fly to Tehran, and then to Manzariyeh without having to refuel. The best plan was to have an aircraft carrier go into the Persian Gulf, but the Navy had ruled that out as too risky. The next best was to use a Turkish airbase, but the State Department insisted that the Turks would never permit us to launch a combat operation from their soil, because Iran is a fellow Muslim nation. This caution did not surprise me. I recalled that the Turks had objected in 1970, when we had positioned some transport forces on NATO bases in

Turkey during the crisis at Dawson Field in Jordan, also a Muslim country.

Still, I argued that we should go ahead and use Turkey, even if we could not get permission. We had people and aircraft already on the bases in eastern Turkey and could launch an operation without advising the Turks. There might be diplomatic repercussions, just as the Thais had objected to our using their bases for the raid on Koh Tang in the *Mayaguez* affair. But the Turks are a tough and pragmatic people. I had worked closely with them as the NATO commander of their forces and believed they would accept what we did and be secretly pleased that we were acting firmly and decisively. However, my argument did not convince anyone. We remained without a way to use helicopters, although Harold Brown announced that he would move Navy minesweeping helicopters to an aircraft carrier in the Indian Ocean.*

I also found out at this meeting that the basic force for the rescue mission would be the Army's Delta Force under Charlie Beckwith. It was just two years since the West Germans' rescue operation at Mogadishu had given impetus to Beckwith's aspirations to create Delta. On October 13, 1977, three men and a woman from the PFLP, which had been behind the incident at Dawson Field seven years earlier, hijacked a Lufthansa aircraft leaving the Spanish island of Mallorca for Frankfurt. The hijackers demanded the release of two of their comrades who were in Turkish jails, eleven members of the Baader Meinhof gang, including Andreas Baader, from West German jails, and $15 million. They ordered the aircraft, *Landshut,* to head to Rome. West German Minister of the Interior Werner Maihofer told the West German counterterrorist force, GSG-9, under Colonel Ulrich Wegener, to prepare for action.

The West Germans had formed GSG-9 after terrorists struck down Israeli athletes at the Munich Olympics in 1972. The Munich state police had not performed well, and the government in Bonn decided to create a first-class national counterterrorist force. They opted for a civilian organization under the Minister of the Interior, not a military one as the British had in their SAS. This was to be its first test.

---

*For this, the helos had to be disassembled, shipped in C-5A transport aircraft to the island of Diego Garcia in the Indian Ocean, reassembled, and then flown to the carrier. When the press detected some of these activities, we explained the importance of having a minesweeping capability near the Strait of Hormuz in the Persian Gulf, and they believed us. Fortunately, the story soon died.

When *Landshut* arrived in Rome, Maihofer phoned the Italians and asked them to keep the plane on the ground, shooting out its tires if necessary. He wanted to send GSG-9 to storm the aircraft. The Italians, however, clearly did not want a German police unit conducting operations on Italian soil. Chancellor Helmut Schmidt, appreciating the Italian predicament, agreed to let the aircraft go on (see Map 5).

The terrorists took *Landshut* to the airport at Larnaca, in Cyprus. Wegener and GSG-9 followed in another Lufthansa aircraft but were required to land at a military base fifty miles away, and missed any opportunity for a rescue attempt.

Landshut next stopped briefly in Bahrein before setting down in Dubai. At that point Schmidt called on one of his close associates, a troubleshooter on terrorism, Minister of State Hans-Jurgen Wischnewski, to board still a third Lufthansa plane and head for Dubai. As Wischnewski rushed out of his office, he asked his private secretary to get him ten million deutsche marks immediately. The secretary predicted that it would be impossible to get that much cash in just a few minutes, late on a Friday afternoon, but he did phone the private secretary of the Minister of Finance. "My minister wants ten million deutsche marks immediately." The retort was "So does my minister!" Wischnewski had to leave without his marks, but he took with him a representative of the Ministry of Justice and the chief pilot and chief stewardess of Lufthansa. He knew he might have to make difficult decisions involving risks to both the crew and the passengers of *Landshut,* possibly involving legal issues.

At Dubai, the government was reluctant to give Wischnewski permission to unleash GSG-9 for fear of appearing to be indifferent to an Arab cause, even though this one had turned to terrorism. As Wischnewski was working on this, the hijackers left for Aden, in South Yemen. Wischnewski was unable to get permission to land there and diverted to Jiddah, in Saudi Arabia, to await developments.

By now the saga was in its third day. The hijackers, hostages, and plane crew were all near exhaustion. In Aden the terrorists, perhaps reflecting their fatigue, killed the pilot of the aircraft, Jürgen Schumann. Conditions for the eighty-six remaining passengers and crew were becoming unbearable, but the terrorists ordered *Landshut* to Mogadishu.

Schmidt held a long, frustrating, inconclusive phone conversation with President Mohammed Siad Barré about the GSG-9 aircraft. It was

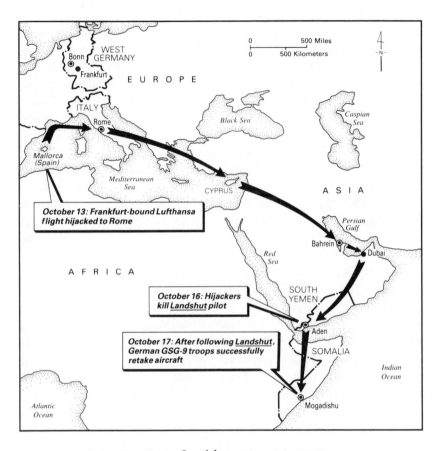

MAP 5. FLIGHT OF *Landshut*, OCTOBER 1977

then Wischnewski's job to get permission to bring in the force and send it into action. Siad Barré, however, wanted to assault *Landshut* with his own troops. Wischnewski agreed, confident that the Somalis would back off when they realized what they were up against. Sure enough, late on the afternoon of October 17, Siad Barré gave Wischnewski the permission he sought. The GSG-9 plane landed without lights just after dark. Colonel Wegener quickly reconnoitered and recommended an assault at midnight. Wischnewski, after staving off efforts by Schmidt in Bonn to give him detailed directions, gave Wegener the go-ahead. He reasoned that the hijackers, who were threatening to blow up the aircraft, themselves, and the hostages, were now so tense that they might just carry out their threat.

Wegener wisely integrated the Somalis into his attack plan as partners by having them ignite large bonfires in full view of the aircraft's cockpit. While the fires burned and three of the four terrorists went to the cockpit to see what was going on, twenty-eight men of GSG-9 scrambled up ladders onto the aircraft's wings, opened the doors, and stormed in.*

The GSG-9 team happened to be very familiar with the layout of the aircraft, because they had practiced on this very one, *Landshut*. Their marksmanship was excellent; they killed three terrorists and seriously wounded the fourth. Only one hostage was wounded, though several were injured. It was seven minutes after Wegener's people opened the doors that Wischnewski could radio Schmidt and tell him it was all over and a complete success. The operation boosted Schmidt's political stock dramatically. He told me years later that he was prepared to resign if the operation had failed and that he defined failure as a significant loss of hostage lives.† When Jimmy Carter sent Charlie Beckwith to Iran, he must have known that he, too, was entrusting his political future to a military rescue force.

The Mogadishu operation marked a turning point in the German struggle with the Baader Meinhof gang. Baader and three of his principal accomplices, who were also in jail, concluded that the outcome

---

*There have been numerous reports that two British officers who accompanied GSG-9 detonated two "stun bombs" as the doors were opened. These experimental bombs were intended to stun everyone in the vicinity, but not to injure them permanently. Wegener told me emphatically in a discussion in Bonn, in October 1986, that he did not use these bombs, because their record in testing was poor. "They were dangerous," he said.

†Discussion in Hamburg in October 1986.

at Mogadishu ended their hope for release. They all committed suicide the day of the rescue operation.

It was the day after the Mogadishu rescue that President Carter, in a note to Secretary of Defense Brown, asked, "Do we have the same capability as the West Germans?" In response to that memo the SCC had debated whether Delta Force would in time be our equivalent.

I had many reservations about using the military for a rescue force. GSG-9, being a civilian force, is dedicated to a single mission. I feared our military, with its many responsibilities, would not give sufficient attention to small-scale, stealthy, and unconventional operations. I thought the CIA would be a more logical organization to set up a unit like GSG-9. The CIA had sponsored, equipped, and trained people from other countries for unconventional warfare, although it had never possessed more than limited capabilities of its own. Although storming a hijacked aircraft, as at Mogadishu, was not within its present capabilities, the CIA, a small, elite organization, would be good at developing untraditional techniques for such operations. But Delta Force was already in existence, the need seemed urgent, and the military would have strongly resisted any move of the CIA in this area, so I had joined the other members of the SCC in recommending that Delta Force be developed into a GSG-9.

The Army had done that well and just in time; Beckwith's graduation exercise came the very night our embassy in Tehran was stormed. But nine days later something was missing. We couldn't find a way to get our hostages out of Iran if Delta did rescue them. We were not ready.

While planning for the rescue of the fifty-three hostages was being done in great secrecy, we were also surreptitiously working on a second rescue operation for six other Americans who had not been captured. One had been outside the embassy, and five others had managed to slip out as the mob stormed in. The Canadian ambassador, Kenneth B. Taylor, soon reported to the Canadian Foreign Office, which in turn informed our State Department, that two of the six Americans were now in his residence and four in the home of his deputy. We were, of course, anxious that the Iranians not learn about these six. Our media reported that there had been seventy Americans assigned to the embassy when it was captured, and they heard from the students that they were holding sixty-six. Some American and Canadian reporters, noting the discrepancy, deduced that four embassy staff must have some-how escaped.* After intervention by both the President and Cy Vance, these newspeople held the story.

I had a group of CIA operations experts studying how to rescue the six people hiding with the Canadians. Since we knew that even a hint that there were six American diplomats loose somewhere in Tehran might lead to their capture, the planning group of State Department and CIA people was kept to only a handful. There would be no SCC meetings. I was compartmenting this project down to a very few, just as Zbig had tried to hold the military planning group to a minimum. I did, however, keep the President, the Secretary of State, and Zbig well informed.

---

*The further discrepancy between the four embassy staff not accounted for and the six hiding with the Canadians comes from the fact that two Americans who were not government employees were inside the embassy when it was captured and were caught up in the affair.

· 6 ·

SEARCH FOR A STRATEGY

Where are Iran's power plants, Stan?

— Jimmy Carter,
November 13, 1979 [1]

AT THE DAILY SCC meeting on November 12, Day 9, the Secretary
of the Treasury, G. William Miller, reported that the Iranians were
about to stop selling us oil. We hastily agreed to beat them to the punch
and announced we would no longer purchase their oil.*

On Day 10 I was in my secondary office, in the Old Executive Office Building next door to the White House, eating lunch at my desk
when my secretary, Cele Velar, stepped in. "The President's appoint-
ments secretary just phoned to ask you to meet with the President at
two-thirty on Iran and the hostages."

I was glad I was downtown rather than at CIA headquarters, eight
miles away in Langley. It was easier to sit back and think in the quiet
of this lovely old building. With fifteen-foot ceilings, massive oak doors
capped with light transoms, deep and elaborate moldings, massive marble
fireplaces, and tall windows, it was, I thought, the most beautiful government building in Washington. My office, facing Pennsylvania Avenue and Blair House, was where I normally made my last preparations for the general intelligence briefings I gave the President twice a
week. Now I needed to set that task aside. What did the President

---

*At this time, any action that might reduce the flow of oil from Iran had to be
considered carefully. The balance between world demand and world supply was very
fragile. At the same time, we were conscious that, because oil is a fungible commod-
ity, Iranian oil would flow elsewhere into the world market.

want? This morning, as on every morning since the hostages were taken, I had sent the President a written intelligence briefing on the hostages. I had nothing new or different to tell him this afternoon.

Fifteen minutes ahead of time I walked across West Executive Avenue, separating the Executive Office Building from the White House, and went to Zbig's office in the West Wing. Zbig sat in on most of the President's meetings on foreign affairs. He told me he was also bringing David Aaron to this one. Neither of them knew what the President had on his mind. We walked down the hall to the waiting room outside the Oval Office. Nell Yates told us to go right in.

As we entered, the President left his desk and motioned us to join him on the couch and chairs in front of the fireplace. As always, he got down to business immediately. He wanted detailed, factual information about Iran, especially its vulnerabilities. What would it take to destabilize the government? How dependent was Iran on imports? What was its relationship with its neighbors? What were the critical points in its electrical power system? Where were the principal power plants? Were the complex F-14 fighter aircraft the United States had sold to Iran likely to be operational?

He fired one question after another at me, measuring his strengths against the Ayatollah's. I answered when I could and noted where follow-up information would help. I wondered whether he was thinking of using the CIA to try to undermine Khomeini. Was he considering whether an economic embargo could strangle the Iranians into giving up the hostages? Did he have in mind a military strike against critical facilities? I was surprised that so many of his questions implied military action.

The President said he knew from reading Zbig's summaries that the SCC was meeting for several hours a day to discuss options. I assumed he was also receiving advice privately from Vice President Walter F. (Fritz) Mondale, Chief of Staff Hamilton Jordan, Press Secretary Jody Powell, Zbig, Counsel Lloyd Cutler, and others close to him. Now he was explicit in asking me not only for facts, but also for my views on the policies being considered. He even asked me to have the CIA's experts work up alternative options. It was unusual for President Carter to forsake the traditional practice of keeping the DCI out of policy formulation. Once an intelligence chief begins to recommend policy, it becomes very difficult for him not to want his intelligence to support that policy. However honest a DCI may be, advocacy creates a mental filter that tends to give less credence to intelligence that does not support his policy choice.

And even if a DCI can both recommend policy and be objective, it may not appear that way to others, as we later learned when President Reagan's second Secretary of State, George Shultz, said he did not trust much of the intelligence he received from my successor, William Casey.[2] In this instance, President Carter was obviously willing to break this rule of intelligence if it would help solve the crisis. The President went so far as to ask me a direct policy question: "Should we put an embargo on trade with Iran?" I told him Iran could circumvent any embargo because many key countries depended on Iran for oil, and even our close allies probably would not cooperate if it hurt them.

This discussion gave me an opportunity to offer the only firm suggestion I had at the moment: to mine the harbors. I pointed out that we could put pressure on the Iranian economy by mining the ports, reducing the country's imports and exports to almost nothing and eliminating most of its outside income. This would not necessarily force the Iranians to release the hostages, but as their reserves of foreign exchange dwindled, they would have to assess the worth of holding our people. The onus for any damage or loss of life would be on those who attempted to run their ships through our minefields despite our warnings; or on the Iranians if they attempted to sweep the mines and encountered trouble.

Our meeting lasted forty-five minutes. Zbig and David Aaron rushed back to their offices and I to my car to take me up the George Washington Parkway to CIA headquarters, where I called together a few key staff members. I told them the President had asked us to come up with options as well as detailed information to help him formulate his own ideas. They understood the hazards of our getting into policy, but we agreed to restrict the effort to a small team that would do nothing else for however long it took. That evening I jotted down: "It's clear that the President of the United States has taken on the role of number one action officer on Iran. He's trying to study the situation so thoroughly that he can come up with his own solution. Apparently he feels we are just not supporting him adequately."

I believed President Carter needed more discussions with a range of knowledgeable advisers. He may have felt he was having full analytical discussions of the issues with his closest White House advisers, but there was a much broader and deeper pool of resources for him to tap. As usually happens when a major crisis is handled informally by an insider group holding ad hoc meetings without full staffing, the bureaucracy is left behind, unengaged. The big loss is the corporate knowledge the bureaucrats possess from having served many administrations. President Carter, in his determination to find something more effective than what we had come up with so far, needed to draw on that expertise. Although we in the SCC were not bereft of ideas, someone in the group opposed almost every suggestion, preventing us from making unambiguous recommendations. When the President wanted to expel Iranian diplomats, Cy pointed out that some of them were our best, most sympathetic lines of communication to Tehran. When the President wanted to ask our allies to break relations with Iran, I pointed out that, because our problem with Iran did not seem important to them, the request would antagonize them and gain us nothing. And on it went.

We seemed able to agree only on retaliating for moves the Iranians made. On Day 10, U.S. banks received reports that the Iranians were about to withdraw the sizable deposits they, along with other Middle Eastern oil producers, had made in the United States since the dramatic rise in the price of oil in 1973. Even while we debated what to do, the telexes would begin whirring and the funds would soon be out of American control. Bill Miller and his people at the Treasury Department moved quickly and gave the President a plan for freezing these assets. At about four the next morning, the Iranians began to withdraw funds. At 8:10 the President signed the order freezing all Iranian government assets in U.S. banks in the United States and abroad.

Bill Miller soon appeared at the SCC to tell us of a complication. Because any funds that the Iranian government placed in United States banks would automatically be frozen before they could reach the intended recipient, Americans exporting to the government of Iran would not receive payment. Cy Vance and Warren Christopher felt strongly that we should find ways to make it possible for the Iranians to continue purchasing our food and medicines. I argued that the Iranians probably had several months' worth of supplies on hand, and if they did not, they could quickly find other sources. It would help us if the Iranians realized they were losing a valuable source of important supplies. My argument fell on deaf ears. Cy reasoned that if the United States abandoned its concern for human welfare, the terrorists in Tehran would have achieved a victory. So before the day was over, the State Department announced that we would work out a way to continue selling food and medicine to Iran.

Next, Bill Miller was back to tell us it was probably illegal to block Iranian bank accounts in the foreign branches of U.S. banks. He recommended that we unblock them. This led to a heated discussion with Hamilton Jordan, who argued that to do so would make the President look weak and vacillating. After prolonged debate, we decided to sound out those allies where U.S. branch banks held Iranian assets. Over the next few days answers came back supporting our freezing of assets but suggesting that the legality of our doing so was questionable and would be brought before their national courts, where we would probably lose. The allies hoped, though, that it would take some time for that to happen. In the meanwhile, they would take no action to unfreeze the funds. The President decided to stand by his decision.

The SCC next accepted a recommendation to require the fifty thousand Iranian students in the country to report within thirty days to the Immigration and Naturalization Service to prove they had not violated the terms of their visas. The idea was to have the INS selectively deport those who were organizing pro-Khomeini demonstrations in a number of larger cities. Singling out Iranians for this visa review troubled no one, yet many of us had sat around the same table just two years before, revising the rules for intelligence collection inside the United States to strengthen the protection of American civil liberties, including the right of visiting foreigners to express their views.

Attorney General Benjamin R. Civiletti then raised another issue of civil liberties. He told us that pro-Khomeini students had asked to demonstrate in Lafayette Park across the street from the White House. The President's political advisers were aghast. They felt the President looked impotent enough in not having got the hostages released in well over a week. How could he have Iranians thumbing their noses at him on his doorstep? Ben estimated, though, that if he denied the permit and was taken to court, he might well lose on constitutional grounds. The feeling in the SCC was that he should take the chance and prohibit the demonstration. There was such a strong sense of urgency that Zbig called the President and asked whether he, Cy, and Ben could come upstairs to discuss the matter. They left, and our meeting ended. Late that afternoon, Ben Civiletti denied the permit.

At the SCC meeting the next day, Ben explained the President's reasoning. A pro-Khomeini demonstration might incite a counter-demonstration, and people could get hurt. If pro-Khomeini demonstrators were hurt, there might be reprisals against our hostages in Tehran. I thought that was stretching matters. The ink was hardly dry when

Ben came back to the SCC to tell us he was permitting a demonstration in Washington by a group that professed to be neither anti- nor pro-Khomeini, only against violence in Iranian-American relations. He said it would be unconstitutional to stop this kind of demonstration because there did not appear to be any logical connection to the safety of our hostages. We were drawing very fine constitutional lines.

On Day 14, November 17, I was distressed that we had yet to come up with an effective way to put pressure on Khomeini. We were still on the defensive. Our only offensive steps, like harassing Iranian students, were weak. There must be other options, I thought, but after two weeks of constant SCC and NSC meetings, plus the countless hours each of us had spent with his own staff, we were not finding them.

At the morning meeting on Day 17, Tuesday, November 20, Zbig told us that President Carter was exasperated by the SCC's lack of responsiveness and was en route from Camp David expressly to meet with us. Whenever he had suggested some new course of action, we had found numerous reasons that it could not be followed. That afternoon, I listened with a sinking feeling as he berated us and read us a list, of his own devising, of detailed actions he wanted to take. He also said we were neglecting such long-range issues as our relations with Iran after the crisis was over. Did it take the President of the United States to get this bureaucracy moving? President Carter was known for his penchant for detail, but his reaction on this day was more than that. He was justifiably frustrated because the process of bureaucratic coordination had caused us to do only what received near unanimous approval in the SCC — and that wasn't much.

Despite the President's admonitions and his presence, we got bogged down for twenty minutes working out the wording of a public statement warning the Iranians that we would feel free to retaliate with military force if any of the hostages was harmed. After only a brief discussion of other items, the President left, but with instructions that the SCC come to Camp David that Friday prepared to discuss both his ideas and the ultimate outlook for our position in the Persian Gulf region.

The SCC, thus, had the rest of Tuesday plus Wednesday and Thursday to prepare for the Camp David meeting. We started right then and met again on Wednesday and on Thursday, Thanksgiving. We discussed all of the President's initiatives. Except for Zbig, we were unanimous in rejecting every one. It seemed almost disloyal, but declaring diplomats persona non grata and breaking relations with Iran were not going to accomplish much. Others, like getting our allies to set a schedule for breaking relations and instituting an embargo, would take so long to effect that we found them not worth considering; we still believed the crisis would not last. If we had let the President down before, we were doing so again. Moreover, we never followed his request to review long-term issues, like how to keep the Soviets from using our contretemps with Iran to their advantage.

Day 20 was a mild autumn Friday. At 7:30 A.M., two helicopters with Zbig, Cy, Harold, Dave Jones, Jody Powell, and me took off from the back lawn of the White House and headed for Camp David. Ham Jordan was waiting at the landing pad and accompanied us into the heavily wooded compound. We passed the small cottage where I had visited with Anwar Sadat during the Camp David talks; then the much larger log cabin–style residence that was the President's. Finally, we entered a lodge in which there was a sizable conference room with a table that would seat about fifteen. The President was waiting.

Navy stewards served coffee. After they left, the President began to talk. His first and major premise was that we had only a matter of weeks to resolve the crisis. We could not let it become protracted. I suggested that while this was a reasonable objective, it did not necessarily fit the Iranians' plan. The most optimistic view we had come up with at the CIA was that following an extended Muslim holiday, Ashura, which was to begin in about two weeks, the Iranians might begin to release hostages. The CIA analysts believed, though, that they would drag out the process over a considerable period of time.

The President asked whether we could induce the Shah to leave the country. Fritz Mondale supported the idea and reviewed the benefits of doing so. I said that it could also be dangerous. If the Shah left, those holding the embassy would quickly recognize that they could no longer use threats to the American hostages as leverage to get the Shah back. Someone else would have the Shah. In frustration they might take it out on the hostages. The President, however, said he had made up his mind. The sooner the Shah left, the better. He wanted to know more about the Shah's physical condition and asked us to find ways to encourage him to leave.

Next he asked why we couldn't break diplomatic relations with Iran, close Iranian consulates in this country, and expel most of its diplomats. Cy, although he knew the President was becoming more frustrated, argued again that maintaining what slim contacts we had with Iran might be the only avenue to a solution. The President, seeing how strongly Cy felt, acceded and moved on.

He then argued that the combination of an economic embargo and mining the harbors could bring the Iranians to their knees. He had concluded that, first, they needed to import various foodstuffs, including corn for raising chickens; second, Khomeini would see the end of all commerce with us as a severe blow; and third, they badly needed military spare parts, especially because of the several armed insurgencies inside Iran. I argued that the Iranians could tighten their belts and hold out for a long time; spare parts for American-made fighter aircraft and naval ships were not necessary for dealing with their immediate military needs, putting down internal insurgencies; and we all knew the allies were not likely to impose an embargo soon. Since no one was enthusiastic about the use of military force, not even the mining, the whole discussion of this subject just died.

We moved on to Khomeini's latest threat of putting the hostages on trial and the students' renewed threat of killing them if we took military action. Both were alarming. The President had already made up his mind on how he would respond. If our people went on trial, we would mine some or all of Iran's ports. If even one hostage was harmed, we would bomb the Abadan refinery. But how could we get this message to Khomeini with maximum impact? I suggested that CIA operatives find a behind-the-scenes emissary. Cy preferred using the Swiss ambassador in Tehran, as the Swiss were representing us there. The President concurred. Later that day, he made a public statement that if the hostages were put on trial or harmed in any way, the consequences for Iran would be "extremely grave."

Next, Cy briefed us on the status of the indirect negotiations that had been going on secretly. Cy was working with Kurt Waldheim, Secretary General of the United Nations, and through him with an unnamed Iranian who had come to New York from Tehran. This person suggested that while the Iranians publicly were demanding the return of the Shah and his wealth, privately they were more interested in a public trial in which the United States would be condemned for having supported the Shah for so many years.

This led to a long discussion of what kind of insults and humiliations we would accept to get the hostages back. National honor, not just the release of the hostages, had become an issue, just as it had with Lyndon Johnson in considering what kind of confession he could sign in the *Pueblo* affair. We decided the United States could agree to a Wald-heim suggestion for organizing a commission to investigate Iran's complaint about past American support for the Shah, but only simul-taneously with the release of the hostages. We were, of course, con-cerned about whether such a commission would produce anti-Ameri-can propaganda, but everyone agreed we would have to take the chance.

I suggested promising to cooperate with such a commission, or al-most anything else, and then, once the hostages were out, reneging, on the grounds that we had agreed under duress. The President imme-diately and peremptorily said, "You know we can't do that, Stan." The aspect of working for Jimmy Carter that I liked most was that one always knew he was going to take the honest and honorable course. Here, though, he'd stuck to principle when I could easily have been tempted to be devious. Did we always have to play by gentlemen's rules when our opponents ignored them? The President was saying something close to yes.

He wasn't the first President to face that kind of choice. In 1790, Thomas Jefferson, as Secretary of State, proposed that we take Alge-rians hostages and trade them for our seamen being held in Algiers. He thought the Barbary States would accept a deal whereby, if the United States released two Algerian prisoners, they would release one American.[3] Nothing ever came of this suggestion, though Jefferson had opened the door to using what we would today call "covert ac-tion," or "dirty tricks," to fight terrorism. The Johnson administration turned in this direction when *Pueblo* was captured in 1968. According to Secretary of State Dean Rusk, "We considered seizing a North Ko-rean merchant vessel in retaliation, but . . . the North Koreans had coastal vessels only, no oceangoing ships."[4] Later, though, a story leaked to the press that the administration was considering capturing two fish-processing ships the North Koreans had purchased from the Netherlands and which were scheduled to begin the long sea journey from Europe to Asia. When this idea surfaced, the *New York Times* editorialized: "The seizure of innocent fishing vessels on the high seas is not a legitimate form of pressure in anybody's book. It would be an act of piracy."[5] Nothing came of this idea either.

The Camp David meeting ended, and we walked to the waiting he-licopters. Back on the lawn of the White House we dispersed, having decided not to meet on Saturday or Sunday. Thus, Days 21 and 22 would be the first without SCC meetings since Day 2. That afternoon, back at the office, I briefed my CIA hostage team on what had come out of Camp David: we would use military force if the hostages were placed on trial or harmed, but the real hope for release was to find acceptable terms for a negotiated deal. The only terms we could see as acceptable were release of the hostages followed by a UN commission of investigation.

On Monday, November 26, Day 23, Cy told us the unnamed Iranian envoy in New York had at first refused even to send those proposed terms back to Tehran. He thought them totally unacceptable. To him the issue of priority was a condemnation of the United States for its past association with the Shah; the hostages were a secondary problem. He relented and did send the terms to Tehran, but his attitude and Khomeini's peremptory refusal to receive Ramsey Clark and William Miller left me very skeptical about the prospects for negotiation. The gap between what was acceptable to the President and what Khomeini would agree to seemed immense. I could see no sign that we could close the gap either by pressure or persuasion.

I kept asking myself why a country of our political influence and economic and military power was even considering making a deal with a nation like Iran. Perhaps there were no other solutions, but I wondered if it was because the Carter team was not working well together. At our SCC meetings the discussion often could not stay on track. I recalled that just before Thanksgiving somebody asked Dave Jones a question on a military matter. He attempted to answer three times, but was interrupted each time by someone different. One person even completed Dave's sentence for him. Dave finally sat back, and no one bothered to ask him to finish his answer. Stress accounted for some of this, but overactive egos played a bigger part than they should have. And the strong philosophical differences between Cy and Zbig were also a key factor.

National Security Advisers and Secretaries of State and Defense had clashed before, notably under President Nixon when Henry Kissinger was the Adviser. But because President Nixon tended to follow Kissinger's advice more often than not, there was no stalemate, and foreign policy moved ahead in innovative ways. However, Jimmy Carter vacillated between Brzezinski and Vance, and they often canceled each other out.

Institutional factors also played a part. Everyone protected his organization's interests and turf. I was no less guilty than the rest. For instance, Zbig was attempting to keep as much control over the rescue mission as possible when he pushed for his Colonel Odom to meet with Ross Perot. I objected to Odom, not just because turning Perot over to the NSC staff was hardly the best approach, but because I wanted to keep the CIA as close as possible to the center of events. Both moves were part of a struggle for power, and neither Zbig nor I gave much consideration to which approach was better for getting the job done.

Normally, though, the departments and agencies should develop recommendations. The National Security Affairs Adviser should lay out for the President objective comparisons of the positions recommended by the departments and agencies. Unfortunately, the President's assistant — first Henry Kissinger and then Zbig — came to be more an advocate than an arbitrator. That change pushed more of the problem upstairs to the President, who had to do all of the adjudicating himself. He also had to determine whether his assistant was projecting a fair representation of the views of others or introducing a bias toward the position he favored. I could see that it must have been difficult for strong personalities like Kissinger and Brzezinski to stay neutral. Lieutenant General Brent Scowcroft, who held the position between those two, was in my view a better fit, because he was more willing to stay out of the limelight and facilitate decision making for the President.*

The fundamental reason, then, that we were not working well as a team was that Cy was pushing in one direction and Zbig in another. Cy believed in keeping the door open for Iran to engage us in reasonable discussions. The Iranians, after all, felt they had a legitimate grievance, and held us responsible for much of what they hated of the Shah's regime. Cy felt that if we antagonized or humiliated them, it would take longer for them to deal with us, even through intermediaries. He wanted to apply whatever pressures we could through third parties, like the United Nations, countries friendly to revolutionary Iran, or world leaders who had rapport with Khomeini. He hoped not to drive more of a wedge between us and the Iranians; rather, he wanted to make them realize the hostage issue could cause them harm by isolating Iran from the community of nations. Cy's approach required considerable patience.

Zbig and, I believe, most of the rest of us felt this instance of hostage taking was so heinous that it had to be solved before we could discuss Iran's perceived grievances. Because we were both the ag-

---

*Brent Scowcroft was reappointed to the position by President Bush in January 1989.

grieved party and a very powerful nation, we assumed we could find a way to apply the necessary amount of pressure to the Iranians. We did not want to wait for them to come to their senses; we wanted to act. That attitude was strengthened on Day 15, when the Iranians released the thirteen black and female hostages, who brought back appalling stories of the conditions of imprisonment: hostages in the same room not being allowed to talk to one another; people bound hand and foot, lacking food and news, and subjected to other psychological pressures. We wanted action — now.

There was a problem, though, in that we activists could not think of pressures that might be effective other than punitive military actions, and those could put the lives of the hostages at risk. We were almost forced to consider Cy's strategy of less obtrusive diplomatic pressures combined with patient negotiations, but that did not stop us from continuing to search for active options.

There was no way to stop riding two horses.

HOIST ON OUR
OWN LEGAL PETARD

No funds . . . may be expended for covert operations until the President finds that each such operation is important to the national security.

— The Hughes-Ryan
Amendment of 1974[1]

WE ALL FELT frustration at our lack of progress, but mine was compounded by legal impediments. The first concerned the Shah. Fritz Mondale, who became the point man to find a way to induce him to leave our country, wanted to know what the Shah's plans were. He assumed the Shah would talk about his plans with his friends and family on the phone, and urged me to tap it. At Camp David the President joined him in telling me to listen in on the Shah's hospital phone.

The CIA had just been through the Church Committee investigations (under Senator Frank Church) of alleged CIA wrongdoings in the 1950s and 1960s, and was still reeling from the beating it had taken in the press, some of it justified, some of it sensationalist. When I took office, there was no question in my mind that the President and the Congress wanted the CIA to operate within the law, and it was my intent to see that it did. One of the first issues in which I became involved, in the spring of 1977, was an administration draft of legislation governing electronic eavesdropping. The law that was subsequently enacted, the Foreign Intelligence Surveillance Act of 1978 (FISA),[2] protected not just American citizens, but American "persons," those foreigners legally residing in the United States. The Shah appeared to be such a person. If he was, then tapping his telephone in the hospital was controlled by the FISA. I asked the CIA's general counsel, Daniel B. Silver, to give me a legal opinion.

Dan said it would be illegal; that is, we could not produce the justification required by FISA. He wanted to get a more definitive ruling from the Attorney General, though. When Ben Civiletti agreed with Dan, I thought that would be the end of it. It was not. Zbig, determined that Ben and I find a way around this interpretation of the law, let me know that I had not made myself popular in the White House by insisting on obtaining a legal ruling. Ironically, it was Fritz Mondale who in 1977 had been in the forefront of this legislation, designed to protect Americans from unwarranted intrusion on their privacy. The law did that not by prohibiting telephone taps, but by creating a system of checks to ensure that no tap was authorized unless there was good cause to believe that the government was in need of *foreign* intelligence. This was a protection against arbitrary or deliberate domestic political spying on Americans. The FISA now confronted the administration with a barrier of its own making.

There were two highly technical issues involved. The first was the status of the Shah as a temporary resident in our country. If we could declare him to be "an agent of a foreign power," the rules were less stringent. I believed that, although the Shah claimed to be the legitimate ruler of Iran, he had, de facto, no authority to speak for his country. He represented only himself. That was a fine line.

The second issue was whether a phone tap was justified, since the law required that we employ the least intrusive means to obtain the needed information. I believed that we could learn of his intentions by the neat expedient of asking him. Then, too, he was in touch with many people, some of whom were bound to talk.

Finally, the Shah was accustomed to SAVAK, his Iranian intelligence arm, tapping phones with abandon and may have assumed his phone was tapped. If so, he would avoid using it for private discussions. I felt strongly that not only was the tap probably illegal, but it was also a bad idea.

Zbig, Ben, Dan, and I debated, researched, and argued for four acrimonious days. Zbig contended that neither we, in drafting the legislation, nor the Congress, in passing it, intended that the FISA tie our hands in important matters of national security. The law was to protect Americans, and the Shah was not an American. What Zbig was asserting was a long-standing constitutional opinion that the Executive has primacy in carrying out foreign affairs (an interpretation later used to justify Lieutenant Colonel Oliver North's excluding the Congress from his efforts on behalf of American hostages in the Iran-contra affair). Tensions were mounting. On Day 24, Zbig gave me an ultimatum: place the tap, write the President to tell him why I would not, or resign.

I searched my conscience. Was I being stubborn? I too believed that violating the Shah's privacy was a small price to pay for helping to secure the release of the hostages. But, like it or not, we had a law that governed our decisions. Ben and I were basing our position on what we believed the law intended. Zbig was insisting on the most technical interpretation. He sent me a memorandum saying that the information the President needed was not just hearsay about the Shah's intentions; he required actual transcripts of what the Shah said about leaving the United States. That all but ruled out our use of less intrusive methods, like reports from third parties. The tap now was not so clearly illegal as to be worth forcing the issue all the way to the President, but it was distressing that the best Ben and I were able to do was slow down the juggernaut of Executive determination.

Ironically, the tap was never needed. The Shah was open and cooperative and told us his plans. This small but vexing issue, though, had consumed an inordinate amount of time and had strained almost to the breaking point the relations of an already poorly functioning team of presidential advisers. Ben and I would face several other legal issues before the hostages came home, and interpretation of conflicts between laws and national security would become a central point in the next administration's handling of terrorism.

My next legal problem concerned preparations for the rescue of the Canadian Six, as we came to call the Americans hidden in Canadian residences in Tehran. The CIA was creating new identities for them, ones that gave them reasons for being in Iran. Whatever means we used to extricate them, they would have to be prepared for interrogation by police, Revolutionary Guard patrols on the streets, border guards, and airport customs inspectors. This was clearly not intelligence work, which is limited by legal definition to the collection and evaluation of *information* about foreign countries. Rather, it was *making something happen*. When an intelligence agency attempts to influence what happens in foreign countries by secret means, it is carrying out a "covert action." By the provision in law cited at the beginning of the chapter, the President must approve of all CIA covert actions. He must also notify the Congress "in a timely manner" each time he approves of one.

In this case we knew that the slightest leak would almost certainly lead to the Iranians' ferreting out the Canadian Six. At the least it would greatly increase the risks for those trying to extricate them. Since we didn't want to tell anyone not vitally involved in this rescue effort what we were planning, I recommended using the loophole of "in a timely manner," waiting for a more timely moment to inform the Congress that the President had approved this covert action. At the same time, I worried about the implications of doing this. When congressional committees are bypassed, they feel strong justification for tightening the law. Already some members had suggested requiring *prior notification* of all covert actions. That, I thought, could make some too risky. Consequently, I had always been as forthcoming as possible with the Congress, so as not to stir up those who would tighten controls too severely.

Next, and complicating the same problem, Dan was carefully monitoring the CIA's expanding activities in support of the possible military rescue of the fifty-three hostages in the embassy and Foreign Ministry. Here again we were doing more than intelligence work, that is, more than the gathering of information. The military's latest rescue plan would send Delta Force to the outskirts of Tehran by helicopter. The CIA was to provide trucks to move the troops from there into the city, so our operatives were now out looking for trucks to buy and a warehouse to store them in. This was a covert action and required presidential approval and notification of Congress. But the President had not yet chosen to inform the Congress that he was planning a military rescue operation, and was not obligated to do so under the War Powers Act of 1973.[3] If we were to inform Congress that the CIA was supporting the planning for a rescue operation, we would, of course, tip the President's hand. Recognizing this, Dan Silver ruled that if the President was eventually going to notify the Congress of the rescue operation under the War Powers Act, we could refrain until then. Dan felt strongly, and I fully agreed, that it was important for us to receive assurance that the President was, in due course, going to notify the Congress. Obtaining a written assurance from Zbig to that effect was difficult, but I insisted and finally prevailed.

Having to deal with these three legal problems made me wonder whether in the previous few years the Ford and Carter administrations, and the Congress, had gone too far in establishing controls over our intelligence activities. Some of the architects of those controls were now chafing under what they had created. What would happen if we returned to the less stringent controls of the past? President Nixon had run into trouble because his White House staff had pressured various agencies of the government, including the CIA, to take actions that were, if not illegal, certainly questionable. Circumventing the law seemed important and justifiable to Nixon and his men. However, Nixon's abuse of the enormous powers of the presidency contributed to his downfall and shook Americans' confidence in their government.

It was partly with Watergate in mind that we had established the rules and passed laws to supervise the secret activities of the CIA in accordance with the democratic principle that all elements of government must be under control. Now the Carter administration was chafing under these rules and laws. And the next administration would go to extraordinary lengths to circumvent them. The pragmatism of dealing with terrorism can run head on into principle.

· 8 ·

GETTING TO TEHRAN

Why not convert a supertanker into a disguised aircraft carrier for helicopters and sail it into the Gulf?

— Suggestion to the CIA from
Charles Rittenbury of
Tulsa, Oklahoma,
November 1979

WHILE we in Washington were wrestling with the legal problems concerning to the CIA's preparations for receiving the rescue force in Tehran, our people on the spot were facing more formidable challenges in obtaining the vast amount of detailed information needed for rescue planning. The first order of business was to scout the embassy, its defenses, and the location of the hostages. The next was to purchase the trucks and find a place to hide them.

Moving our people in and out of Tehran to direct these operations was no simple task. Westerners were harassed at the airport when arriving and departing, Khomeini's Revolutionary Guards accosted foreigners on the streets, and Iranians staged riots in front of our embassy every day, whipping up an anti-American fervor that made just being in the vicinity dangerous for non-Iranians. We looked desperately for CIA people whose cover would hold up under rigorous scrutiny. Most who went into Tehran once during this period would not volunteer for a second shot because the chances of being recognized — and brutalized — were too great. We found "Bob," though, a retired officer of foreign origin and irrepressible self-confidence. He was perfect for what had to be done. Fortunately, he was also willing. Bob traveled in and out of Iran repeatedly during this period to make the necessary arrangements for Delta Force.*

---

*Because Bob took such risks, and his contribution was so important, when it was all behind us, I took him to the Oval Office to receive thanks from the President.

Then on Day 25, November 28, Zbig shocked me when he mentioned off-handedly that the President had ordered all planning for a rescue mission to cease. The Joint Chiefs of Staff had met with the President at Camp David six days earlier, largely to talk about the military budget. Not surprisingly, the rescue planning had come up. The Joint Chiefs were so pessimistic that the President did not think the benefits of continued planning justified the risk that a leak might jeopardize the negotiations Cy was conducting. He ordered an all-stop. It was now clear it was Zbig who had been pushing the pace of the rescue planning, not the President. I suspected it was only in his discussion with the Joint Chiefs that the President learned how much effort was going into the planning.

That the President's decision had been made during a meeting on quite another subject, and no one bothered to notify the rest of us, was a typical lack of coordination. What the President did not know was that I was on the verge of authorizing some high-risk entries into Iran. If we stopped collecting intelligence and searching for trucks, the loss of time could not be recouped should he later change his mind. We couldn't catch up by simply doing things faster; if clandestine operations are going to work, they must be done at a natural tempo lest they attract attention. I pondered whether to lay this out for the President or to proceed with the preparations. There was no doubt in my mind that our sending operatives into Tehran posed a greater risk to Cy's negotiations than the planning in Washington that the President had stopped.

What, though, if the students killed a hostage a day until we delivered the Shah to them? One option for us was a military attack, but that would probably lead to the death of more hostages. Another option was an immediate rescue effort, but we in the CIA were not ready to provide the support necessary for such a mission, and I did not know how long it would be before we were. Wanting the CIA to be ready to play its role whenever the President gave the green light, I decided not to slow down what we were doing, but to keep an even closer eye on how we were doing it. I knew I was sticking my neck out, but at such times I often recalled what Chief of Naval Operations Admiral Arleigh A. Burke had told me when I was a young naval officer: "No commanding officer is worth his salt, Turner, who does not occasionally exceed his authority." Fortunately, it wasn't long before Zbig apparently brought the President around, because the rescue planning group gradually resumed its regular secret meetings.

At one of those, Dave Jones informed us that the Joint Chiefs had selected Army Major General James B. Vaught to command the overall rescue force and Charlie Beckwith to lead Delta Force. Beckwith would be out in the field with Delta, practicing on a mock-up of the embassy in Tehran. Jim Vaught would be in the Pentagon, developing the operation plan directly under Dave Jones, and would be responsible for bringing in the Navy, Marine Corps, Air Force, and CIA as needed. It was routine to appoint a single commander when several of the military services were involved. In this case, having a general officer in charge would ensure that the operation received the attention it deserved. It was unusual, though, for the commander of such a small operation to work directly for the Joint Chiefs of Staff. The more normal arrangement would have been for Vaught to report to a four-star theater commander, in this case, the Commander-in-Chief, Pacific (CincPac), whose zone of responsibility stretched to Iran. But the special command arrangement under which Vaught reported to Dave Jones was expressly designed to keep this operation, with its highly political implications, under tight control in Washington. Also, by narrowing the number of people involved, it reduced the chance of leaks.

I thought the choice of Jim Vaught a good one. In 1976, when I was Commander-in-Chief of NATO's forces in Southern Europe, Jim was a brigadier general assigned to a subordinate command in Izmir, Turkey. He briefed me once on plans for the defense of Turkey. While he did not seem particularly comfortable in the role of a briefing officer, he was forceful and direct, and I could easily envision him out in the field, driving his troops hard but commanding their respect. And I was glad to have in this position someone I knew.

When Jim came out to Langley and called on me, on Day 30, he described in detail his idea for the operation. He had ruled out the Ross Perot approach of having the troops infiltrate through the airport. As I suspected when watching Beckwith's display in the summer, it would be almost impossible for fifty to sixty athletic young American soldiers not to draw attention to themselves in this area of the world, whatever disguise we might dream up for them. He had also ruled out hiding the troops in large cargo trucks and driving them into Iran from Turkey. Border inspections were too thorough. And he had eliminated the option of parachuting his troops into the outskirts of Tehran. The risk of their landing scattered or injured was too great.

That's why Jim had decided to send his troops into the area of Tehran by helicopter. Anyway, helos seemed to be the only way to get the hostages from Tehran to the airfield at Manzariyeh, whence they would be airlifted out of the country. The sticking point was that we did not have helos that could fly the thousand miles from an aircraft carrier in the Arabian Sea to Tehran without refueling. The Navy still refused to risk taking a carrier into the Persian Gulf, and the State Department was still not willing to ask Turkey for permission to launch from its territory.

Jim's approach to refueling was to drop bladders of fuel by parachute into a remote desert area between the Arabian Sea and Tehran and then have the helos fuel from them en route to Tehran. He was also weighing the idea of capturing a remote, little-used Iranian Air Force airfield at Nain, about two hundred miles short of Tehran, and refueling there. Either way, the helos would have to fly at night to avoid detection. However, even in winter, the nights were not long enough to enable Delta Force to fly from the Arabian Sea all the way to Tehran, rescue the hostages, fly to Manzariyeh, and then out of Iran (see Map 6). The men would have to lay over somewhere the first night and complete the operation on the second. If the rescue force stopped at Nain on the way in, for the next twenty-four hours they would somehow have to prevent anyone from finding out they had been there. Jim's plan was to have enough troops stay behind at the airfield at Nain to capture and lock up anyone who might come out to the base. It would, though, take only one telephone call to Tehran to sound the alert. The students would then have time to scatter the hostages around the city, kill them, or man the machine guns they had mounted on the embassy walls, and wait for an unsuspecting Delta Force to arrive.

At just this time, Charles Rittenbury, an oil man from Tulsa, Oklahoma, approached the CIA with an idea for getting a rescue force into and out of Iran. Like Perot, Rittenbury was a millionaire who was inquisitive and ingenious enough to assume we would be planning a rescue mission. He deduced we would need helicopters and that range would be a problem. He came to Washington to suggest converting several very large oil tankers into disguised helicopter platforms. These pseudo-helo carriers could move up into the Persian Gulf without risk of attack and without arousing suspicion. It was an imaginative idea, and we discussed it with him for some time, but I concluded that the hostage crisis would be over well before we could modify tankers and get them to the Persian Gulf. That was a bad judgment, one based on a continuing view that this unprecedented affront to the rules of diplomacy could not go on much longer.

Thus we continued with Jim's plan, under which the helos would be refueled in the middle of the first night, either from the bladders in the

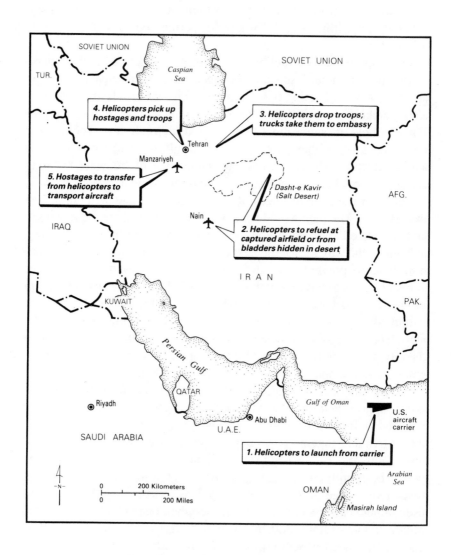

MAP 6. PROJECTED RESCUE PLAN

desert or at the Nain airfield. They would then carry Delta Force to a remote area Bob had found about seventy miles east of Tehran. Bob thought the men and their helos could hide there undetected during the next day. On the second night, the CIA would send the trucks it had obtained and hidden to pick up the troops and drive them into the city. Once at the embassy, Delta Force would scale the wall around the embassy compound, storm the building or buildings where the hostages were being held, and gather them up to leave. The helos would arrive from the hiding spot east of Tehran, land on the embassy grounds, load up the hostages, and carry them away to Manzariyeh.

Satellite photographs soon revealed, however, that the Iranians had erected what looked like telephone poles on the only open area inside the embassy compound where a helicopter could land. However, one of our agents in Tehran noted that a soccer stadium right across the street from the back of the embassy would be a satisfactory alternative. Once the hostages were freed, Delta could guide them to the stadium, and the helos would lift everyone to Manzariyeh, which an Army unit would have captured after landing in large transport aircraft. Everyone would then depart from Iran in those aircraft, leaving the helos behind.

It was a good plan but a complex one, with many points of potential failure. The trick would be to lower the risk of failure at each point. But there were two big problems. The first was the refueling of the helos. The second was knowing whether the hostages were still in the embassy compound and, if so, where. We remembered that a well-executed U.S. raid on a prison camp at Son Tay in North Vietnam in 1970 had failed because the prisoners were not there. Getting information from inside the embassy compound was proving to be very difficult. There were rumors that the students had taken some of the hostages to other locations in Tehran to foil a rescue effort, but we were not sure. We knew that some of the Americans had been shifted from building to building within the compound, but we needed to get someone inside the compound to verify exactly where every person was being held.

Jim Vaught also needed to know the precise route the trucks should take from the hiding place to the embassy. If trucks with troops had to shoot their way through even one checkpoint, the alarm would be sounded. But Bob, and the Iranians he had recruited to help him, were doing a good job of scouting those roads. They felt sure there were ways around the checkpoints. It worried Jim, however, that Bob was neither American nor military. He wanted one of his own people on the scene.

Because of Jim's concern, I anticipated the likelihood of friction developing over the reliability of our intelligence. I wanted to prevent any misunderstandings or recriminations. I was also worried that if Jim was not confident of our people, he might turn to other sources, which I knew would be less reliable. I asked him to give me a list of the intelligence data he needed in order of priority and told him I would send him our best answers in writing twice a week, along with an assessment of our level of confidence in each item.

Jim and I met several times during December, and the White House group meetings continued in Zbig's office several times a week. But by the end of the year, Day 58, the Joint Chiefs still did not have a plan they would endorse or a rescue force fully trained. Nor were we in the CIA ready to play our role.

Only once did the NSC or SCC discuss military options other than a rescue. That was at the Camp David meeting just after Thanksgiving, when we talked about bombing the refinery at Abadan and mining the principal Iranian ports. Harold Brown and Dave Jones showed no interest in discussing other military operations, even in a small planning group, composed of Harold, Dave, Zbig, and me, that met periodically to evaluate possible military attacks on Iran. I understood the reluctance of military men to put too many options on the table lest civilian leaders patch together a military action that might be clever but unsound. But I believed the President deserved a longer menu from which to choose. He also needed to be informed of where punitive military action might lead. What would happen if he tried mining harbors, bombing Abadan, or both, and the Iranians still hung on to the hostages? He would then have to choose between widening the operation and retreating. I was concerned that Jimmy Carter might be dragged, slowly and almost involuntarily, into an increasing use of force, as we had been in Vietnam.

Because Cy Vance's negotiations were being held very quiet, and a rescue mission and punitive attacks were discussed in very small groups, there were only a couple of people who could give the President advice on the relative merits of all of his options. At one SCC meeting, I suggested we lay out and compare all the possibilities, military and other, to see exactly where we stood. Immediately, Jody Powell and Ham Jordan got up to leave, saying they could not be part of any discussion of military options. I did not see why Jody and Ham, two of Jimmy Carter's closest advisers, could not be involved when the political implications of any military action were immense. Zbig, however, was extremely distressed that I had raised the subject when they were present. He said he had rigid orders from the President on the matter.

STRATEGY BY DEFAULT

The Security Council urgently calls, once again, on the Government of the Islamic Republic of Iran to release immediately all persons of United States nationality being held as hostages in Iran.

— From Resolution 461,
December 31, 1979 [1]

M Y V I E W that we were not serving the President well was reinforced at an SCC meeting on November 28, Day 25, when Zbig read us a list, compiled by the President, of six approaches, in sequence of severity. Again, the President seemed to be the only one taking time to think about strategy. His list included two political, two economic, and two military initiatives.

1. Obtain condemnation from friendly countries and the United Nations of Iran's holding of hostages. The objective would be to make Iran feel isolated.
2. Effect the earliest graceful and humane departure of the Shah from the United States.
3. Establish an economic embargo on Iran and request friendly nations to join us.
4. Ask the United Nations Security Council to impose economic sanctions on Iran under Article VII of the UN Charter.
5. Mine some of Iran's harbors and threaten stronger military punishments if any hostages were harmed, but promise to lift the blockade when the hostages were released.
6. Make visible preparations for punitive military action in case any of the hostages was harmed.

After digesting these points, I was encouraged. At least we had a basis for looking at a solution as more than a series of reactive steps.

But I was also discouraged. Two key options were not included on the President's list: a rescue mission and a negotiated release. We all knew that the primary thrust of our current strategy was to negotiate, even if it was not being discussed in the SCC.

As chief of intelligence I had the advantage of keeping abreast of what was going on in the negotiations; I could read the intelligence reports about foreign reactions to them. They were not going well. All sorts of intermediaries and would-be intermediaries were popping up. In the main they were secular "moderates" in the Iranian government who wanted to resolve the hostage problem. Unfortunately, none had the authority to fulfill promises he might make. And in time, any moderate who favored release found himself outflanked by radicals, who accused him of being soft on what Khomeini had labeled us, "the Great Satan." Our hostages had become part of the continuing internal Iranian power struggle.

On Day 31, December 4, the President called a meeting of the NSC to review his proposed six points. On the first, the condemnation of Iran, we had already asked the International Court of Justice in The Hague for a ruling that Iran's action in holding the hostages was illegal. The President decided at this meeting to send Ben Civiletti to The Hague to press the case. As it turned out, on December 15 the court, with remarkable speed, unanimously issued a preliminary ruling in our favor. Iran announced that it would ignore the court.

Also, as a result of a petition we had previously filed, the United Nations Security Council on the same day passed a resolution calling for a "peaceful settlement of the hostage problem" through immediate release of all Americans being held in Iran. Iran's Foreign Minister, Sadeq Ghotbzadeh, quickly responded that achieving a "peaceful settlement" would require that the United States extradite the Shah. This revealed the extent of the problem we were facing. Ghotbzadeh simply did not understand that we would never give up the Shah to certain death. But it made no difference; Iran ignored the resolution. On Day 39, December 12, President Carter used this as a reason to reduce the number of Iranian diplomats in the United States from 218 to 35, something he had been wanting to do all along, but which the SCC had backed Cy in resisting.

There was no discussion of the second point, encouraging the Shah to leave. All dealings with the Shah were being handled separately and secretly, but at an SCC meeting on December 15, Zbig announced that, as the result of several trips Ham Jordan and Lloyd Cutler had made to Panama to persuade General Omar Torrijos to accept him, the Shah had decided to leave that very day for Panama. I was still concerned that the Iranians might see this as our way of making it more difficult for them to get their hands on the Shah, but his departure had no visible effect on them, good or bad.

On the two economic alternatives, everyone thought a unilateral economic embargo would be ineffective. Some believed it would push the Iranians into breaking off further negotiations. The only hope anyone saw was that if the allies joined in sanctions, the Iranians might see the situation as extremely serious. Consequently, the President decided to limit our immediate action to pressing friendly nations to join us. He approved sending a team to Europe to cajole our key allies. Representatives of both the State and Treasury Departments were to leave immediately to pave the way for Cy, who would follow a week later in conjunction with a NATO meeting.

Under the President's rules, the two punitive military options could not be discussed, even in as restricted a forum as the NSC.

The meeting then took an unusual turn. The President, in effect, dismissed Dave Jones and me by announcing that only "statutory members" of the NSC were to remain. He made an exception of Zbig, a non-member, as secretary of the NSC. At first I took this as a personal affront, but after reflection thought the President may have wanted to discuss the domestic political aspects of the hostage situation. It would have been inappropriate for the Chairman of the Joint Chiefs and Director of Central Intelligence, both of whom must be strictly apolitical, to be present.

Two days later, however, I found that more than political concerns had been covered. I received a copy of a follow-up memorandum from Zbig reminding Cy to explore with some of our allies the possibility of joint undercover efforts to strengthen the opposition to Khomeini and to bring about a more moderate government in Iran. This would involve providing advice and financial support secretly to so-called moderate political elements.

I was dumfounded. What had been agreed upon was clearly a covert action, and the CIA would have most of the responsibility.* I should have been given the opportunity to offer an opinion on the risks and

---

*There was also agreement to explore the possibility of obtaining military-base rights in several countries around the Indian Ocean, a topic on which Dave Jones's expertise would have been very useful.

probabilities of success of the covert action, especially since CIA people might have to put their lives on the line. Zbig was trying to shift control of this action to the NSC staff, turning the advisory staff into an action agency, something we would see in spades in the Iran-contra affair.

Some move toward covert action was almost inevitable. Historically, when there are no open options, Presidents and their staffs turn to covert ones. The Carter administration had inherited virtually no continuing covert actions from President Ford and DCI George Bush. Until now there had been only limited enthusiasm for changing that. This sudden shift indicated how desperately we were casting about for ways to solve the hostage problem. It also showed a naïveté about what could be accomplished covertly, springing from one of the CIA's better known covert successes, the overthrow of Prime Minister Mohammed Mossadegh in 1953. What made this new idea naïve was that the situation in Iran in 1979 was so different from that in 1953. Covert actions to overthrow governments work best when the situation is unstable and only a small push is needed to change it, as was true with Mossadegh. Covert action is far less likely to bring about the reorientation of a government that enjoys wide support, as did Khomeini's.

When I showed Zbig's memo to the covert action specialists at the CIA, they were very doubtful. They did not think we could get help from our allies without the plan leaking. Nor did they believe any foreign intelligence service was capable of manipulating the Khomeini government covertly. I urged Cy to play it in low key with the allies, neither alarming them nor drawing too much attention to our move toward covert action. On December 9, Day 36, Cy headed off to Bonn, Rome, Paris, London, and Brussels. In his discussions, he found no enthusiasm for trying to install a more moderate government in Iran through covert influence. Nor did the Europeans have helpful ideas on how we might do so. That left the ball in the CIA's court, where it should have been in the first place. We had already contacted anti-Khomeini Iranians but were skeptical of their usefulness. Those living outside Iran held exaggerated beliefs about being able to return home and become contenders for power. They were all talk. Those inside Iran could not risk drawing attention to themselves; they were unwilling to talk.

On Cy's trip to Europe, he urged his counterparts to stop arms sales to Iran and ban new financial credits, suggesting that we might resort to military force if they did not help us solve the problem in nonmilitary ways. This did not move the Europeans, who refused to jeopardize their commercial positions in Iran. The best they would promise was participation in an embargo if one was mandated by the Security Council.

When Cy returned, then, we only had two choices on economic pressure: ask the Security Council for a resolution or do nothing. The risk was that if we forced a vote in the Security Council and the Soviets vetoed it, the U.S. Senate in retribution might kill the SALT II treaty then under consideration. Just as our political stake in Iran had made the President reluctant to close down the embassy in Tehran when he admitted the Shah, so we now had a clash between political objectives and dealing with terrorism. President Carter, who wanted very badly to see SALT II ratified, knew a Soviet veto of sanctions against Iran was quite possible, because tension with the USSR was increasing because of its military buildup on the border with Afghanistan. Nonetheless, he took his chances on the treaty and chose to help the hostages all he could by pressing the UN for an embargo.

When Cy approached Waldheim on December 19, the Secretary General asked for a delay of several days because he was involved in "intensive discussions" with the Iranians.[2] Nothing came of those discussions, so on December 21 we formally requested the Security Council "to consider measures which should be taken to induce Iran to comply with its international obligations."[3]

Waldheim, though, was determined to continue talking with the Iranians. After numerous sessions with him both in New York and Washington, Cy finally worked out a compromise. Waldheim would go to Tehran, not to negotiate a settlement, but to determine whether there was a chance for useful discussions. He was to report back to the Security Council on January 7. If there had been no progress, the council would "adopt effective measures" against Iran, meaning economic sanctions. Resolution 461 confirming this plan passed the Security Council on New Year's Eve.

With Waldheim flying off to Tehran, our fifty-eight-day hostage crisis passed into 1980.

· 10 ·

TAKING STOCK

It wasn't until I saw the grief and hope on the faces of their wives and mothers and fathers that I felt the personal responsibility for their lives. It's an awesome burden.

— Jimmy Carter,
November 9, 1979 [1]

ON JANUARY I, 1980, Day 59, I had the opportunity to step back and look at where we were after almost two months of the crisis. Unfortunately, I had to fly to the West Coast to deliver the eulogy at the funeral of Commander Walter D. Williams, a Navy pilot who had been my aide for several years, including a brief period at the CIA. He had been killed in an accident at sea. The loss of Butch Williams, for whom I had profound respect and affection, was a terrible blow. I found myself unable to open my briefcase and plow through the stacks of paperwork I always took on long flights. In the uninterrupted hours on the plane, though, it was inevitable that I would reflect on the problem that had absorbed so much of our time since November 4. There had been, for instance, thirty-six meetings of the SCC, ranging from forty-five minutes to two hours, and countless meetings within our departments or agencies.

What struck me first was that we were still so thoroughly disorganized. Secretly, one team was trying to negotiate; another was planning a military rescue; still another was assessing punitive military operations; and covert action was being discussed without the benefit of those most knowledgeable and experienced. Openly, we were trying diplomatic and economic initiatives and hoping the public would see these as significant actions. I was sufficiently concerned about the lack of direction and coordination that back on December 12 I had asked for a private meeting with the President.

I first stressed to him the danger of compartmented groups. Many people with important contributions to make were frequently excluded from meetings, and those of us in charge of departments or agencies were constantly told not to tell anyone in our organizations about a particular activity or plan. I suggested that he was not benefiting from the full expertise of his advisers, let alone their staffs. The proof that we were not giving him adequate support was the number of times he had had to bring his own proposals to the table. I did not feel, however, that this argument had much effect.

Second, I said I was seriously concerned that the controls over the intelligence apparatus established by President Ford and himself were being abused. I was frustrated at having been pressed to skirt the law to tap the Shah's telephone; if we allowed ends to justify our means, and bypassed the law, we were repeating abuses of the past. The CIA can be strong, I argued, only if it has congressional and, ultimately, public support. And that will come only if it does not indulge in the kinds of activities that undermined public trust before. The President said he agreed completely.

Third, I emphasized our inability to launch a rescue operation, even five weeks after the hostages had been taken, largely as a result of the U.S. military's concentrating almost exclusively on the defense of Europe since the end of World War II and neglecting preparations for possible problems elsewhere, like the one we now faced. I hoped that once this crisis was behind us, the President would examine carefully what our military should do to be ready for likely challenges in a world much changed since 1945. I thought the President accepted this as something to consider, but not during the current crisis.

Within days of my getting these concerns off my chest, though, I saw that we would continue to pursue the compartmented approach to decision making. The President was certainly entitled to his own style, which had made him as successful as he was. I was probably underestimating the importance to him of curtailing leaks that could scotch the negotiations or risk incensing the hostage holders. And he was undoubtedly getting a broad range of views during his various private meetings. For instance, after his meeting with me of November 13, when he asked for options from the CIA's experts, I had taken two of them to meet with him. We gave him a few ideas. None was earthshaking, but if other people had been in on that discussion, our ideas might have sparked still better suggestions from them. What worried me most about the lack of dialogue and interchange of ideas was that we were not admitting to ourselves that nothing we had done seemed to hold any promise of success.

Zbig continued to push for covert action. After his failure to involve the Europeans, he set up a new steering group to develop and oversee covert actions against Iran. The committee was just another attempt to circumvent the CIA because of our low estimate of the prospects for successful covert action in this instance. Sure enough, Zbig soon put before the committee a sizable list of covert actions developed by the NSC staff. All of them seemed unrealistic to me. Most were feats of derring-do, such as sabotaging public facilities in Iran, though there was little hope that any such action would seriously affect Iran, let alone achieve the release of the hostages. When we in the CIA effectively vetoed all the items, Zbig surely saw this as bureaucratic resistance to new, imaginative ideas. We saw it as the professionalism of the experts keeping the political leadership from undertaking ventures that would be embarrassingly unsuccessful. The only appeal from such a veto is to higher authority, in this case the President. Zbig did not see his case as solid enough to try that course, and covert action floundered about, with Zbig continuing to push and we continuing to be cautious.

Despite endless quiet discussions of military options, it was clear we were not going to try any of them. Cy strongly opposed the use of force, and the President viewed it only as a response to maltreatment of the hostages. Whenever the discussions came close to being serious, no one could assure the President that we could get the hostages back alive if we took punitive action. We were in the same quandary as President Johnson when the crew of *Pueblo* was being held in North Korea. Our nation's immense advantage in military power was of little use.

As far as diplomacy, Waldheim's effort was all that was left; as far as economic pressure, that depended on whether the Security Council would vote for sanctions on January 7 if Waldheim came back empty-handed from Iran. These were slim reeds. What might have been seen as a fall-back, a rescue mission, was not in the cards because the military and the CIA were still not ready.

Yet concern over the hostages was not diminishing. Probably the most significant development in the fifty-eight days since they were seized was that the President's commitment had become deeper and more personal. Considering how much emotion the plight of one hostage, Sergeant Kraus, had aroused in him ten months before, this was not surprising. On Day 5 the State Department had held a meeting for the families of hostages who lived in the Washington area. The President had gone over to Foggy Bottom and made a surprise appearance.

On Day 12, having heard there was to be an interfaith church service for the hostages, he attended, receiving national attention. And on Day 33 when the families of all of the fifty-three hostages were invited to a meeting at the State Department, he talked with each family.

I knew in a small way how heart-rending such meetings could be. I periodically had discussions over luncheon with the wives or mothers of CIA members being held hostage. I obviously could not tell them everything I knew, like the planning of a rescue operation, but it was difficult for me to withhold information they wanted and which I felt they had a right to have. What was even more difficult was that I could not honestly express much optimism; I knew it would be unkind to encourage them with unfounded hope.

The personal emotional involvement of the President with hostages was not unique to Jimmy Carter. Lyndon Johnson had agonized over the crew of *Pueblo*. "If I had to pick a date that symbolized the turmoil we experienced throughout 1968," he wrote, "I think January 23 would be the day — the morning the U.S.S. *Pueblo* was seized. The *Pueblo* incident formed the first link in a chain of events — of crisis, tragedy, and disappointment — that added up to one of the most agonizing years any President has ever spent in the White House."[2] And Richard Nixon's press secretary commented, in the midst of the Dawson Field incident, "It's been a while since I've seen the President as deeply concerned with a problem as he has been with . . . the innocent victims who are going through this terrible ordeal on the desert."[3]

One other factor intensified the pressure on President Carter — public opinion. At the end of November, the President's popularity rating had gone up sharply. The public respected his restraint in dealing with the Iranians and his commitment to the people being held. His political standing, though, was something we never discussed in the SCC; our recommendations were based on what we considered best for the country, no matter what the domestic political implications might be. We all recognized that the public's forbearance on the hostage issue would not continue unless there were results and that it would be difficult to ignore public opinion indefinitely.* After all, it seemed inconceivable that the United States could not make a small nation like Iran abandon

---

*While the President and his political advisers must have been extremely conscious of the effect of the crisis on Jimmy Carter's prospects for re-election, I never saw any hint of his placing that consideration above what was in the best interests of the hostages.

an indefensible action that flouted every rule of international behavior, or that we could not go in and retrieve our hostages.

By the end of 1979, the public's approval of the President's handling of the crisis had dropped from 75 percent to 61 percent. A Gallup Poll noted the growing impatience with the lack of movement. The survey said implicitly that even though the public did not have specific actions in mind, it did not understand why we could not find a solution. There seemed no likelihood that public interest would abate, as sometimes happens when a crisis drags out, witness the matter of *Pueblo*.

Now, Americans were furious with the Iranians. Starting as early as Day 3 and continuing for weeks, hundreds of anti-Khomeini demonstrators assembled in front of the Iranian embassy. In a number of cities there were tense moments when pro-Khomeini Iranian students organized protests, like the one the Attorney General had prohibited across the street from the White House. Anti-Iranian demonstrations broke out in unexpected places: in Newark two Iranian flags were burned in front of City Hall by city employees; in Houston and Los Angeles there were fistfights between American and Iranian students. The country was galvanized in December when Penelope Laingen, wife of the most senior foreign service officer being held hostage, tied a yellow ribbon around a tree on the lawn of her Maryland home. Yellow ribbons sprouted all over the country, and the song "Tie a Yellow Ribbon Round the Old Oak Tree" was revived with a new meaning that helped unite the country against Khomeini. At Christmas, hundreds of thousands of Americans sent cards to the hostages. The outpouring of sympathy for those victims had become intense.

The public's concern stimulated the media, and the media, in turn, fed full coverage to the public. As early as Day 5 ABC aired a late-night special, *The Iran Crisis: America Held Hostage.* By March this show covered much more than the hostage issue and had become *Nightline,* hosted by Ted Koppel; it went on to become a TV institution. On Day 74, Walter Cronkite concluded his nightly news broadcast by announcing the number of days the hostages had been held captive, and he maintained that practice. James Reston in the *New York Times* later suggested that this had had a heavy impact:

> One simple idea was put directly to the President — that he should just wait for the inevitable collapse of the squabbling factions in Iran and then maybe get the hostages back home. President Carter rejected this notion. He was being criticized for being indecisive and for letting time

go on without "doing something." Oddly, but seriously, one of the innocent villains in motivating Carter to want to ''do something'' was my old buddy the Ayatollah Walter Cronkite. It seems slightly mad, but it happens to be true, that those characters in the White House really felt some pressure from Uncle Walter's announcing every night the number of days of captivity of the hostages.[4]

Whether intentionally or not, the Iranians also contributed to the hype in the United States. In Tehran they continued to drive thousands of Iranians to our embassy to demonstrate, and when these scenes were shown on American TV, the American public became even more incensed.

The President's own actions also stimulated the public's sense of crisis. After canceling his trip to Canada on Day 5, he decided it would be inconsistent to go off on scheduled campaign trips to Pennsylvania and Florida. This led to what was described as his campaigning from the Rose Garden. On Day 40, responding to an idea Cy Vance had transmitted to him from a friend, he surprised the nation by leaving some lights out on the National Christmas Tree. He proclaimed Day 46, December 19, as National Unity Day; the flag was to be flown as a demonstration of concern for the hostages.

January 1, 1980, ushered in a presidential election year. Political sniping had begun not long after the hostages were taken. Alexander M. Haig, Jr., a candidate for the Republican nomination, on November 21 "lambasted the [Carter] Administration for impulsively ruling out the use of force against Iran."[5] In late November Ronald Reagan, also campaigning for the Republican nomination, claimed that Carter's policies of "weakness and vacillation" had made possible the taking of the hostages. He intimated that once the hostages were returned he might make the Iranian issue a major theme of his campaign.[6]

Clearly, the pressures on the President, personal, public, and political, were building, but the conclusion of my stock taking was that we did not yet have any leverage in dealing with the Iranians, and therefore the end was nowhere in sight.

· 11 ·

ON TO THE

NEGOTIATING TRACK

[I am] glad to be back, especially alive.

— Kurt Waldheim,
Secretary General of the
United Nations [1]

NINETEEN-EIGHTY did not open auspiciously for the hostages. Waldheim came back empty-handed on January 5. Not only had Khomeini showed his disdain for the United Nations by refusing to meet with him, but twice the Secretary General believed his life was threatened by angry mobs.

In light of Waldheim's failure, the Security Council, following its earlier resolution, voted on January 13 to impose sanctions on Iran. The vote was 10 to 2, but one of the two negatives was a veto by the Soviet Union, apparently in retaliation for our having voted a few days earlier to condemn it for having invaded Afghanistan on December 26.

Cy Vance attempted to persuade the allies to enforce the sanctions anyway. After all, the Security Council had clearly favored applying sanctions, and the veto was in no way related to the merits of sanctions. But the allies were technically off the hook; they had found a convenient excuse for delaying. And they had still another reason to stall. The Iranians were about to elect a President, and the man expected to win was Abolhassan Bani Sadr, a secularist who appeared to favor releasing the hostages. Why not wait to see what Bani Sadr might do? Economic sanctions moved to the sidelines leaving negotiations all that remained in active play.

President Carter authorized Cy to brief the SCC on Day 82, January 24, on eight current lines of negotiation. There were several groups of Iranians who had offered to negotiate with Waldheim, several Americans who knew members of Khomeini's entourage, and the Chargé d' affaires, Bruce Laingen, who, though in custody in Tehran at the Ministry of Foreign Affairs, was talking with Iranian officials. However, whenever Cy got close to a deal with any of them, either the Iranian negotiator could not produce or the negotiator changed and Cy had to start all over.

I thought Cy's briefing might be in response to the complaints, by me and others, that the severely restricted access to information was hurting our combined effort. But the occasional wrap-up briefing like this seemed to me almost as bad as no access at all. We in the SCC were now supposed to be up-to-date on the negotiations, yet since we came to the meeting without any idea of what Cy had been doing, we had not been able to discuss with our staffs the merits of these particular approaches, nor could we assess how the negotiations fitted into other possible approaches. By the time we digested Cy's synopsis, consulted our staffs, and developed opinions, the negotiations would have taken new turns. Presumably we would be briefed on those one day, but we would always be behind, unable to give the President timely advice.

Even more distressing, I knew Cy's briefing was significantly incomplete; he had not been authorized, it seems, to tell us about the most promising negotiation. A week earlier, Ham Jordan had included me in a meeting with two Panamanian officials, whom he had first met during the work on the Panama Canal Treaty in 1977. They were now intermediaries between him and two lawyers, a Frenchman and an Argentinian, who were in touch with the Iranians. The lawyers claimed they could arrange the release of the hostages and were interested in doing so for humanitarian reasons.

Knowing of this, I could see why Ham had begun arguing for a relaxation of our negotiating terms. He suggested that we let a commission from the United Nations investigate the relationship of the United States with the Shah, without insisting on the prior release of the hostages. This was contrary to the position outlined at Camp David just after Thanksgiving, which the Iranians had turned down on the grounds that condemnation of the United States was the more pressing issue. They also feared that they would lose out if they released the hostages first and the commission then issued only a mild condemnation of the United States.

Their stance on the second count made sense, but no more than our concern that they might not release the hostages even after a commission report. I opposed making any concession at this time, reasoning that the real bargaining had not yet begun. We were dealing in a Middle Eastern bazaar and could not afford to concede too much too early. However, enthusiasm for negotiations was building, and no one shared my concern. The crisis had stretched another two months, the country was losing prestige abroad, and we were willing to risk an injury to our national honor to get this problem behind us.

We were soon down to the one secret negotiating track between Hamilton Jordan and the team of lawyers. There was little for the SCC to discuss; meetings were reduced from five or six a week to two. Cy even stopped coming and instead sent his deputy or the third senior man in the department, David D. Newsom. Zbig looked tired, distraught, and discouraged. He and his NSC staff were off to the side while Ham Jordan, a politician not versed in foreign affairs, carried the ball. With the tight secrecy around the operation, Ham was almost cut off from professional advice. Fortunately, he was wise enough to keep Cy informed and to accept Harold H. Saunders, a career foreign service officer and one of the State Department's true experts on the Middle East and South Asia, as an assistant to work closely with him.

Ham also needed help from the CIA and we gave him all we could, but because we were not privy to all he was doing, we could not help him as much as I would have liked. We sent him special updates on the situation in Tehran and provided intelligence reports on the two lawyers, describing the Argentinian as "at least an opportunist and possibly a scoundrel." Ham decided not to tell this to the President, because he could see no alternative to relying on these two.[2]

While Ham was proceeding in secret, the rescue planning group was making quiet progress. By mid-January the CIA's intelligence was good enough for us to be reasonably sure that all the hostages were in the embassy compound. The Agency had procured eight trucks to transport Delta Force into Tehran and a warehouse to store them in until needed. Reconnaissance of the embassy's exterior was thorough and continuing. We knew where the guard posts and machine gun positions were and when they were manned. And we knew how best to navigate Delta into the city from the outskirts without arousing suspicions. Though it had taken us too long to be ready, we were finally there.

The training of Delta was also going well. There were two problems with the helicopters, though. First, the Navy pilots who came with the Navy helicopters were not up to navigating precisely over land at night; they were accustomed to flying low over water while towing minesweeping gear. Nor were they motivated for this mission; one pilot even refused to continue with the training. In early December a group of Marine Corps pilots replaced them — probably because two of the officers most responsible for the helicopter side of Jim Vaught's operation were Marines, who knew where and how to find suitable pilots quickly. The heat was on from Zbig in Washington to be ready immediately.

The other problem was refueling. Jim Vaught had tested dropping bladders of fuel into the desert but found that cumbersome and unreliable. He had fallen back on using the airfield at Nain. The necessity for holding this airfield for twenty-four hours without being detected bothered me greatly. I did not think the President should or would accept the risk. Until we found a way around this, I did not think we were ready to conduct a rescue.

I decided to have the CIA covert action people look for an alternative and asked them to think of a way to enable the helicopters to reach Tehran. Within a week they were back, and I could see that one of the veterans of special operations was excited. In satellite photographs they had seen a desert area in eastern Iran near the town of Tabas, some 300 miles southeast of Tehran and about 650 miles from where the aircraft carrier would be operating in the Arabian Sea. It might be possible, they thought, for fixed-wing aircraft to carry the fuel bladders and land on the desert. There, the helicopters could refuel on the way to Tehran. The desert seemed sufficiently level and smooth. The only question was whether it was firm enough, and the team believed it was.

Then, the big news! To test whether the desert site was acceptable as an airfield, a CIA crew would fly a small airplane to it from Oman over the Persian Gulf. They would land near a road that passed through the area, check the terrain, and take core samples of the ground that would be tested for larger, heavier planes carrying fuel. When I asked about the risk of the crew being caught while involved in this activity, the operations specialists said the plane would go in at dusk and come out before dawn; it was so small that the Iranians would be hard put to see it in the dark. And it would fly low enough to stay under Iranian radar coverage. The pilot would, though, need a full moon to see for landing. They hoped he could avoid damage from boulders and gullies and not jeopardize his ability to take off when the survey was finished. They believed car and truck traffic would be very light in such an isolated area in the middle of the night; but the aircraft would taxi out of the way once it landed. If, despite all precautions, the plane was disabled on landing, the crew would walk across the desert toward the Arabian Sea until the aircraft carrier could send in a helicopter to pick them up.

I thought the idea was ingenious. It could overcome what I saw as the fatal flaw in the rescue plan — the need to capture a conventional airfield. We adjourned, but I asked "Dick," the principal architect of the plan, to come back the next morning. I mulled over the plan most of the evening. The next morning, after asking Dick some more questions, I decided that the exploratory flight was just what was needed. It was Day 81, January 23. I went immediately to see Zbig, who wanted to go directly to the President for permission so that the flight could take place on the full moon of February 1. I said no and was adamant about not going forward until Cy was informed. If this mission was detected, it could severely damage his negotiations. Zbig agreed, and it was decided that he tell Cy and Harold Brown at a scheduled luncheon the next day.

After that luncheon, Cy asked me to have breakfast with him the following morning. I then went through the plan step by step; Cy readily approved. I found, however, that he was asking more questions about the rescue mission itself than about the proposed reconnaissance flight. He had only a sketchy idea of the rescue plan. Either he had not been told the details or he had chosen not to involve himself in a plan he did not favor. Feeling strongly that the Secretary of State should be completely informed, I readily told him all I knew about it.

I was extremely disappointed late on Day 83 when Zbig phoned to say the President did not want to proceed with the exploratory flight; he believed we should not go that far in rescue planning. I had agreed all along with Zbig that a rescue capability ought to be ready as soon as possible. It was not that I favored using it yet, but I wanted the President to have as many options available as possible. Also, we needed to weigh a rescue mission in our assessment of all options. With the President's negative decision, we would have to wait another month for the next full moon.

Everything, then, was now in Ham Jordan's lap for the time being.

・ 12 ・

THE CANADIAN SIX

My middle name is Hitler.

— CIA operations officer at
the Tehran airport,
January 1980[1]

ALTHOUGH we were not accomplishing much toward the release of the fifty-three hostages, we were making headway on the case of the six Americans hiding in Canadian residences, the Canadian Six. It was slow and painstaking work. The operations experts at Langley began by taking an inventory of each of the diplomat's professional skills, language capabilities, general interests, available photographs, and whatever other data they could collect from the State Department's personnel records. They then gave each a new name, birthplace, and occupation, and developed a rationale that tied the six together as part of a business group with a legitimate reason for being in Iran at the time. The Canadians were particularly helpful with all the documentation needed to support the new identities. Every detail had to be exact lest one error or inconsistency give the game away. One mistake was found on a set of documents, and the Canadian ambassador, Ken Taylor, went to work in Tehran correcting it with the deftness of a professional forger. All the while, the Canadian Foreign Office in Ottawa served as a relay point for secret messages between Washington and Tehran.

Only a handful of people in Washington and Ottawa knew of this operation. Surprisingly, one of the Canadians was the leader of the opposition, Pierre Trudeau. With an election imminent, Trudeau was criticizing the Canadian government for not doing more to help the Americans. He quieted down after Prime Minister Joe Clark took him aside and told him there was more going on than met the eye.

・ 90 ・

While the new identities were being fabricated, the CIA team in Washington and Ken Taylor in Tehran exchanged ideas on how to organize the escape. Taylor went back and forth between his residence and his deputy's, holding discussions with the two groups of Americans. They devised four escape options. The first was to smuggle the six hostages out of the country, either across a land boundary with Turkey four hundred miles to the west, where they would bribe their way past the border guards as Perot's people had done, or across the Shatt-el-Arab River to Iraq, some three hundred miles to the south. The second option was to take them in disguise right through Tehran's Mehrabad Airport and onto a commercial flight out of the country. The third was to move them only a short distance outside Tehran and have a U.S. military helicopter come in and pick them up. Finally, some of the hostages thought the safest course would be just to wait it out, since everyone expected the Iranians would come to their senses and release the fifty-three hostages downtown before too long.

Although the idea of waiting it out seemed the safe course, it too was risky. How would the Iranians react once they learned these six had hidden from them? They might well refuse to include the six in any deal made for the others. One of them pointed out that the Iranians, with their paranoia about the CIA, might decide that they were all CIA people.

In Washington, we were less than enthusiastic about the plan of using a helicopter to pick up the six near Tehran. Helicopters were figuring so prominently in the rescue mission planning that we did not want to overwork that angle. That narrowed down the choice to smuggling the six individually across one of Iran's borders or sending them right through Mehrabad Airport on false passports.

As we came close to a decision, I briefed the President, telling him I thought using the airport would be the better choice, but suggesting we let each hostage decide which way he or she should go. Each could take into account the physical stamina needed to make the long trip to one of the borders and perhaps across the mountains into Turkey, or the cunning needed to deceive the inspectors at the airport. The President, however, thought the burden of making that choice would be too great for people under stress and suggested that we decide for them. Since Bob and other agents were using the airport repeatedly, and we were reasonably familiar with the routine there, we chose that option.

There was hesitation among the six as to whether they could pull it off at the airport, so the CIA operations experts recommended that several of them go to Tehran to train the six. By having our men on the spot, we could better evaluate the chances and determine whether it would be wise to shift to the overland plan. Having experienced CIA people there to lead the six people through the airport should also increase the chances of success. The negative side was that it would place more Americans at risk. But I agreed this was the way to go.

The Canadians in Tehran were becoming anxious; it was difficult for everyone. The six Americans were like guests who had come to dinner and would not leave. Each movement had to be carefully guarded so that it would not be seen from the outside. The Iranian gardener at the deputy's house was not trusted, and the four hostages there had to scurry out of sight whenever he was around. Although the Canadians were standing staunchly by us, there was concern that our people would be found while in hiding or while attempting to escape. If the Canadians became implicated in our hostage problem, their diplomats might end up being hostages too. Even if our plan worked perfectly, the Canadians had to expect retaliation when it became known, as it likely would, that they had abetted the escape. In anticipation, they began withdrawing their embassy personnel from Tehran in late January and were ready to close down about the time the CIA's chief planner for the operation, accompanied by a State Department official, flew to Ottawa to describe the plan in detail and ask permission to attempt it.

We were delighted when the Canadian government gave firm approval to go ahead. In view of the lackluster responses we had had from most allies on economic sanctions, this was a heartening affirmation of friendship. In late January, the CIA experts headed off to Tehran. When they reached Mehrabad Airport, the entire operation almost came apart. One of them was traveling on a West German passport under an assumed name that included the middle initial H. An alert customs inspector stopped him, noting that he had never before seen a West German passport in which the middle name was not spelled out in full. Our man, with magnificent aplomb, replied that he was ashamed of the middle name his parents had given him and had obtained special permission to use only his initial in his passport. The H, he said, stood for Hitler. No further questions were asked. Quietly, and without attracting any more notice, the two experts left the airport and made their way to the Canadian residences.

For the next two days, the CIA team and a Canadian diplomat put the six hostages through rehearsal after rehearsal. One hostage still favored waiting it out, but after the CIA men said the six were ready to leave, and after a final check with the State Department and the

Canadian government, I gave the go-ahead. Our men on the spot would decide on the exact timing.

Reservations were booked on an early-morning flight on Air France on Monday, January 28, Day 86. At four o'clock that morning, a Canadian embassy van picked up the six and their CIA escorts from the residences and headed for the airport. The drive there was uneventful. The city was still quiet and the road had little of the traffic that would quickly build up after first light. Shortly before five, the van pulled up in front of the nearly deserted terminal. Bags were unloaded and good-byes and thanks said to the driver. Inside, the group passed the ticket counters and approached the customs desks. As each American appeared before an inspector, tension was at its peak, but soon they were all through. The gang walked casually to the waiting lounge by the gate. Suddenly their ears perked up at an announcement that their flight would be delayed three hours. This, they thought, was surely because they had aroused suspicion and the inspectors wanted time to do more checking, perhaps with records back in the city; that would be fatal. Or perhaps the Iranians had finally noted the discrepancy between the number of diplomats in our embassy on November 4 and the number of hostages they held. The group waited apprehensively, saying little to one another. What would happen next?

But after only twenty minutes, the gate to the field opened, and the Canadian Six with their CIA mentors walked across the tarmac toward the aircraft. As they started to climb the steps to the plane they were startled to see that the name painted on the plane's nose, with a French variation in spelling, was the same as the CIA's code name for the operation to get them out! It had to be a good omen. After a few minutes, and without further incident, the plane took off. Once airborne, the ex-hostages ordered Bloody Marys, but they were hesitant to toast their freedom until the aircraft left Iranian air space. When they arrived in Switzerland, one stamped his foot so hard on the free soil that it hurt. Their documentation was accepted by the Swiss immigration authorities. They were welcomed by waiting State Department officials, who cautioned them against public exuberance; we had hoped to keep this Canadian caper secret lest it complicate our problem with the other fifty-three hostages. The following morning a Canadian newspaper broke the story, however, and both governments confirmed the report. Canada hastily closed its embassy in Tehran and withdrew its diplomats.

We had treated this as a covert action and obtained a presidential

finding back when we first started the planning.* Again, though, secrecy was so critical that I had used the escape clause "in a timely
manner" to withhold notification of Congress. But before the story
broke, I had the intelligence committees informed, because this was
the first time we had not notified Congress immediately after a finding
was signed. To my relief, the committees understood and accepted our
delay. There is no doubt that the operation's success helped to smooth
the way.

The nation was euphoric. There was a surge of pride that Americans, assisted by Canadians, had finally outsmarted the Ayatollah. On
March 15, at the annual Gridiron Club dinner in Washington, there
was a warm display of the appreciation we all felt for Canada. As the
toastmaster introduced each dignitary at the long head table, the audi-
ence applauded politely and automatically. But just as the applause for
Canadian Ambassador Peter Towe began to fade, people suddenly realized which country this man represented. Within seconds everyone
rose and gave Canada a standing ovation.

---

*In retrospect, I believe the Congress, in writing the Hughes-Ryan Amendments of
1974, did not intend to define operations like this or those in support of Delta Force
as covert actions. At the time, however, we gave no consideration to such an interpretation.

A Fling with
Iranian Moderates

Politically, it was important for the President to be seen taking
every possible action against Iran.

— Hamilton Jordan,
January 12, 1980[1]

HAM JORDAN'S negotiations were more than alive on Day 102, February 13, when he phoned to ask me for a disguise. He said he was
going to use it on a forthcoming trip to Paris to meet with an unnamed
Iranian official. The Argentinian and French lawyers had worked out
with this man a new, complicated scheme to combine an investigation
of the relations between the United States and the Shah with the release
of the hostages. Ham was excited at the prospect of obtaining a commitment to this plan from the official. People from the CIA's disguise
section outfitted him quickly with a wig, mustache, and different glasses,
and gave him some tips on altering his bearing and style of walk. Ham
thought even his mother wouldn't recognize him. He was a bit taken
aback when I asked for his assurance that the disguise was to be used
in support of the hostage problem. Then I reminded him that the last
White House man to borrow a disguise from the CIA, specifically a
red wig, had been E. Howard Hunt of Watergate notoriety. Ham's
response was "This is not for a break-in; it's for a break-out."[2]

The same day, President Carter stated at a press conference that the
United States had agreed to the creation of an international commission
with the "carefully defined purpose" of investigating the Shah's regime
and eventually leading to a resolution of the hostage crisis.[3] The most
encouraging development was that the Iranian demands had narrowed
to just a condemnation of the United States by the commission; there
was no mention of the return of the Shah and his wealth, which we

could not undertake. I couldn't help noting that the Iranians at this time and the North Koreans at the time of *Pueblo* were determined to secure a public reprimand of the United States. It was a reward they obviously coveted, very likely to save face for having taken the controversial action in the first place.

Subsequent public statements made it clear that, despite what had been said, the commission's purpose was not well defined. On February 20, the White House issued a statement welcoming a UN commission that would explore the United States' grievances against Iran; Iran's President sent a telegram to Waldheim welcoming a commission that would investigate American intervention in Iran's internal affairs under the Shah; and Waldheim termed the commission a "fact-finding mission" to hear Iranian grievances and seek an early solution to the hostage crisis.[4] We were in this ambiguous situation because we had abandoned, as Ham had been urging, our insistence on the release of the hostages before the start of an investigation. That enabled the Iranians to treat the commission as separate from the hostage issue, which was the way they saw it.

Ham, on his trip to Paris with the disguise, sought to join the two issues back together by gaining from the Iranian official a promise that the hostages would be released. (Ham has stuck to his word not to reveal the identity of his interlocutor.) The Iranian almost refused to discuss the question, noting that "holding fifty-three Americans is a slight injustice compared to the killing and torturing of thousands and thousands of Iranians by the criminal Shah!"[5]

I do not believe any of us understood how wide was the gap in outlook behind that statement. What we saw was that kidnaping Americans and invading U.S. diplomatic property were deliberate violations of international law and human rights. Whatever the Iranians' complaints about the Shah, we could not believe they truly thought the United States should be held responsible for the actions of their former chief of state. But the Iranians' animosity toward the Shah was so great, and included us, for they saw us as his ally. Moreover, it has always been a normal Iranian perception to see outside forces shaping much of Iran's destiny, and the United States was the principal such force in the post–World War II period. Nor was the attitude limited to the Khomeini extremists. About this time, I had luncheon with an Iranian friend who was former chief of his country's navy. He stunned me by saying that he and his friends felt that we, the United States, were behind the rise to power of Khomeini. Had we better understood this view, we might have rated the chances of compromise through negotiation as considerably less than we did.

As it was, we hoped that our letting a commission investigate us and the Shah would strengthen the hands of the moderate Iranians. Ghotbzadeh and Bani Sadr, now President, were among them; each had made statements about the desirability of ending the hostage crisis. Ham asked his contact in Paris whether Khomeini knew about and approved the idea of an investigation that would lead to the release of the hostages. The reply was that after Khomeini had been briefed, he had nodded.[6]

Then, on Day 112, February 23, Khomeini spoke out publicly just as the UN commission arrived in Tehran. He said the Majlis, the Iranian Parliament, would decide on the release of the hostages, and "any concessions they should obtain for the release."[7] This was not quite a Catch-22, but almost, because there was no Majlis. The last one had resigned in February 1979. Elections were scheduled, but it would be a good two months before there was any hope of getting a new Majlis organized and ready to address the question. Despite the prospect of further delay, we did not withdraw our support for the UN commission. We hoped someone would induce Khomeini to change his mind or would effect the release without his approval.

Not long after Ham returned from Paris, he called me to request false documentation to complement his disguise. On his next trip he wanted to be completely incognito. He might have to go to Tehran to work out the final details of the release and was understandably anxious that he not be recognized by an angry mob. Ham never went to Tehran, though, because negotiations never reached that point. The commission encountered one stumbling block after another. After two and a half weeks it went home, on Day 129, March 11, without filing a report.

Why had the United States fallen for this scam? First, because Jimmy Carter had as little leverage over the hostage holders as Presidents Washington, Jefferson, Theodore Roosevelt, Johnson, and Nixon had had: there were not many feasible options. Second, because the President's hand was growing weaker every day: the primary election season was beginning and the presidential election was less than nine months away. Ham's Iranian contact in Paris had expressly pointed out that he was well aware of this. Ham, who was running the President's re-election campaign, said, "Politically, it was important for the President to be seen taking every possible action against Iran."[8] At this point, the negotiations were the most hopeful course we could find, but because we were counting so heavily on them, another possible course was being shunted aside: the rescue mission.

On February 14, well before Ham's negotiating efforts failed, I asked the President for permission to fly the CIA's exploratory flight into the desert on March 1, the next full moon. I suggested that he talk with Dave Jones and Harold Brown about my fear that the plan to capture and hold the Nain airfield was too risky.

The next day, Dave, Harold, Cy, Zbig, and I had breakfast with the President and reviewed the plan. President Carter was still concerned that word of our planning a rescue might get out and drive the Iranians away from the negotiating table. I said the worst that could happen as a result of the flight would be that the CIA's light aircraft would crack up and the crew would be captured or killed. We would take steps to disguise the fact that the plane was connected to rescue planning. And with the desert site about three hundred miles from Tehran, the Iranians might never make such a connection. Dave favored making the flight, but Harold, Cy, and even Zbig argued for holding off, since the negotiations looked so favorable at that moment. To my disappointment, the President said no to a flight on the next full moon.

By the time the negotiations crumbled, we had missed the early March full moon. It would be almost April before the next chance.

THE DIE IS CAST

I told everyone that it was time for us to bring our hostages home.

> — Jimmy Carter at a National
> Security Council meeting,
> April 11, 1980 [1]

I WAS WITH the President on March 12, the day after the UN commission left Tehran. I had never seen him show such signs of stress. He had been concentrating for over four months on this one problem, and to no avail. To make the pressures worse, our intelligence had detected Soviet military maneuvers and paper war games in the Transcaucasus region, just north of the Iranian border and to the west of the Caspian Sea. Were the Soviets letting President Carter know that we had better not use military force in Iran? Even for a rescue operation? Or were they planning to move into Iran on the assumption that we would not support the Iranians under the present circumstances? When we uncovered these activities, I hated to add one more concern to those on the President's mind. Fortunately, it all ended with nothing untoward, and we shall probably never know whether the maneuvers were a coincidence of timing or a deliberate message.

The tension the President felt was getting to almost everyone at the top. Zbig was visibly discouraged by his inability to persuade the President to take a more militant stance. Cy was clearly in the doghouse because of a mistake that had been made in casting a wrong vote in the United Nations, one that had angered Israel and might have domestic political repercussions in an election year. Finally, Ham Jordan, although relatively young and physically vigorous, had been pushing the limits of his endurance. Here he was, deeply involved in foreign affairs when his plate was already full with the primary election campaign, let alone his normal duties as Chief of Staff. For weeks he had shuttled back and forth to Europe on the hostage issue and was right now on his way to Switzerland for still another attempt to salvage the negotiations through the two lawyers. The top leadership of the United States was stretched to the breaking point, and there seemed to be nothing the rest of us could do to lighten their loads.

Toward the end of my meeting with the President, he asked me a curious question. Was I getting sufficient information about policy decisions to provide good intelligence support? When I told him I did not feel adequately informed, he indicated that I should be getting what I needed at the meetings of the SCC. I responded that I found those meetings a charade; all the decisions were being made elsewhere and we were simply going through the motions.

Six days later I could see why the President had asked his question. He called an unexpected meeting of the NSC and opened it by saying he felt we weren't working together as a team. We were not, for instance, exchanging enough different views and opinions. He wanted us all to come to Camp David the next Saturday, Day 140, for a thorough discussion of the Middle East, Afghanistan, and the Soviet Union, as well as the hostages. He was looking for ways to increase the pressure on Iran. The American people, he said, were sick and tired of the stalemate.

I was ecstatic. It appeared he was going to open up the compartments and draw on the full resources available to him. But then he told us emphatically not to consult our staffs in preparation for the meeting, but to think the issues through ourselves. On my way back from the White House to CIA headquarters, I wrestled with that stricture, but by the time I reached Langley I had made my decision. I gathered three top analysts, the head of the CIA's operations branch, and Deputy Director Frank C. Carlucci in my office. They were the same people I had consulted the previous November when the President asked me to put the best minds in the CIA at work to devise solutions to the hostage problem. I wanted the President to have that kind of advice again; he needed it even more now. After a long discussion, I asked the others to give it some more thought, even consulting with their colleagues, though without disclosing the impending meeting at Camp David. We scheduled another meeting two days later and spent several more hours going over the key issues confronting the United States in foreign policy. I then sat down and distilled my thoughts into written outlines.

· · ·

March 22 was eleven days after the United Nations commission had failed in Tehran. Cy, Zbig, Harold Brown, Dave Jones, Jody Powell, David Aaron, and I went by helicopter to Camp David. President Carter was waiting in the conference room, and we began right away. The President kept emphasizing that we were not working well as a team but were "drifting," not focusing on the real problem. As if to prove his point, we once again reviewed the economic and diplomatic pressures we had gone over so many times before, though they had never offered much hope.

As the discussion meandered on, it was obvious that the only useful options left were military ones. I was dismayed, however, at the timidity with which we approached military action. The proposals Harold presented ranged from dropping strips of aluminum down the intakes of Iranian power plants to sending high-altitude aircraft over Tehran to "intimidate" the Iranians. In part this timidity must have been related to the recent Soviet military maneuvers and the risk that they might use strong military action on our part as an excuse to move into Iran themselves.

Mining was the only truly punitive action discussed. It was the one the President seemed to favor, perhaps because it was nonlethal and therefore less likely to bring harm to the hostages. But Harold and Dave opposed it. They pointed out that Iran might turn to the Soviets to sweep the mines for them and that we could not close the Iranian port of Khorramshahr on the Shatt-al-Arab River without also cutting off Iraq from her principal port, Basra. They added that there was a potential for repercussions in the Islamic world and that the hostages might be harmed. There was some justification to these objections, but it seemed to me that the Joint Chiefs of Staff had decided they preferred a rescue mission to any kind of punitive attack, especially mining.

I understood but did not agree. Mine warfare is a poor stepchild in the Navy and receives little attention and not much money. Few admirals know enough about it to be its advocates. Laying mines and waiting for ships to run over them is neither decisive nor aggressive. The Joint Chiefs did not want to put the fate of the hostages and the military's reputation on what the Navy saw as an essentially passive and uninteresting tactic.

Dave Jones gave a thorough and positive review of the rescue planning. He wanted two authorizations from the President. The first was to send Army scouts into Tehran. This was in response to Jim Vaught's desire to have his own people double-check the information they were receiving from the CIA. He needed to feel absolutely confident, so I did not object. I did worry, though, that the Army men might be caught and would tip our hand.

Second, Dave wanted the CIA to fly the exploratory mission into the desert on Day 148, March 30, when there would be another full moon. I said we would need to move quickly to make that date, only eight days away. The President responded that he had not given up hope on the negotiations and wanted to wait another ninety days before considering a rescue. Dave pointed out that the nights were becoming shorter and soon the rescue mission would have to be stretched to three nights: one to reach a refueling location, one to move to the outskirts of Tehran, and one to conduct the assault and pull out of Iran. This would greatly increase the risks. Cy continued to oppose any rescue effort, believing some hostages would almost certainly be killed. Although the President shared Cy's concern, he noted that hostages might be killed by the Iranians for other reasons. Reluctantly, he told me to go ahead with the flight, but noted that he might change his mind in the days before the full moon.

Discussion on the hostages ended. We had come closer than in any of our previous meetings to laying all the options on the table, only because we had run out of anything else and had to address military options. The range was narrow: the President and Cy objected to such punitive actions as bombing, and the military objected to a passive option like mining, leaving only the rescue mission. And now, if the CIA's flight showed that refueling in the desert was feasible, we would at last have a rescue plan that could work. Still, I was far from convinced that the President would order the mission.

We spent the rest of the day at Camp David discussing the situation in Afghanistan, the Middle East, and our relations with the Soviet Union. The President was adamant about not backing down on his strong response to the Soviet invasion of Afghanistan, yet he did not want a confrontation with the Soviets. The previous June he had invested a great deal in reaching an agreement with Secretary General Leonid Brezhnev on the SALT II nuclear arms treaty. It was exasperating for him to see how quickly the tension between our two countries had built up again. I wondered whether any of us could understand the pressures on the President: release of the hostages, efforts to ease tensions with the Soviet Union, domestic prosperity and well-being, and an impending campaign for re-election. How could we support him better? We did not seem to be doing well at the moment, despite all the talent available. When, on our way back from Camp David, Zbig mentioned that my contributions at the meeting had been particularly helpful, I felt vindicated for having broken the President's stricture against consulting our staffs.

When we returned to Washington late in the afternoon, I told Dick from the operations team to move the light aircraft into position in the Middle East. The crew had barely started on the long journey to the jump-off point in Oman when Dick reported that Jim Vaught was telling his staff he would not use the desert refueling site, no matter what the flight revealed. Frustrated, I called Dave Jones and arranged to meet him and Vaught in Dave's office, where I told them I could not in good conscience risk the lives of these men in landing on an unlit desert at night if they had no intention of using the site. Dave had obviously gone over this with Jim and assured me that if we found the conditions in the desert "very good," he would rule for the operation.

That still left me with a difficult decision. What were the odds that Vaught would evaluate the conditions as "very good," no matter what we found? His opinion would carry considerable weight with Dave Jones, but I knew Dave to be a thoroughly honest man and I trusted him to be objective when making the final decision. I decided to let the flight proceed.

The next morning I asked for a last briefing on the emergency procedures for rescuing the crew if something happened to the aircraft. They would head off by foot across the desert carrying a beacon that a search aircraft could detect. We would also have our photographic satellites look for them. After we had gone through this in detail, Dick said, "Admiral, I've got to tell you one more thing. The pilot of this aircraft has an artificial leg." My first reaction was that this was surely a bad joke, but I saw that Dick was dead serious. He then convinced me that this pilot, by virtue of his experience, was decidedly our best man for the operation. Since all of the plans had been built around him, I did not have much choice, and consented. But what if the crew was forced to walk out of the desert!

I then went to the President and asked for final permission to go ahead. It was Day 145, March 27, still three days before the full moon. Without hesitation he said yes. I heard nothing more from him and gave approval for the aircraft to take off on Sunday evening, March 30, Day 148. That morning, I received a phone call telling me there was a mechanical problem and the mission would have to be postponed for twenty-four hours.

At noon on Monday, March 31, just before going to the White House for a meeting with Zbig and two congressmen, I received word that the aircraft had taken off. When the meeting was over and I could talk to Zbig privately, I told him the plane should be crossing the Iranian coastline just about then and heading into the desert. To my surprise, Zbig expressed consternation. He said he had expected me to get a final approval from the President. I reminded him that I had made it quite clear on the previous Wednesday that I was asking not for contingent approval but for a go-ahead. I had no sense that the President wanted to give last-minute approval.

As confident as I was that Zbig was misreading the President, I became anxious. If I had misunderstood my instructions and everything went well, it wouldn't be too serious. But what if something went wrong? My concern mounted that afternoon when the President called a meeting of the National Security Council on short notice. He told us that President Bani Sadr had been sending him messages, rekindling hope for negotiations. I was shocked. What if Zbig was right and I had done something that might end up blowing the negotiations and preventing the release of the hostages? Not everyone at the meeting knew of the flight, so I could not mention it, but I was relieved not to have to tell the President; he rushed right out of the Cabinet Room when the meeting was over.

Back in my office, I immediately called in Dick. He had no news. We hoped that meant all was going well. At 6:00 P.M., on my way home, I stopped by Dick's office for one more check. Still no word. A few minutes later I was home and changing to go to a dinner party when the CIA phone rang. The aircraft had successfully taken off from the desert for the return flight to Oman. Our greatest concern — that the plane would not be able to get back in the air — was behind us. It would still be several hours, though, before the mission was complete and the crew safe. As soon as I got home from the dinner, I picked up the secure telephone and with great relief learned that the plane had landed safely in Oman. As far as the pilot could tell, no one had detected them. I called Zbig and told him we could breathe easily again.

By the next afternoon we began learning the details of the mission. When the pilot had the aircraft about fifty feet off the desert floor ready to land, an alarm went off, warning that radar had detected the plane. There was almost no chance that an Iranian radar could have seen this small aircraft so close to the ground and in such a remote area. Nonetheless, the pilot was distracted and he let the plane drop on the desert too hard. It bounced back into the air — but fortunately came down again in one piece. A quick inspection showed no disabling damage. The pilot, the co-pilot, and an Air Force officer, whom we had taken on the mission expressly to reassure the military, reconnoitered two prospective airstrips, three thousand feet long by ninety feet wide, one on each side of the road. They took core samples and planted remote-controlled landing lights that the CIA had provided. Five cars passed by while they were doing all of this. We had not anticipated that much traffic, but none of the cars stopped or slowed down. The crew was confident it had not been seen. Overall, the conditions were more than "very good" for C-130 aircraft carrying fuel bladders to land on this desert airstrip.

A CIA officer who had been waiting in Oman was on his way back, aboard a commercial flight, with the core samples. The CIA pilot and co-pilot would ferry the little aircraft home later. I felt the entire team, from the innovative planners who first sketched out what would be done to the skilled crew who actually did it, had reason to be proud of a job very well done. I couldn't have been more proud of the CIA. Now, how would Jim Vaught react?

But I was never to talk with Jim about it again. It took almost a week to get the data to the Air Force experts and to have it analyzed. Then, at an NSC meeting on Day 156, April 7, Dave Jones told the President he had shifted the refueling stop for the rescue mission from Nain to what was now called Desert One.

The President had convened this meeting because, he said, he was totally exasperated. He felt we had leaned over backward with the Iranians, to the point of being inept. He was through negotiating with Bani Sadr, who had gone from being a white knight to being a villain. The President was ready to proceed immediately with a series of diplomatic and economic actions we had been considering for some time, among them expelling the rest of the Iranian diplomats.

He wanted to review all his options, and we started with the familiar litany of minor diplomatic and economic sanctions. Suddenly I realized we had spent forty-five minutes discussing how to expel Iranian diplomats and another forty-five on financial claims against Iran. I was dumfounded. President Carter, who usually would not sit still for long, rambling discussions, was displaying an uncommon tolerance for our groping. He was obviously facing a decision he did not want to make. Although he could theoretically have waited it out some more, perhaps for a more genuine offer of negotiations, public impatience at home had made that difficult.

The President then closed the NSC meeting to all but the statutory members plus Dave Jones, Zbig, and me. That removed Ham Jordan and Jody Powell from the ensuing discussions of military options — now the only forms of pressure we had left.

The President said he was willing to consider mining but not a rescue operation; that, he thought, would almost certainly involve the loss of some hostages. Fritz Mondale, Harold, Zbig, Dave, and I all spoke in favor of the rescue operation. I thought that mining, though the preferable punitive option, would require considerable time to take effect, but a rescue mission would succeed — or fail — in one swift stroke. The risks were greater, but so was the payoff, and I was convinced that we could do it now that we had established the feasibility of refueling at Desert One. Dave Jones added that the Desert One option had increased the confidence of the JCS in a rescue mission. Warren Christopher, speaking for Cy, proposed limiting ourselves to the diplomatic pressures we had just discussed. The meeting adjourned without any indication of whether the President had shifted from mining to a rescue mission.

It was ironic that Jimmy Carter, whose personal political fortunes depended on resolving the hostage issue as quickly as possible, should prefer mining, which could take months to have an effect, while the rest of us, with much less personally at stake, opted for a quick solution. The impulse to "do something soon" was what brought most of us to favor the rescue mission; the hostages had been dominating American foreign policy for 156 days. Every evening we winced when Walter Cronkite signed off with yet a higher number of days. Although no one raised it in the NSC, a recent Gallup Poll showed that approval of the President's handling of the crisis had fallen to 40 percent, down from 75 percent in November and 61 percent in January. The public expected something more than having its expectations alternately raised and dashed.

A few days later, on a secure telephone, Ham Jordan had a revealing conversation with Harold Brown:

"We're in a box, Harold. We've broken relations with Iran and imposed sanctions, but we still have no leverage on Khomeini. We've got to do something."

"That's right," Brown replied. "Neither the naval blockade nor mining the harbors will bring the hostages home."

"Except in boxes."

"And if they begin killing our people, then we'll have to take punitive measures — and God only knows where that will lead," Brown
reasoned.

"The rescue mission is the best of a lousy set of options."[2]

On April 11, Day 160, the NSC met in the Cabinet Room over
lunch. Warren Christopher stood in for Cy, who was out of town. The
President opened with two comments. First, he did not want to wait
around for our allies much longer: "It is time for us to bring our hostages home."[3] Next, he pointed out again that our national honor and
reputation were at stake. He asked each of us for an opinion on a
course of action. His patience was obviously wearing thin.

Warren argued articulately against the rescue operation. One by one,
all the rest of us except Ham and Jody, who did not comment, spoke
in favor of it. Jody and Ham's counsel would likely be given in a
private meeting. I added to the pressure by mentioning a recent CIA
report, which concluded that the increasing number of incidents on the
Iraq-Iran border might soon distract the Iranians from the hostage issue.

The President repeated that we had been disgraced by our handling
of the crisis, and that he had been stung recently when Mrs. Anwar
Sadat told him she could not understand how we could have acted so
supinely. Still, he said he did not see what we could have done differently. Noting that recent threats by the students made the hostages'
situation even more precarious, he agreed that the rescue operation
should go ahead as soon as the military was ready. The tone of the
meeting was subdued. Harold recommended the mission go on Day
173, April 24. The President approved. Jimmy Carter had just crossed
his Rubicon. •

What finally pushed him to the reluctant decision he had so long
avoided? The Ayatollah had shut all the doors to a negotiated solution.
We, the President's advisers, had boxed him in by voting against, or
watering down, most other options — though there weren't all that
many good ones. Punitive military action appeared to threaten the lives
of the hostages. The only choice left was to wait it out, and the pressure of public opinion was making that difficult. It is easy to jump to
the conclusion that the President, with the Gallup Polls in mind, was
looking ahead to the November election, and that this was a political
decision. No President, of course, can ignore his electoral prospects.
But it was clear that Jimmy Carter had agonized over this decision and
had tried every way to postpone making it.

The President also had to consider other Americans still residing freely in Tehran. How could we encourage them to leave before April 24 without jeopardizing the secrecy of the mission? But if we did not warn them, and the rescue succeeded, we might find we had emptied the embassy of hostages one day only to have the Iranians fill it again on the next. Some of those Americans were married to Iranians and might refuse to leave. News reporters were a different and highly visible problem. When we discussed what to do about them, someone blithely suggested, "Absolutely nothing, after all the problems they cause us!"

A few days later, Ham Jordan picked up on this problem; he told me that Foreign Minister Ghotbzadeh planned to be in Paris in a few days. Ham intended to meet him there and, by professing continued interest in negotiations, hide our decision on the rescue mission. He wondered whether he should also try another ploy with Ghotbzadeh to help get the newspeople out of Tehran. He could tell him that one of the constraints on President Carter in negotiating was the rage Americans felt toward Iran and that this was fueled by the nightly television clips and daily press stories filed by our correspondents in Tehran. If Ghotbzadeh would expel American media representatives, matters might cool before we went into the next round of serious negotiations. It was a good idea. I offered the CIA's help in providing still another disguise so that he could travel to Paris without alerting the press.

On April 19, Ham returned from Paris very optimistic. Ghotbzadeh had been enthusiastic and had canceled a trip to Algiers so that he could return to Tehran and set the plan in motion. But it was not until April 23, the eve of the rescue operation, that Ghotbzadeh made his move. And then what he did was announce that the credentials of American journalists in Iran would not be renewed when they expired. It could be months before all the journalists were forced to leave. Ham Jordan's ploy had worked, but not quickly enough.

Four days after the President's decision, Cy returned to Washington, and there was a sudden call for a meeting of the NSC. The President, more somber than usual, told us that Cy had strong reservations about proceeding with the rescue mission. He then gave Cy the floor. He started by saying he believed that the considerable investment we had made in the negotiating process would pay off in time. He pointed out that our allies were going to meet in just a week to formulate a new position on economic sanctions and that a date had been set for the election of the Iranian Majlis, to which Khomeini had given jurisdiction over the hostages. He saw no immediate danger to the lives of the hostages but was afraid there would be one if we attempted to rescue them. He added that our resorting to force could turn the Muslim world against us and possibly drive the Iranians into the arms of the Soviet Union.

It was a calm, powerful argument, but the subsequent discussion was brief. The President wound it up with a revealing statement: "Cy, my greatest fear all along is that this crisis could lead us into direct confrontation with the Soviets. The chances of that are much greater if we exercise any of the other military options — a punitive air strike, mining the harbors, or a blockade — than if we go in, rescue our people, and get out."[4] Though I often disagreed philosophically with Cy, I had immense respect for his capability, forthrightness, and integrity; there was no one of higher caliber in the Carter administration. Now, he offered no rejoinder or suggestion for compromise when the President decided against him. I felt certain that what we had seen was a reprise of a more emotional private meeting between him and the President earlier that morning.

Then, on Zbig's initiative, we started discussing whether to launch punitive military attacks if the rescue operation failed. Cy became agitated. He had come to this meeting to discuss whether we should try a rescue operation and was taken aback to find that one of the factors in the final decision was the possible use of military force against Iran. Zbig, Harold, and I felt that if the mission failed, we could not walk away with our tail between our legs. The President approved drawing up plans, but stressed that he wanted as few casualties on both sides as possible. He stated that the reputation of the United States would suffer if we caused much bloodshed.

Zbig suggested that the rescue force should deliberately capture and bring back Iranian hostages. While this might have given us some advantage if the Iranians subsequently captured media people or other Americans in Iran, I thought it extremely unwise. What would stop the Iranians from killing their hostages? Would the United States kill its hostages in return? President Carter rejected the idea out of hand, just as George Washington had not picked up on Thomas Jefferson's proposal in 1790 with regard to capturing Barbary pirates, and Lyndon Johnson had rejected the idea of seizing North Korean fishing boats.

It was momentous for the President to rule against his Secretary of State on a major decision of foreign policy. Never before had there been a showdown like this in front of so many of us. I thought it signaled more than the resolution of one specific issue; otherwise, the President would not have let it come to a head this way.

The next morning, Day 165, eight days before D-Day, I received word that the military men who would lead the rescue operation would brief the President at the White House that evening. Unfortunately, I was to host a dinner for the head of a foreign intelligence service that evening at my home. Since I could not miss my own dinner party without indicating that something very significant was happening, I asked my deputy, Frank Carlucci, to substitute for me at the briefing. The next morning he gave me a written report of what had taken place.

Jim Vaught, Charlie Beckwith, and an Air Force lieutenant general, Philip C. Gast, arrived at the Situation Room in civilian clothes to avoid arousing the attention of newspeople around the White House. Gast, though recently promoted to a rank senior to Vaught, had been Vaught's assistant for air matters almost from the beginning and was now designated as his deputy. The meeting got off to a good start when the President recognized the Southern twang in Beckwith's voice and learned that Charlie came from a county near his own in Georgia. They compared notes for a few moments before the President opened the meeting by praising the dedication of Delta Force and emphasizing how important its mission was to the prestige and honor of the country. After assuring the men of his full backing, he asked to be walked through the operation step by step.

Dave Jones turned it over to Jim, who, with help from Charlie, started with the flight to Desert One and the subsequent move to the hiding place on the outskirts of Tehran, called Desert Two. He proceeded to the assault on the embassy and release of the fifty hostages, a secondary assault on the Foreign Ministry and release of the three hostages there, and the flight by helicopter to Manzariyeh, followed by the escape from the country by fixed-wing aircraft (see Maps 7 and 8). The President listened carefully and stopped the briefing at each step to ask questions.

- How would Charlie handle any cars that passed through Desert One? Charlie explained they would establish two roadblocks, each to include a Farsi-speaking person. These sentries would turn back travelers by saying that an Iranian military exercise was taking place. If necessary, they would detain people and transport them out of the country on the refueling aircraft, disabling the cars to make it look as though they had broken down.

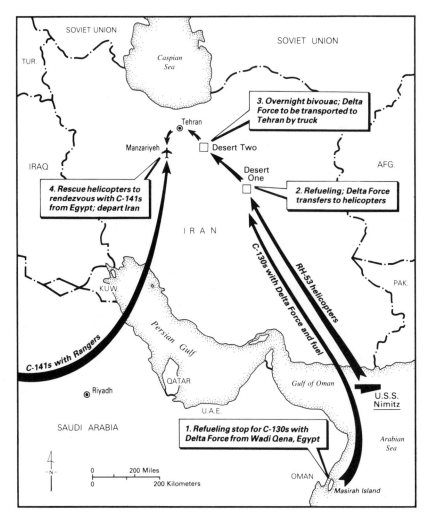

3. Overnight bivouac; Delta Force to be transported to Tehran by truck

4. Rescue helicopters to rendezvous with C-141s from Egypt; depart Iran

2. Refueling; Delta Force transfers to helicopters

1. Refueling stop for C-130s with Delta Force from Wadi Qena, Egypt

C-130s with Delta Force and fuel

RH-53 helicopters

C-141s with Rangers

SOVIET UNION

SOVIET UNION

TUR.

Caspian Sea

Tehran

Manzariyeh

Desert Two

Desert One

IRAQ

AFG.

I R A N

KUW.

PAK.

Persian Gulf

QATAR

Gulf of Oman

U.S.S. Nimitz

Riyadh

U.A.E.

SAUDI ARABIA

Arabian Sea

OMAN

Masirah Island

0   200 Miles
0   200 Kilometers

MAP 7. OVERALL RESCUE MISSION PLAN

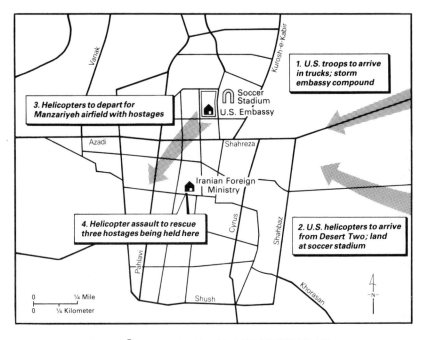

Vanak

Kurosh-e-Kabir

1. U.S. troops to arrive in trucks; storm embassy compound

Soccer Stadium

3. Helicopters to depart for Manzariyeh airfield with hostages

U.S. Embassy

Azadi

Shahreza

Iranian Foreign Ministry

4. Helicopter assault to rescue three hostages being held here

Cyrus

Shahbaz

2. U.S. helicopters to arrive from Desert Two; land at soccer stadium

Pahlavi

Khorasan

—N—

0   ¼ Mile
0   ¼ Kilometer

Shush

MAP 8. TEHRAN PHASE OF RESCUE PLAN

- Would Delta Force bivouac the first night at Desert Two, where the helicopters would drop them, or in the warehouse in the city where the trucks were hidden? The President's questioning indicated his preference for the former plan because it would be easier to withdraw from the outskirts if the mission were called off for any reason. (The briefing had emphasized that there were contingency plans to retreat at almost every step of the mission.) Charlie understood the President's point but wanted the freedom to decide on the spot. The President assented.

The most hostile questioning came from Zbig after Jim Vaught revealed that he was planning to lead the force that was to capture Manzariyeh airfield. Jim said he would direct the withdrawal operation from there. It was unusual for a general officer to be in command on the scene of such a relatively small operation. Normally, he could exercise his command responsibilities better, including the referral of decisions to higher headquarters, from a rear headquarters with good communications facilities. Zbig felt Vaught was just being macho, but Jim vigorously defended his plan, and again the President assented.

The closest the President came to giving direct operational orders was during the discussion of possible loss of life. "I think it is important to keep your mission simple. It will be easy and tempting for your men to become engaged in gunfire with others and to try to settle some scores for our nation. That will interfere with your objective of getting our people out safely. In the eyes of the world, it is important that the scope of this mission be seen as simply removing our people. If innocent people are killed, the Iranians will make a great public spectacle of it and will say we murdered women and children."[5]

Jim estimated that four hostages and eight members of the Delta Force would be wounded. Both Jim and Charlie made it clear that some Iranians would be killed. CIA agents had reported that there were normally three sentries posted along the wall of the embassy that Delta Force was going to scale. These sentries were to be killed with weapons equipped with silencers just before the Delta lead element stormed over the wall.

Perhaps the most important part of the meeting for Jim and Charlie was the President's assurance that he would not harass them with requests for information while the operation was taking place and that they could make their own decisions. The President said he would be available if they wanted to refer a particular decision to him. He would, though, get his information through the chain of command; that is, they would report to General David Jones directly, he to Secretary Harold Brown, and Brown to the President.

As the two-and-a-half-hour meeting went on, the participants became more optimistic and enthusiastic. Even jingoistic. It was punctuated with comments from Charlie such as "Sure, people get killed, but I should have been killed six times, judging by the number of times I've been in combat"; and "I shoot ten thousand rounds of the taxpayers' money every day"; and "Mr. President, we're going to get these people out, you can be sure of that."[6]

Just before closing, Frank told the President the CIA planned to infiltrate agents into Tehran for a last-minute check, especially on conditions around the embassy. They would be taking somewhat greater risks to get the best and latest data. We needed to know very soon whether they should do this or not. The President said he had made his decision and the operation was to proceed. Only if there were some unexpected development would he call it off.

As the meeting closed, the President drew Charlie Beckwith aside and said, "Colonel, I want to ask you to do two things for me. And one of them is very difficult. Before you leave, I want you to line up everybody that's going to Tehran, all the Delta guys, and I want you to tell them that if this operation is not a success, it's not their fault, it's not your fault, it's my fault . . . the buck stops here. I'd also like to ask you if there's an American that gets killed inside the embassy grounds, if it's a hostage or one of your guys, if you possibly can, without costing the life of someone else, try to bring his body back. I know what I'm asking is a tall order." Beckwith replied, "Mr. President, you know my track record. I ain't gonna leave anybody if I can help it."[7]

Charlie Beckwith, who acknowledged that before this meeting he had been no "big Carter fan,"[8] was obviously pleased with the President's decision; as the President was walking out of the Situation Room, Charlie turned to his Commander-in-Chief and said, "God bless you, Mr. President."[9]

FAILURE IN THE DESERT

Ask "Eagle" [radio call sign for Colonel Charles Beckwith] to consider going on with five.

— Jim Vaught to Charlie
Beckwith at Desert One,
April 25, 1980[1]

THERE WAS only one matter left for our White House rescue planning group: to ensure that the Iranians did not find out about the rescue operation before it took place. There were bound to be opportunities for leaks in the next eight days. Delta Force had to move from Fort Bragg, North Carolina, to a staging base at Wadi Qena, Egypt, and then on to Masirah Island, Oman. Besides the more than a hundred men who would actually go to Iran, plus all their equipment, there was a headquarters unit for Jim Vaught and support personnel like meteorologists and chaplains. The numerous aircraft sorties required to transport them all might well attract attention. CIA agents doubling their reconnaissance around the embassy in Tehran might also be noticed. And the Army's plan to send its own three scouts into Tehran could easily backfire. After spending almost a month working with the CIA to develop cover that would hold up under scrutiny, they were ready to head in.[2] New activities were being established and old patterns broken. We were vulnerable.

Our planning group had been excessively secretive thus far. Now we became almost paranoid. Zbig came to me with a story about a CIA officer who was suspected of being a mole for the Soviets. He wouldn't tell me where he got the story, but was worried that the man might inform the Soviets, and they might alert the Iranians, who could then be waiting for Delta at Desert

One.* Zbig wanted the officer placed under twenty-four-hour surveillance until after the rescue. The CIA's counterintelligence people were familiar with the case, which was based on suspicious behavior some twenty years before without any new evidence since. Dan Silver advised me that under rules promulgated by President Carter, we did not have grounds for placing the officer under surveillance. Though security of the rescue mission was extremely important, it disturbed me that we were again ready to ignore the rules.

There were other, more substantive concerns about security. On April 22 we intercepted a radio broadcast in Farsi from Moscow which said that beginning May 1, the U.S. Navy would blockade all Iranian ports. That same day a broadcast from Tehran claimed the government had uncovered a CIA plot to rescue the hostages, and we had indications that an Iranian gendarmerie unit in southern Iran had been placed on alert. All this was worrisome, but we believed much of it was tied to a story in the *Washington Star* two days before by a former CIA officer describing a plan he had concocted for a rescue operation that was, unfortunately, similar to the real one.[3]

Then we went into a near panic over a report from one of our CIA agents who had gone in and out of Tehran several times. While scouting the perimeter of the embassy, he noticed that the guards were more alert than before. He thought the operation could not be conducted safely. When Cy heard this, he argued that the President should reconsider his decision. But the momentum was by now too great to reverse course on the basis of a single report.

Next, the Omanis complained that we had misled them in explaining that we were placing aircraft on Masirah Island, just off the entrance to the Gulf of Oman, in order to conduct ocean surveillance. They had deduced exactly the true reason. The State Department put them off by changing the story to one of an airdrop to the Afghan insurgents, believing it was better that the Omanis be able genuinely to deny having known we were staging a rescue mission from their territory.

Finally, we debated how to maintain security while also informing the Congress. Although the President was not required to notify Congress in advance, doing so would help win its support whichever way the mission turned out. It seemed prudent to let at least the congressional leadership know. The President decided to invite them to the

---

*In the late 1940s the CIA infiltrated agents into the Ukraine and into Albania. The British mole Kim Philby was given this information, which he passed to the Soviets. The CIA agents were met and captured on arrival.

Cabinet Room on the second day of the operation, just as Delta Force would be scaling the embassy wall. I did not think this a good idea. It would place the President, as Commander-in-Chief, alongside a group of congressmen at a time when he might have to make operational decisions. If he left the room to consult his advisers privately, the congressmen would be offended. If he included the congressmen in his consultations, he might be inhibited by partisan political concerns.

There were a few encouraging reports about security along with the alarming ones. An amusing one came from a CIA officer who had gone to the aircraft carrier *Nimitz* in the Arabian Sea. He and a naval officer accompanying him were to install a special, CIA-procured navigational system in the helicopters. En route to *Nimitz*, they had to stop at the island of Diego Garcia in the Indian Ocean to transfer to an aircraft capable of landing on the carrier. While they waited, a Navy enlisted man stationed there boasted to them that he had figured out, from the people and aircraft going through Diego Garcia, that a rescue operation was imminent. Taking no chances that this deduction might spread, the naval officer ordered the surprised sailor to board the aircraft going to *Nimitz*. That would keep him and his ideas out of the way until the mission was over.

One piece of good news was that on April 21 the three Army scouts, headed by Major Richard J. Meadows, arrived safely in Tehran. Meadows verified Bob's information and checked the trucks and the warehouse. He had good military communications equipment and was ready to take charge of the movement of Delta Force from the outskirts of Tehran to the embassy. In the two days they had to prepare, however, they almost tipped our hand. Driving around Tehran, they became involved in a minor traffic accident. When the police asked to see the driver's license, he realized it was in the trunk of the car, along with a good bit of highly compromising communications equipment. Fortunately, he managed to retrieve the license without the policemen looking inside the trunk.

The really good news came from Bob in Tehran. With two days to go, he sent word that the Tehran portion of the operation would be "a piece of cake." Bob was well respected, and I had more confidence in him than in the agent who had suggested calling off the mission. The day before the mission I had a scheduled half-hour meeting with the President. It was a warm, sunny spring day, and he suggested we sit outside in the Rose Garden. He had made a lonely, fateful decision, which was now almost out of his control.

I wanted to let him know I was fully behind that decision. I told him

I thought it would be six to nine months before we could get the hostages out any other way. We had no intelligence that indicated the operation had been compromised, and I was confident our agents in Tehran would be able to warn Charlie Beckwith of any last-minute change of conditions at the embassy. Although this would be a high-risk operation, I believed the Iranians were disorganized and there was a good chance of our pulling off the series of complex actions involved without their being able to react decisively. Finally, I continued to think the rescue attempt was our best alternative, the only one that would solve the problem soon.

And then we had splendid good luck. On the evening of April 23, the cook from the embassy decided to leave Iran. By chance, he was on the same commercial flight as one of our agents. When they arrived in Rome, the agent took the man aside and questioned him about the location of the hostages. The cook said he had delivered breakfast to them that very day, and that approximately forty-five were in the chancery and four or five were in the ambassador's residence. (The remaining three were still in the Ministry of Foreign Affairs.) We immediately sent this information to Jim Vaught at Wadi Qena, and Charlie Beckwith modified his assault plan. Although the cook's report was not much different from the CIA's twice weekly written reports, Charlie could now concentrate his forces on the chancery with greater confidence.

The final meeting of our rescue planning group convened in Zbig's office on Day 173, April 24, at just about the time the first aircraft carrying Delta Force took off from Masirah. We had agreed that, as part of our deception, we would all carry on with business as usual until late the next afternoon, when the troops would be over the embassy wall and secrecy broken. Then we would gather in the Cabinet Room, along with the leadership of Congress. Harold Brown reminded us the President had stated unequivocally that only the President and he would give orders to Dave Jones. All of us understood that this comment was pointed directly at Zbig. Jimmy Carter, a former naval officer, was not going to let even a trusted assistant break into the chain of command during a military operation.

Our spirits and hopes were high. But it was not easy to carry out my normal routine while waiting anxiously for word of the operation's progress. I spent the morning on Capitol Hill testifying on the intelligence budget. As important as this was, I had difficulty concentrating. When I returned to my office, word had come in that one of the eight helicopters launched from *Nimitz* had crashed inside Iran. I was worried that this might tip off the Iranians, but I knew the remaining seven helos were sufficient for our needs. Only six were necessary to go forward from Desert One.

In the afternoon, I had a scheduled meeting with a professor who was an expert on the Middle East. Because of our problems with Iran over the preceding two years, I found it useful to meet from time to time with academics who specialized in the region. This was my first meeting with this man. My secretary, Doris Gibbons, interrupted to ask me to take a phone call. An officer in the makeshift CIA war room passed on the good news that the C-130 aircraft carrying both the Delta Force personnel and the fuel for the helicopters were arriving at Desert One on schedule. The bad news was that as the first C-130 dropped its rear ramp and a Ranger unit drove out to take control of the road, a large bus had appeared. The Rangers had brought it to a halt with gunfire and off-loaded forty-some passengers. That situation was no sooner under control than more traffic appeared. The reports were incomplete and confusing, but one vehicle had managed to turn around and escape the roadblock. In addition, a gasoline truck had caught on fire. Since the refueling aircraft were not carrying fuel trucks, only hoses and pumps to deliver directly to the helicopters, it was hard to imagine what truck was burning.

I put the phone down and turned back to the professor, who delivered his principal message: "Avoid any form of military action against Iran if you want to get the hostages out soon."

In a few minutes Doris interrupted again, and the war room officer told me they presumed the gasoline truck belonged to gasoline smugglers. Our people had fired at the truck and had ignited it. The driver had escaped in another car and sped away before the Rangers could react. On the assumption that the smugglers were likely to believe they had encountered a police trap and would not report what they had seen, the President decided the mission had not been compromised, and did not abort it.

At a little after 5:00 P.M., Doris interrupted still another meeting. The message was brief. The mission had been aborted. I brought my meeting to a close as quickly as I could without revealing why and dashed down to a very confused war room, where we were receiving periodic reports from a CIA officer in the Pentagon war room. Even though this officer was right at the center, he had difficulty keeping abreast of the rapidly changing picture, and there were not enough secure telephones to permit him to remain on the line with us.

We learned that a second helicopter had turned back. But that still left six operational helos and did not explain the decision to abort. It was unrealistic, yet I desperately wanted to pick up the phone and call Dave Jones and offer advice. But as I was responsible for only a small part of this operation — the CIA operatives in Tehran — I had no justification for interfering. I knew Dave must be frantic, between talking to Jim Vaught at Wadi Qena and the President at the White House. What he did not need was a kibitzer.

My frustration turned into despair when a report came in of a fire in one of the aircraft. I hoped this was confusion with the fire in the gasoline truck, but no, we were soon told the situation was so bad that the men were abandoning the helicopters in the desert and withdrawing in the C-130s. All hope was dashed.

The planning group had never discussed the possibility of total failure, though we made plans for retreat at each stage. Now the rescue force was moving out pell-mell and was bound to leave lots of evidence behind. Together with two key officers, I retreated to an office across the hall from the war room in the hope of quietly thinking through where we stood. But we had scant information as to why the mission was aborted, and we were so despondent at having failed that we just sat there, looking at one another forlornly.

We had to buckle down. We had both CIA agents and the Army scouts in Tehran to worry about. Some of them would soon be going out to meet Delta at Desert Two. Others would be at the warehouse with the trucks, and some would be reconnoitering the embassy. Once the Iranians pieced together a picture of what we had attempted, they were almost certain to conclude we had positioned people in Tehran to assist Delta when it arrived. Their lives were suddenly very much in danger.

We needed to warn them to get off the streets as soon as possible and then to get out of the country under what would surely be tight surveillance at all border posts and airports. We could not communicate with the CIA people until early the next morning, Washington time, when they were scheduled to listen for us. Our agents used a communication system that was small and easily hidden, but it had its limitations. The Army people had taken a greater risk in bringing in more substantial equipment with capabilities for unscheduled communications. The problem now was to get through to both groups, one way or another. Until we had done that, the less the Iranians knew about what was going on, the better.

I kept trying, without success, to phone Zbig to ask for a delay in making a public announcement. In desperation, at eight o'clock that evening, still not having heard from him, I dictated a note:

> Zbig: We have operatives in Tehran. Dave Jones and I share responsi-
> bility for these people. We urge that no public statement be made about
> what has happened until we are forced to do so. This will give the people
> in Tehran maximum opportunity to protect themselves and get out. Please
> call if this is too cryptic. I will amplify.[4]

My executive assistant, Bob Gates, telephoned this to Zbig's secretary on a secure phone and asked her to deliver it to him immediately,
even if he was with the President. Within minutes I received word that
I was to come down and join the President in the Cabinet Room. When
I arrived, the President was not there, but I found Lloyd Cutler, Harold
Brown, Jody Powell, Ham Jordan, Cy Vance, Warren Christopher,
and Fritz Mondale. Every few minutes a secretary or an aide would
appear in the doorway and pass a note to one of us, who in turn would
dash out of the room, only to reappear a few minutes later. Because
there were no secure telephones in the Cabinet Room, each of us had
to go to someone's office to find one.

While waiting for the President, I asked Harold to fill me in on what
had happened. With a number of interruptions, he outlined the sequence of events as he understood it. A second helicopter, after developing problems, had returned to *Nimitz*. Another helicopter arrived at
Desert One with a hydraulic failure. That left us with only five helos.
And that was when Charlie Beckwith, goaded by Jim Vaught to go on
with five, made his fateful decision not to do so. This was reported to
the White House as the joint recommendation of Vaught and Beckwith, and the President accepted it. There was also a subsequent fire
in which an undetermined number of people were killed.

When the President returned, he asked me to describe the situation
of our people in Tehran. I told him who they were, why they were
vulnerable, and the difficulties we had in communicating with them.
Just then Harold came back from a phone call and said that Jim Vaught
had been able to get through to Major Meadows to tell him the operation had been called off. Whether Meadows would or could seek out
our Bob and his people, we could only guess. I explained that getting
out of Tehran would take these men time. They might opt to lie low
for a number of days, or they might try to get out immediately. Only

they could judge which course gave them the better probability of success. In any case, the more time they had before the Iranians deduced that they were there and started looking for them, the better their chances of escape.

We then debated how much the fate of these agents should affect the timing of the public notification. Lloyd Cutler and Cy made good arguments for an early announcement: when the Iranians found the six helicopters we had left at Desert One, they might easily draw an exaggerated conclusion as to what was going on and possibly harm the hostages. And the Soviets, who, after all, had been conducting maneuvers in the Transcaucasus, might overreact to partial information. Nonetheless, with the backing of Zbig and Jody, I argued that we owed it to our men in Tehran to give them every opportunity to get out.

Harold interrupted with a new report that eight men had died when a helicopter and a C-130 collided on the ground. In the resulting fires and explosions, several more were seriously burned and were already en route to Masirah. Medical experts on burns were on their way there also. A pall settled over the room. There was nothing any of us could say. The President was ashen, but he turned back to the business at hand.

He was torn between his responsibility to our agents and his desire to avoid a confrontation with either the Iranians or the Soviets. Finally, in spite of Cy's and Lloyd's objections, he decided to delay the announcement until 6:00 A.M. That was six hours away and would give the agents some time to hide or to get out.

Bob Gates, who had accompanied me, came in and handed me a report indicating that the plight of these agents was even worse than we had thought. Numerous classified materials had been left on the helicopters in the desert. If these documents revealed that trucks were to be brought to the outskirts of Tehran to carry the troops into the city, the Iranians would know for sure that we had agents there. The President suggested I use the secure telephone in his private office to get additional information. When I came back, I told him the situation looked as bad as we had imagined. Then Harold received a report indicating that the authorities in Tehran were aware of some incident in the desert near Tabas. That meant they might react, perhaps against the hostages, sooner than we had thought likely. When the President looked at me and asked whether I would agree to moving the announcement up to 2:00 A.M., I could only say yes.

Not long after, Jody Powell told us an NBC reporter had come into his office demanding to know what was going on when at this late hour the official vehicles of "all the foreign policy biggies" were in the driveway outside the West Wing of the White House. He suspected a rescue operation was under way. Jody had put him off but pointed out it would not be long before speculation would begin to hit the street.

After reports that all the C-130s carrying the rescue force had taken off for the trip back to Masirah, news slowed to a trickle. Before we left the White House, we agreed to begin notifying the leaders of the congressional committees with which we dealt. Jody Powell was drafting a public statement to be made at two o'clock, and we were all to be back for a seven-thirty breakfast with the President to review a statement he would make to the nation.

At 1:00 A.M. I tumbled into bed, physically exhausted and emotionally drained. I could not remember a more disheartening experience in my life. I spent what was left of the night tossing and turning, worrying about the hostages, our people in Tehran, the dead and wounded, and what would come next.

At seven the next morning, still tired, I got into the official car to head back to the White House. I asked Ennis Brown to turn on the radio. Much to my surprise, I heard the President telling the American people the tragic story of the failure at Desert One.

In his brief announcement, Jimmy Carter stressed that this had been a humanitarian rescue effort and that he assumed full responsibility for what had happened. Yes, I thought, as the Commander-in-Chief he was responsible — but how very much he had been at the mercy of those of us who planned the operation. His composure at breakfast was impressive. More than that, he emphasized that he was pleased with the way we had all gone about our tasks and that he had no recriminations.

As far as I was concerned, Jimmy Carter had been a textbook Commander-in-Chief. He had left the planning to us; reviewed it thoroughly, without making changes his commanders in the field opposed; had not interfered during the operation, other than to concur in the recommendations he received through the chain of command; and now was shouldering with grace the responsibility for failure.

The President told us he had just received a heartwarming phone call from Henry Kissinger, giving his full support and saying the President had been right in attempting the rescue effort. He further added that the President could publicly state that he had called to offer his support. There had not been much love lost between the Carter administration and Henry Kissinger, but the President said he did not want to hear anyone knocking Kissinger again, and if we ever heard him doing so, we should remind him of what he had just said.

Dave Jones filled us in on what additional information they had received in the Pentagon. The troops were already heading to an American base in West Germany. It was not at all clear what had caused the helo to crash into the C-130, setting off the fire and explosions. The casualties were the five crew members of the C-130 and three men in the back of the helo. Troops who were already loaded into the C-130 managed to escape, though some were badly burned.

There was much speculation as to why the forces had left Desert One so rapidly, had not removed the classified materials, and had failed to recover the bodies. Dave said they had abandoned the helos and retreated in the C-130 aircraft so as to get out of Iran before daylight. There was anguish about the bodies of American soldiers having been left behind. None of us, of course, knew whether the fire and explosions prevented Charlie from recovering them, as he had said he would.

The President then asked me about the status of the agents in Tehran. I was pleased to report that we had talked with Bob right on schedule. He did not feel under pressure. Several of his people believed they now required different documentation, which would take some time to get to them. The Army people had planned to leave from Manzariyeh as part of Delta Force, but now they needed a new scheme, which they were working on.

The net result was that the President told us not to discuss with the press or with Congress what the operations at Tehran and Manzariyeh should have been. He wanted to minimize any discussion that could hint of our having agents in Tehran. He also wanted to preserve the plans we had made in case we tried a rescue operation again.

That was certainly a good idea as far as the agents were concerned. It put me in a difficult position, though, with respect to informing the congressional committees on intelligence about the CIA's role in the operation. The morning after the failure, Senators Daniel Inouye and Birch Bayh of the Senate Intelligence Committee came to see me. I had no trouble telling them of the CIA's flight into Desert One. But I was under a presidential injunction to withhold information about the preparations we had made in Tehran. The senators, though, believed they should have been told everything in advance. I didn't see how I could hold out on them now and preserve the good working relationship the Agency had painstakingly developed with their committee.

But what if they insisted that I tell the entire committee? That would be risking a leak. Happily, after I gave them the full story, Dan Inouye solved my problem by volunteering, "This is far too sensitive to give to our committee."

We had a lot more to do before we could piece together what had actually happened and explain it to the entire Congress and the American people.

· 16 ·

WHAT HAPPENED IN THE DESERT

The rescue operation was feasible. It probably represented the plan with the best chance of success under the circumstances. It was a high-risk operation. People and equipment were called on to perform at the upper limits of human capacity and equipment capability.

> — Report of the Special
> Operations Review Group[1]

THE RESCUE MISSION aborted Thursday night. On Saturday morning, Day 175, April 26, as I walked into Zbig's office, he said, "We're going to try it again." I had been thinking of this too and knew that it would have to be as soon as possible. Once the Iranians scattered the hostages, it would be too late. But there was no time to talk it over. Zbig said we were meeting with the President in a few minutes.

Harold Brown and Dave Jones were already outside the Oval Office. Jim Vaught was also there, just back from Wadi Qena. As Zbig and I arrived, Nell Yates motioned us all into the office. President Carter got up from his desk, on which, appropriately, was Harry Truman's carved wooden sign THE BUCK STOPS HERE. He came over to shake Jim Vaught's hand and tell him how proud he was of the tremendous effort he and his men had made. Jim remained at attention after the President and the rest of us took our seats. He began speaking while looking down at the President. In a deep, measured voice, he told the President his troops had given their all and had performed splendidly. He assured the President that even though he did not believe the American people would appreciate what these brave men had attempted, every last one stood ready and eager to go in again. He then saluted and sat down. It was an extraordinary performance, one that I, as a military professional, found extremely embarrassing. The Commander-in-Chief was due an apology from a military commander who had led a mission that had ended in dismal failure. Instead, he had received a lecture about how well his commander had done.

We were all startled into silence. Finally, the President, instead of responding, asked for ideas on a new rescue plan. Harold and Zbig articulated their concepts forcefully, but because of constant interruptions we were repeatedly sidetracked. The problem was largely Jim Vaught, who interrupted everyone, even the President. Exasperated, President Carter said that if he could just be allowed to finish a thought, we might make some progress.

Amidst the confusion, it was easy to see where the new rescue planning was headed. Having failed in a surreptitious entry into Tehran, we were now turning toward the use of direct force. Zbig wanted to assault the Manzariyeh airfield and then drive trucks right to Tehran, shooting our way if necessary. Vaught instantly upped the ante by suggesting the use of armored vehicles, not trucks. I could see it would soon be a full-scale invasion by several divisions, and kept trying to interject that if the Iranians scattered the hostages, no plan would work. But it was almost impossible to speak. Dave Jones, whose military opinions should have been valued, found it equally difficult to be heard. The President grew more and more frustrated. At last, he simply terminated the discussion.

Before we left, though, the President said he wanted to meet with the rescue force the very next day at a secret CIA base in Virginia, where the troops had been brought for debriefing. We were using this location to keep reporters from finding and interviewing them and perhaps revealing too many details. I worried that if the President did visit them there, the press corps would pursue him and the base would no longer be secret. He assured me that he would sneak down in a helicopter without anyone's knowing!

When I got back to the office just after noon, I called my Iranian planning group together to tell them we were going to host the President the next day and that we were to plan a new rescue effort. The chief of the Iranian branch told me the students in the embassy had issued a statement that the American attack had been assisted by "mercenaries" inside Iran, that the hostages were to be moved from the embassy to other Iranian cities, and that if there were another rescue attempt, the hostages would be killed. If the Iranians did scatter the hostages to several locations, and we rescued only one or two groups, the remaining hostages would most likely be killed in retaliation. It looked as if our only chance at a rescue was behind us. Nonetheless, I told the planning group to stay together and work with the military on a second attempt.

The next day I learned more of what had happened in the desert. When Dave Jones and I flew down to the CIA base in advance of the President, some of the helicopter pilots from the rescue force hitched a ride with us. On the base itself we had several hours to talk with other officers and men before the President arrived.

It was a delicate situation. The emotions of these people were mixed. Just three days before they had been as tightly strung and enthusiastic as a college football team playing for the national championship. They told me of the dramatic finale at Wadi Qena before Delta Force boarded the aircraft to head for Masirah and Desert One. They had assembled in a Russian-built aircraft hangar and their chaplain had read to them from the Bible: "And there went out a champion . . . named Goliath." When he finished, they broke out singing "God Bless America." The Delta team was flying high.[2] Now, they were home and back down firmly on the ground. They were both excited and anxious about meeting the President. Although proud of having risked their lives for their countrymen, they knew they had failed but didn't quite understand why. My questions were bound to place some of them in a difficult position, because military people are inherently loyal to their organization and commander, and are loath to tell tales out of school.

I quickly sensed, though, that while there was this kind of loyalty among the Delta Force, it was not the same with the helicopter pilots. They were discontented. As contrasted with Delta, they were not a normal military unit. Three different officers had played roles in training the helicopter unit and planning its employment on the mission: Air Force Major General Gast, Marine Corps Colonel Charles H. Pitman, on loan part-time to Vaught from the staff of Dave Jones, and Lieutenant Colonel Edward R. Seiffert, the senior Marine Corps pilot assigned to the mission. This must have been confusing for the pilots, as none of the three was ever put expressly in charge. But the more I talked with the pilots, the more I sensed that this was not the major problem. What bothered them was their relations with Beckwith and Vaught. When these had got off to a bad start, the pilots did not have anyone designated as commanding officer who could stand up for them or explain their case. They were orphans, never able to get in favor with their boss. Part of the problem was that Beckwith and Vaught were under pressure to build a rescue capability quickly, and the helicopter pilots were a particular problem for them. Even after the original group of Navy pilots was replaced with Marines, one-third of the Marines had to be replaced before long.

I asked about the helos on the mission, and what I heard about the first one that dropped out was straightforward. When it was about a hundred miles inside Iran, an alarm in the cockpit indicated a possible problem with one of the rotor blades. The pilot landed by moonlight on a dry lake bed. The pilot of his buddy helo noted his plight, landed, and took him and his crew and their classified materials aboard his aircraft and proceeded to Desert One.

At this time, no one knew for sure what had happened to the helo that turned back to *Nimitz;* that crew was still on its way back to the United States. Other helo pilots, though, spoke with awe about the two *haboobs* they had encountered. *Haboob* is Arabic for a large cloud of fine white dust. The helo pilots had been forced to fly in *haboobs* for several hours, without lights and in radio silence, relying totally on instruments and at low altitude to avoid radar detection. They constantly worried about colliding in midair or crashing into a hillside, and they were so exhausted when they arrived at Desert One that several wanted to reconsider whether to go forward.

One of the Delta Force men told me that when the last helicopter arrived, the pilot shut down the helo's rotors. To conserve the canisters of high-pressure air carried for restarting their engines, the pilots had been told to keep the engines running while at Desert One. In this particular case a cockpit warning indicator had alerted the pilot several hours earlier to problems with the aircraft's hydraulic systems. With the engines off, the pilot was able to inspect the systems carefully. He determined that all the hydraulic fluid had leaked out of one of the two systems, causing the pump in that system to burn up. As best as I could piece it together, Air Force Colonel James H. Kyle, who was in charge of the C-130s and the fueling operations, discussed the hydraulic problem with Ed Seiffert, the flight leader. Seiffert decided that the helo would not go on to Tehran, and Charlie Beckwith decided he would not go ahead with only one.

Harold Brown had told me the night of the disaster that when the message reached the President recommending an abort, the President had asked whether Vaught and Beckwith agreed. After Harold assured him they did, the President concurred. Now, as I chatted with Charlie over luncheon, I wanted to ask him what had gone through his mind. There he was, close to the fulfillment of an ambition, having campaigned for over a decade and a half for the creation of Delta, spent two years nursing it into being, and then brought it over the past six months into fighting form for what lay just a few hours ahead. How could he have resisted not taking a chance and going on when he had assured the President he was ready to do whatever was needed to get the hostages out? It must have been the most wrenching decision of his life.

I couldn't find a way to put my question directly to Charlie without the risk of sounding critical, and criticism was the last thing he needed at this moment. Besides, while the men of the rescue force around the luncheon table that day were tense, there were some amusing stories to lighten the atmosphere. A Delta officer, moving his troops from their C-130 to the point at Desert One where they were to wait for their helicopter, became disoriented in the dark. He was relieved when he saw another group of people across the road and decided to find out who they were so that he could get his bearings. After marching his troops over to them, he found they were forty-five Iranian pilgrims lying flat on the ground beside their bus, with several Americans keeping guard over them. Not quite the reference point he had in mind!

Another wry twist to the sad event was what would have happened to these pilgrims if the operation had proceeded on schedule. The plan was to load them into one of the C-130s and fly them to Egypt. The next night they would have been returned to Iran in the aircraft carrying the troops who would storm and capture the Manzariyeh airfield. One can only imagine what kind of a miracle the pilgrims would have recounted when it was all over. There they were, heading across the desert of eastern Iran toward their shrine on one night; then, after being spirited away in several flying machines, they ended up the following night some four hundred miles west of where their journey had been interrupted.

And there was the story of a near disaster during the haste to evacuate. With two runways, one on either side of the road, one of the C-130 pilots lost his bearings in departing. Heading down one runway, he veered toward the lights of the other. As his aircraft gathered speed, it struck the shoulder of the road, shuddered, and, after rising slightly, bounced down onto the other runway. Fortunately, it bounced back up and gained enough airspeed to lift off.

The pilot who had led the C-130s to Desert One and made the first landing was at the luncheon. I asked him how the CIA's remote-controlled landing lights worked. He said that when he pushed the button and the lights came on, it was easier to see where he was going than at Washington's National Airport.

Lunch ended and the President's helicopter arrived. The base commander led us all into the hangar where the troops were assembled. The President spoke to the men about their bravery. He reminded them of the importance of the mission and said he had no recriminations for an outcome that could not have been foreseen. And he expressed his regret and personal sorrow for the loss of their eight comrades.

Dave Jones, Jim Vaught, and I followed the President down the line as he shook hands with each of the hundred or so men who were there. When the President came to Beckwith, Charlie burst out with the apology the President deserved: "Mr. President, I'm sorry we let you down. Will you let us go back?"[3]

FAILURE AT THE TOP

Two factors combined to directly cause the mission abort: unexpected helicopter failure rate and low-visibility flight conditions
en route to Desert One.

— Report of the Special
Operations Review Group [1]

The cancellation of our [hostage rescue] mission was caused by a
strange series of mishaps — almost completely unpredictable.

— Jimmy Carter's Diary,
April 24–25, 1980 [2]

NEITHER THE PRESIDENT nor the country had a good explanation
of why the rescue mission failed. I thought it important that the President appoint a small, high-level commission to analyze what went wrong
and derive lessons for the future. This was our third successive failed
rescue operation following Son Tay in 1970 and the *Mayaguez* in 1975.*
Were there failures of leadership? Of planning? Of equipment? Or was
it fate? The public deserved to be able to judge whether rescue operations could be employed in combating future terrorism, for there was
no reason to believe this would be the last time the United States would
have to consider dispatching a military rescue force.

Beyond that, as a military officer I believed thorough accountability
was essential. Eight men had died in the collision as the force was

---

*Although President Ford's overall handling of the *Mayaguez* hostage problem was
a success in that the hostages were released quickly, the rescue mission launched on
Koh Tang Island must be judged a failure, because eighteen Marines lost their lives
and no hostages were rescued.

preparing to retreat from Desert One. We owed it to those men, and to others who would be asked to place themselves in jeopardy in the future, to be certain those lives had not been lost needlessly.[3] Our military had let the country down. We needed to take whatever steps were necessary to ensure it would be ready to do better the next time.[4]

I wanted the role of each of us who was involved in the planning and execution of the rescue operation to be investigated carefully. The President was standing very much alone. Only Cy submitted his resignation. I hated to see him go; he is a man of wisdom and probity. I thought the President needed him. It now looked as though he may have been more right than the rest of us in how to approach this problem. At the least, the rest of us were going to have to find some of his patience.

It was soon clear there would be no close study of the lessons to be learned from Desert One. The President was in the midst of the primary election campaign, with Senator Edward M. Kennedy challenging him for the Democratic Party's nomination. His advisers tried to push the failure of the rescue mission out of sight, even insisting that we delay briefing the Congress on what happened. That was a problem for me because of my responsibility for informing the intelligence committees of covert actions "in a timely manner." I went to the President directly, pointing out we were going to lose more than we gained by stalling. We had worked hard to deserve the trust of Congress and did not want to jeopardize it.

President Carter was not nearly as concerned about going to Congress as was his staff. On May 7, thirteen days after the rescue attempt, I received approval to go to Capitol Hill. By then, all of our agents were out of Iran, which made it easier for me to discuss the CIA's several roles in the operation. During the more than two hours I spent with each of the two intelligence committees, the members expressed great satisfaction with the Agency's performance, but at the same time let me know they were annoyed at not having been informed sooner.

Near the end of May, Dave Jones announced the appointment of retired Admiral James L. Holloway III to head the Special Operations Review Group, to study the rescue effort and draw lessons from it. I was confident that Jim Holloway, whom I knew well, would be thorough and honest. However, it was not likely that any group appointed by the Joint Chiefs of Staff, and composed entirely of military officers, would cast blame on the Joint Chiefs if that were warranted.[5] In addition, the review group had no authority to investigate anyone outside the purview of the Joint Chiefs, principally Harold, Zbig, and me. Moreover, when Jim came to the CIA to get our views on the operation, he made it clear that his mandate did not call for allocating blame. The final report of the review group made that point explicit: "The group's charter was not to find fault or to place blame; it was . . . to make 'evaluations and specific recommendations.' "[6]

That limitation was unfair to Jim Holloway and his fellow officers. It was like asking a doctor for a thorough diagnosis of a patient's health, but prohibiting mention of any one of several diseases that might be causing the patient's illness. The report of Holloway's review group, nonetheless, has great value for understanding why four officers made four decisions that brought the rescue mission to a halt.* In each case, the consideration of safety overrode the need to take risks.

Three calls independently determined that helicopters capable of flying would not continue with the mission. The first of these was helicopter number 6, which set down on the desert a little more than two hours into the flight. The cockpit instrument panel displayed a BIM warning. This is an indicator that one of the rotor blades that lift and propel the aircraft may have a crack that would cause the blade to fracture, sending the aircraft plummeting into a certain crash.† Both a primary and a backup indicator in the cockpit said the same thing. After landing, the pilot climbed atop his aircraft and, by inspecting the indicators on the blade itself, confirmed that he was not receiving false signals in the cockpit. The pilot not only had five lives at stake, but if he went on and crashed in an inhabited area, he might give the entire mission away. He elected to abort.

The review group report points out, though, that in this type of helo, the Navy RH-53, every BIM indication recorded had been a false alarm, probably caused by faulty seals. The pilot of number 6 was a Marine, experienced with a different model of this helo, the CH-53. There had been hundreds of BIM indications in the CH-53, all but thirty-one of which had proved to be false alarms. Three of the thirty-one, though,

---

*An unclassified version of the report was published on August 23, 1980, 121 days after the rescue attempt.

†BIM stands for Blade Inspection Method. A BIM indication does not necessarily mean a rotor blade is failing. Each blade is filled with nitrogen under pressure. The indicator tells if the pressure drops, but that can be from a crack in the blade or from a poor seal on either the filler cap or the joint where the blade is attached to the engine shaft.

resulted in crashes and fatalities. But even with the CH-53, the record showed that a pilot could expect from two to eighty hours of safe flying after a valid BIM indication, depending on airspeed. The Air Force had published a rule that after a BIM warning, a pilot could fly a CH-53 up to five hours at speeds no greater than 130 knots — about the speed they were flying en route to Desert One, which was then about three hours away; Desert Two was two to three hours further.

Although this Marine pilot may have been unaware of either the record of the Navy's RH-53s or the rule the Air Force had for CH-53s, it is difficult to believe that an experienced pilot could think a BIM indication was a go or no-go situation. He and the other pilots had been reminded of the BIM issue during their training flights for the mission, when there had been two BIM indications. It also is significant that this pilot had been a presidential helicopter pilot. Although the President's helos were not CH-53s, his position had called for him to steep himself in safety data. On the one hand, that experience may have created a bias toward safety, but on the other, it should have made him aware of how to stretch his aircraft to the limit whenever doing so was critical.

The second helo to abort was number 5. When it was about forty-five minutes inside the second of two *haboobs,* several navigational instruments apparently failed. Flying in formation in near-zero visibility was already hazardous, and the pilot and co-pilot were becoming disoriented. They dropped down to 150 feet and climbed up to 9000 feet without breaking out of the dust storm. Knowing there was a 9000-foot mountain between them and Desert One, on reaching the point where he would not have sufficient fuel to return to *Nimitz,* the pilot decided to return. When he reached the ship, his number 2 engine flamed out for lack of fuel.

As noted earlier, some of the six other pilots, who persevered through the dust storm, were exhausted when they arrived at Desert One. In this helo, though, because the pilots were forced to rely on backup instruments, conditions were even more difficult. Why the instruments failed remains a mystery. An aviation trade magazine reported: "Turbulence encountered in a dust storm . . . may have thrown a duffel bag and flight jackets against a vent feeding the cooling system of the electrical motor that powered navigational instruments."[7] The Chief of Naval Operations confirmed that the failure was due to "inadvertent blocking."[8] I inspected an RH-53 at the Sikorsky factory and concluded that it was physically impossible for a duffel bag or flight jacket to obstruct the cooling system. The opening of the ventilation intake is vertical, not horizontal, and it is located only inches away from a structural rib of the aircraft's frame, making it difficult for anything sizable to be wedged between vent and frame.

But it doesn't matter much whether the pilot's instrument problems were perception or fact. He testified to the review group that, regardless of the difficulties he was facing, had he known either that he was only twenty-five minutes away from Desert One or that the weather was clear there, he would have persisted.[9] In short, faulty instruments and the mountain did not seem insurmountable problems to him in retrospect. He did not break the prescribed radio silence to ask about the weather, though he did so to ask *Nimitz* to steam at full speed in his direction lest he run out of gas. Again, the pilot opted for safety rather than mission accomplishment, but it is only fair to recognize that the pilots of helos number 5 and 6 could each have reasonably assumed his aircraft was not critical to success of the mission, since there were two spares.

The last helicopter to drop out was number 2. Its pilot persevered to Desert One, only to find the supplementary stage of his aircraft's hydraulic system totally inoperative. Should the first stage fail in flight or the demand on it exceed its capacity and require supplementary support from the backup system, a fatal crash was certain. Operating instructions called for an immediate halt in this circumstance, especially when the helo was loaded as heavily as this one was.

Still, the helicopter had just flown for several hours on one hydraulic system with this load and under these conditions. The question was whether to risk doing it for two or three more hours. The pilot wanted to go, but the flight leader, Ed Seiffert, said no to Jim Kyle. I have asked a good many pilots about the pros and cons of flying an RH-53 helo with only one hydraulic system. The best answer I received was from retired Vice Admiral James B. Stockdale, hero of many missions over North Vietnam and the winner of a Congressional Medal of Honor. He wrote:

> I made a couple of phone calls to senior H-53 pilots I knew to get the "feel of the fleet" on that sort of thing in that particular airplane. They both clammed up and started talking about regulations prohibiting it and so on. It wasn't until this fall at a Congressional Medal of Honor get-together, when I and my good friend Colonel Jim Fleming were being transported to a war museum in an H-53, that I asked him if he had ever

launched in one of these planes with one hydraulic system out. Jim calmly told me that in the H-53, if you're flying on one hydraulic system and that system fails, everybody in the plane is going to die; that's a given. But he went on to say that he had launched in an H-53 on one system more than once when the mission was crucial, like the rescue of people down at sea. So, like so many other things, I finally found out that it's all a matter of who's calling the shots. And what I'm saying is that what those shots *are* in history-making situations has a lot to do with the shot-caller's *sense* of history.

It would be unfair to say that any one of the decisions by the three helicopter pilots was wrong; none of us can reconstruct the pressures those officers felt. What is disturbing is that each officer made his choice on the side of safety. While I think it may be unwarranted to draw large conclusions from this, the choices are consistent with other decisions in other contexts I have known of over the past twenty years or so. Together they push me toward the conclusion that an understandable emphasis in the U.S. military on safety in peacetime has carried over even to combat situations. A major difference between leading forces in peacetime training maneuvers and in combat is the level of risk one must accept. Successful field commanders certainly do not expose their men recklessly, but they do take calculated risks. If they carried out only the no-risk initiatives, they would achieve few brilliant combat victories. Truly successful antiterrorist offensives, like Entebbe and Mogadishu, called for a high level of personal and national risk.

We should also be concerned, I believe, that since Vietnam our military services have lost the element of derring-do that marks first-rate combat organizations. This should be interpreted not as a call for recklessness but for more serious dedication. Soldiers, sailors, and airmen tend to believe today they have the right to decide when to place their lives at risk. In this instance, as we saw, one Navy pilot refused even to continue training for the mission, claiming he was not qualified. Apparently he decided this was not a war he wanted to fight, and got away with it. Of course, the country was ostensibly at peace and we were asking men to risk their lives in an operation that, because it was secret, lacked the support which goes with a national commitment.

I believe these generalizations still deserve study, though I must acknowledge that another important factor was the absence of adequate command effort to motivate the helicopter pilots for this mission. First, they had no commanding officer and had been in the doghouse with Charlie Beckwith from the beginning. In the words of the review group, while the Marine Corps flight leader "was responsible for the total performance and welfare of his men, [he was] not provided adequate staff or administrative support."[10] In contrast, Vaught and Beckwith, as Army officers, had Delta Force at a fever pitch. When the rescue force stopped at Masirah island, Jim Kyle told his C-130 pilots not to go near Delta's tent area because he thought the people there were about to explode.[11] Within the complete rescue group, Delta remained an elite segment into which most of the motivational effort went, much as it would into the varsity football team rather than its bus drivers. Unfortunately, motivation of the bus drivers was needed in this case to be sure the team arrived at the stadium. In addition, the pilots must have known of the emphasis the President placed on minimizing the loss of life on this mission, and their lives were legitimately part of that concern.

Still, the Delta team could have reached Tehran if Charlie Beckwith had been willing to go with only five helos. Doing so would have meant dropping some people, some equipment, and maybe some fuel. Charlie had considered carefully what people, equipment, and fuel were necessary. However, any military commander tries to make provision for the unexpected. There is no question in my mind that Charlie could have found some items to leave behind that would have lightened the load yet would have had only a marginal effect on the mission. Among those, I would have considered the antiaircraft missiles, which he took along as insurance against the remote chance of an attack by the dilapidated Iranian Air Force. But if he started dropping such items, his flexibility to meet contingencies would have been diminished. Another consideration was that the last helo arrived eighty-five minutes behind schedule. This pushed the mission against the deadline of arriving at the Desert Two site before daylight. Every minute Charlie took to calculate what to leave behind, and every minute required to locate and unload it, enlarged the risk of being detected.

Still, there is no question that the mission could have gone forward in five helos at increased risk. Charlie and two or three of his subordinates are the only ones qualified to estimate fairly what the increase would have been. What I question, though, is whether Charlie even assessed the risk before he said no. When Jim Vaught asked over the radio whether he would go ahead with five, Charlie fumed. As he put it later:

I lost respect right then for General Vaught. Damn, I thought, how in the hell can the boss ask me that! He should know it will be a disaster if we go forward with five. There isn't any way. I'd have to leave behind twenty men. In a tight mission no one is expendable *before you begin!* Which twenty would I leave? [12]

Charlie's decision was not that black or white, however, and it is curious that it was not one of the issues addressed by Jim Holloway's group. I assume that was because there was no way to discuss Charlie's performance without implying criticism. In retrospect it truly was *the* crucial decision. Zbig has written that he was prepared to urge the President to let the operation proceed with five helos if Charlie had recommended it. [13] The fact that the President wanted assurance from Charlie before aborting the operation indicates that he placed much weight on Charlie's opinion.

Charlie Beckwith's record of three years of combat in Vietnam, including a near-fatal chest wound, is clear evidence that he was a man willing to take risks. Throughout his career he demanded total dedication from his subordinates, as in the flier he used to recruit men to go to Vietnam with his Green Beret unit — "WANTED: Volunteers for Project DELTA. Will guarantee you a medal, a body bag, or both." [14] And when he briefed the President on this operation, he certainly took a tough line. What this situation demanded, however, was a cerebral evaluation, a careful calculation involving aircraft payloads, flight times, and probabilities of failure. Although he was the kind of soldier who will climb fearlessly over the top of the trench, he was not well equipped to lead a complex multiservice operation like this. There is need for men of valor like Charlie Beckwith, but modern warfare demands a broad understanding of the military profession. That includes not only a leader's own specialty — infantry, armor, submarines — but familiarity with other specialties that will also play a role. Today's military leader must be a master of any number of technologies, able to calculate probabilities quickly and with analytic rigor.

The country owes Chargin' Charlie Beckwith a debt for creating Delta Force, but he was the wrong man to lead the operation. Jim Vaught was skeptical of Charlie's flamboyant style and probably would not have chosen him if Charlie had not just brought Delta Force into being. It was not a moment to change leadership. If the students in Tehran had waited a week or two to seize the embassy, Charlie would have been on his way to Europe, relieved of command of Delta. It all might have been different.

Even so, Charlie played the critical role he did at Desert One because Jim Vaught failed to designate anyone to be in command there. That was the most fatal of a number of errors in organizing the rescue operation. The review group came closer to open criticism here than anywhere: "From [Vaught] downward, command channels were less well defined in some areas and only implied in others." [15] Never should troops be sent into combat with only an implied commander.

At the last minute, Jim Vaught assigned Jim Kyle to be " 'on-scene' commander at Desert One, responsible for supervising the refueling operations." [16] Kyle believed this did not give him authority over Charlie Beckwith or Ed Seiffert. [17] Nor did others understand him to be the on-scene commander at Desert One, as indicated by confusion during the operation as to who he was and whether his orders carried weight. The review group pointedly noted that Jim Vaught had made no provision for Kyle to have a command post, a staff, messengers, and backup radios for directing operations at Desert One. [18]

Thus, there were three separate commanders at Desert One: Beckwith, Kyle, and Seiffert. Each made his decisions from a limited perspective: Beckwith on whether he could do the job in Tehran with only the load from five helos, Seiffert on whether he could get six helos to Tehran, and Kyle on whether he could put the fuel where it was needed.

An overall commander would also have asked some different questions, like what were the consequences of sending on helo number 2 with its faulty hydraulic system. One answer is that if it had failed, we would have lost some lives, but the bulk of Delta Force would still have been at Desert Two. Charlie could then have judged whether that force was sufficient to assault the embassy. If it was not, he could have retreated back through Desert One the next night, consolidating fuel into just a couple of helicopters and leaving behind heavy equipment if necessary. Mission planning had emphasized the need of readiness to retreat. Whether it would have been worth risking the lives in helo number 2 would have been a difficult decision, but it was a reasonable alternative that was not even considered.

That failure to address the alternatives for mission accomplishment lies squarely on Jim Vaught's shoulders. Jim Kyle was the logical man to be the on-scene commander, but Vaught had not prepared him for that. The reason was simply that Vaught intended to be there himself. Dave Jones, quite rightly, vetoed that idea. Vaught's responsibility was to pull together the efforts of a number of disparate elements: the rescue force itself, the force going into Manzariyeh for the exfiltration, and the *Nimitz* fighter, which would launch the helos and provide cover for the exfiltration. And he was the point of contact between the operations and the Pentagon. He could best have carried out those responsibilities from a location where he had worldwide communications, not from Desert One.

But Vaught's having toyed with going to Desert One left no time to prepare Jim Kyle for the job. It would have been vital for him to understand thoroughly the role of Delta and of the helicopters if he was to make decisions such as whether to go forward with only five helicopters. These parts of the mission had not been his province at all during training.

Perhaps Jim Vaught thought that his going to Desert One was one way to show the troops he was willing to take the same risks he was asking them to take. Perhaps he wanted to be part of the action. In any case, he insisted on at least being in command at the Manzariyeh end of the operation and had managed to hang on to that despite Zbig's objections at the final briefing for the President. Jim's desire for personal involvement got in the way of the proper organization of his force. He did not rise to the challenge of being the commander of a joint task force.

But it was not only Jim Vaught's fault. Many of the obstacles Jim faced existed because the U.S. military establishment could not give him what he needed to do the job. We lacked helicopters that could fly the required distance or that could be refueled in flight and go almost any distance; we did not have enough satellite communications sets to give more than one to a flight of eight helos. It was not because these requirements could not have been met. The long-distance helos, the aerial refueling capability, and the radio sets all could have been found, but they had not been given sufficient priority. Had any one of them been available to the rescue operation, the probability of success might have changed markedly. Also, because the military establishment did not have plans that fitted anywhere close to this contingency, it took, according to the review group, four to five months to draw up a plan and train a set of forces to execute it.* That is a long time to leave the

---

*The report states two views. On page v, "The first realistic capability to successfully accomplish the rescue of the hostages was reached at the end of March." On page 7, "By 8 February . . . the commanders and planners for the first time had confidence that a capability existed for the rescue." The essential point was that it took from early November to at least early February for our military to be ready to conduct a rescue.

nation's President without a rescue capability. The planning and training should have been "on the shelf" items.

The reason they were not is that we admirals and generals had neglected the requirements of unconventional and low-intensity warfare for too long. We were absorbed with the big problems of nuclear deterrence and the defense of Western Europe. We assumed that if we were ready for the big wars, we could handle the smaller ones, despite clear evidence in Vietnam that we could not. It was not that giving attention and money to lesser forms of conflict would have drained significant resources from the preparation for big wars. The needed resources were inconsequential. It was a matter of myopic neglect of the lesser, more likely contingencies in pursuit of the bigger, more catastrophic ones. The two recommendations of the review group confirmed this attitude.

The first read: "A Counterterrorist Joint Task Force be established as a field agency of the Joint Chiefs of Staff with permanently assigned staff personnel and certain assigned forces."[19] It is always tempting to correct a problem by reorganizing. This proposal, which was eventually carried out in substance, took us in the wrong direction. Our military has two forms of organization. The first is the three military departments, Army, Navy, and Air Force, which acquire, train, and maintain the people and equipment needed for the conduct of war. The second is the Joint Chiefs of Staff, who, under the President and the Secretary of Defense, direct the operations of all military forces in peace and in war. They do so through subordinate commanders, principally the theater, or geographic, commanders for Europe, the Atlantic, the Pacific, and the Persian Gulf region.* This recommendation of the review group would take counterterrorist operations away from this usual chain of command and create a new commander, with worldwide responsibility, also reporting directly to the Joint Chiefs. The implicit message of the recommendation was that this type of warfare is too specialized to be handled by the normal chain of command; we need specialists, experts.

The second recommendation was: "The Joint Chiefs of Staff give careful consideration to the establishment of a Special Operations Advisory Panel, comprised of a group of carefully selected high-ranking officers."[20] The JCS should have been insulted. They were being told

---

*This description of the Unified Command System is abbreviated and simplified to avoid a number of detailed, complex provisions. It is not distorted, however.

they needed special advisers for warfare down at the lower level of counterterrorism. They certainly would have been insulted if the recommendation had been for a panel of experts on how to defend Western Europe or invade Panama or deter nuclear war. *They* are the President's experts on war, across the entire spectrum.

Thus, the review group's report, because it could not lay blame where it belonged, inadvertently misled the public into believing there were organizational problems rather than the one of entrenched attitudes toward this type of warfare. The hostage rescue mission failed not for lack of a separate command or a group of advisers, but for three clear reasons: (1) three pilots and Charlie Beckwith each opted for the safe course of action, (2) Jim Vaught organized the total force poorly, by failing to motivate all of his people and by not designating anyone in command at Desert One, and (3) the U.S. military establishment had not thought out or prepared for rescue operations, despite the rapid rise in terrorism against Americans overseas and the increased attention to counterterrorism throughout the government since the early 1970s.

The review group was not allowed to come to these conclusions. The military establishment did not want to, either. We need look no further than the fact that Jim Vaught remained rescue task force commander, doing the planning for a second mission. There is a reasonable argument that both the JCS and the President knew it would look like punishment if they fired him. However, I thought the JCS went too far when they later promoted him to lieutenant general and assigned him as deputy commander of U.S. Forces in Korea. The message to younger officers surely must have been that success in battle does not matter.

Of course, there had to be a scapegoat if neither Vaught nor anyone else in the military was to be blamed. In time, the impression the American public received was that the failure was due to a combination of factors: the helicopters, the weather, the intelligence, and the White House. But, on examination, none of these explanations holds up.

- The helo failure rate was almost precisely what the planners predicted. They forecast that two of the eight would not make it past Desert One. As to the third helo, number 5, the pilot admitted his aircraft could have gone forward on the backup navigational systems.
- The low visibility in the *haboobs* certainly did not help, but six of

seven pilots who flew into them were able to make it through. In any war situation, adverse factors, such as poor weather or erroneous intelligence, must be taken into account. Nearly two hundred years ago, Clausewitz, whom every professional officer reads, wrote about the "fog of war" and the unexpected "friction" inevitably encountered on the battlefield. Nor does it seem fair to blame the meteorologists. The review group looked thoroughly into the weather forecasting and concluded it would have been impossible to predict the *haboobs* or to observe them developing that day, because the flight was in a remote area for which there were few historical weather data and no current reporting.[21]

- The overall intelligence given the rescue force was excellent. The CIA's agents had located the guard posts around the embassy compound and described when and how strongly they were manned; they had determined how many students were occupying the compound; they had ascertained that helos could not land inside the compound but had located and thoroughly scouted the soccer stadium across the street, where they could; they had acquired the needed trucks and the warehouse; they had selected the Desert Two hiding position and scouted possible roadblocks between it and the city. The largest intelligence obstacle was that the minimum amount of necessary information was not available until mid-January. Had the rescue force been ready before then, lack of intelligence data would have been a problem, but the force was not ready that early. Much has also been made of the fact that the CIA provided high-confidence intelligence on the location of the hostages within the embassy compound only at the last minute. Although that meant Charlie Beckwith had to take along additional troops to search for the hostages throughout the compound, it need not have delayed his readiness to conduct the operation.

- An accusation of undue White House interference was readily leveled at a President who had a reputation for going into detail. But it is untrue and wholly disingenuous. Jimmy Carter did not make changes in the rescue plan nor did he interfere with the operation. The only other possible White House interference with the rescue planning was from our secret group operating out of Zbig's office, but that group took no votes and had no authority over Harold Brown or Dave Jones. If Harold and Dave had felt encumbered by the rest of us, they would surely have told the President they were not ready to go.

There were, though, three problems at the White House. The first was Zbig's constant pressure to get ready and stay ready. If the military had known they had several months in which to prepare, they could have done a number of things differently, like screening more widely for helicopter pilots familiar with the specific aircraft or providing them time to organize and become a team. But no one could have predicted when the President would turn to a rescue option; and without Zbig's pressure, who knows when the military would have been ready?

The second was the President's delay in authorizing the CIA's flight into the desert to confirm and prepare the landing site at Desert One. Had he done so earlier, the military would have had more time to adjust its plans and rehearse; or the operation could have been conducted sooner, when the nights were longer. The trade-off was with the negotiations. They were never quite as promising as they seemed, yet the temptation to hope for a peaceful solution was great. As it turned out, the next administration also put a great deal of stock in negotiations, even though they were negotiating with essentially the same people.

The third was the President's reluctance to discuss rescue planning until the last minute. His emphasis on minimal bloodshed must have raised questions in the military as to whether the mission was a high-priority national commitment.

Still, above and beyond any problems with helicopters, weather, intelligence, or the White House, there is the hard fact that it took three to four months for the military to come up with a barely acceptable rescue plan. Rescue operations were not high enough on the military agenda. Shortly after the failure at Desert One, one citizen, Ronald Reagan, said, "It is very difficult to understand why it took so many months to take any action at all. I support the President in his attempt to rescue our people in Iran. As a matter of fact, I would have supported it six months ago." [22]

CARTER'S DEAL — TOO LATE

Now my political future might well be determined by irrational people on the other side of the world over whom I had no control.

— Jimmy Carter
November 2, 1980 [1]

HAVING RESORTED to a rescue mission largely because we had run out of alternatives, we now had to study those alternatives all over again. Were any options we had discarded viable now? Were there any new ones?

The most obvious was a second rescue attempt. Unfortunately, on the day the President told us to plan for one, the students announced they were scattering the hostages around Iran. In time they claimed they had sent them to sixteen different cities, and named nine. They also said they would rotate the hostages. The best our intelligence could do was to confirm that most of them had been taken from the embassy, but we never could locate the majority until they were brought back to the compound in October.

The inability to locate the hostages led to growing criticism of me and the CIA. Unfortunately, I found it was partially justified. The CIA professionals saw the task as almost impossible and were not trying as hard as they could; and I was no longer keeping up the pressure by holding daily meetings on the hostage situation. Zbig had his solution: the CIA should flood Iran with agents, and Harold offered to cull the military for people of Iranian background to do that.

The problem was that Tehran continued to be an intimidating place for foreigners. Justice was being meted out arbitrarily on street corners, often based only on the suspicions of the Revolutionary Guards. Anyone discovered snooping around or questioning people was likely to find himself the subject of an inquisition. There was an unquestioning fervor for Khomeini and his theocratic standards of dress and behavior. The CIA professionals did not think amateurs at spying, like Iranian-American soldiers, would survive scrutiny for long. Since we no longer had diplomatic relations with Iran, anyone we sent in would be on his own, without the protection, such as it was, of a diplomatic passport. The penalty for being caught spying would probably be death.

The CIA professionals did get back up to full speed, but the task of locating small groups of perhaps two to five hostages sequestered in sixteen cities around a large country was a daunting one and just locating them would not be enough. We would have to keep continuous watch on them lest they were moved before a rescue operation, as had happened in the Son Tay raid in 1970. In retrospect, I do not think we in the CIA did nearly as well as we should have in supporting a possible second rescue attempt, but complaints about the intelligence are somewhat beside the point. Even with precise information on all the hostages, it would have been nearly impossible for the military to conduct sixteen simultaneous rescue operations in Iran.

The Special Coordinating Committee also reviewed the idea of punitive military attacks. The threat of the students to harm the hostages in retaliation for any attack remained an overriding concern, however. I alone argued for some forceful action, like mining, both to regain the initiative and to pressure our allies into supporting economic actions to preclude our making further military moves.

Just before the April 24 rescue operation we had severed relations with Iran, imposed unilateral economic sanctions, and canceled all visas for Iranians to visit the United States. There were not many other diplomatic or economic options left without support from our allies. Some of them were dismayed that we had gone ahead with the rescue operation without waiting for their decision on economic sanctions. The sanctions they announced on May 22, however, were almost meaningless. The only trade embargoed was that under contracts signed after the hostage taking the previous November 4. The British even explicitly told their business community that contracts arranged before November 4 could be expanded. That meant there was virtually no need for new ones. It was obvious that the allies did not want to give up the possibility of lucrative trade with Iran, such as they had had during the Shah's buying spree.

Having our allies consider their pocketbooks before all else was

nothing new. Even when Thomas Jefferson advocated naval cooperation against the Barbary pirates and some Europeans were willing to
join us, Great Britain and France would not. They had navies that
protected their own shipping and found the pirates useful in hampering
rival commerce. Benjamin Franklin reported a saying in London: "If
there were no Algiers, it would be worth England's while to build
one."[2] Lyndon Johnson advocated economic sanctions against North
Korea during the *Pueblo* incident. The blatant act of piracy should
have been seen as an alarming precedent to any nation with a navy or
merchant marine. But even though few nations had significant economic stakes in North Korea, none would cooperate on sanctions.

Then the SCC discussed the possibility of stepping up covert action.
Again, there was no clear sense of direction. We in the CIA had been
nurturing a particular group of contacts. Now, though, Zbig and Warren Christopher were worried that these were people who favored a
return of the Shah and that it could be politically damaging if the United
States were known to be associated with reactionary elements. I was
less interested in such long-term political concerns than in getting the
hostages out, no matter whom we employed to help us. Once again, I
was told to call off the show and find new contacts. That was absurd,
but it did not make much difference, since none of the groups we were
working with or that Zbig wanted us to work with had a solid political
base inside Iran. In contrast, we were carrying on a successful covert
support program with the insurgents operating against the Soviet occupation of Afghanistan. The difference was that an indigenous political opposition did exist in Afghanistan.

The SCC's review narrowed to only one option: wait for the Iranians
to be willing to negotiate on reasonable terms. We never discussed this
explicitly, though, because none of us would admit that the United
States could be stymied by a theocracy run by a group of extremist
clerics. And we certainly did not want to acknowledge our impotence
before the American public.

SCC meetings dropped off to about two a week, but there was little
to discuss even then. Late one afternoon in early June, I noticed that
my IN basket was empty. When I asked Doris to bring in more work,
she said there was nothing that needed my attention. In the six months
between the capture of our embassy and the aborted rescue mission, I
had spent about 70 percent of my time on the hostage problem, and
that had forced me to delegate as much other work as I could. Now
that the hostages were receiving less attention, I had time to spare.

Feeling rather nonplussed, I decided to take the rest of the day off and went home!*

On July 27 the Shah died in Cairo. We waited anxiously for reaction from Iran, but there was none of significance. What did catch the Iranians' attention was a clash that very day in Washington between pro- and anti-Khomeini demonstrators. When 192 Iranians were arrested, many of them Khomeini supporters, the newly elected Speaker of the Majlis, Ali Akhbar Hashemi Rafsanjani, took notice. Claiming that some of the demonstrators had been beaten and that several were critically hurt, he proposed putting the hostages on trial in retaliation. Fortunately the crisis passed when all the Iranians in our jails were released, as a matter of law, within ten days. The previous November, I had questioned the President's decision to deny a permit for a pro-Khomeini demonstration in Lafayette Park. He had done so on the grounds that if clashes resulted in injury to pro-Khomeini people, there might be action taken against our hostages. Here was proof that the President had been right.

There was another twist to this event. The new Secretary of State, former Senator Edmund S. Muskie, said he had considered offering to swap the 192 Iranians for the 52 remaining hostages.† He decided against it because doing so would equate the illegal action in Tehran with our lawful arrest of unruly demonstrators. As has so often been the case, the United States chose not to stoop to the tactics of terrorists in fighting terrorism.

Waiting it out paid off more rapidly than I had predicted when, on the eve of the rescue operation, I told the President it would be six to nine months before we would get the hostages out any other way. On September 9, Day 312, the Iranians, through the West German gov-

---

* I am chagrined to admit that six months later, just before I left the position of Director of Central Intelligence, my IN basket was perpetually overflowing. In pure bureaucratic fashion, I had taken back most of what I had delegated.

† The number of hostages was down to fifty-two from fifty-three because Richard I. Queen had been released by the Iranians on July 11. He had developed multiple sclerosis, and the Iranians were apparently concerned that they might have his death on their hands. We, of course, quizzed Queen on the location of the other fifty-two, but he had been kept in the embassy, and was so isolated that he did not even know that others had been moved. He also had heard nothing of the rescue effort. During the early part of his captivity he was in a room where he was able to read and talk with other hostages and had been treated fairly well. He did, though, describe a cruel mock execution that took place in the courtyard of the embassy.

ernment, let us know that they wanted to talk. The prospective negotiator, Sadegh Tabatabai, was a relative of Khomeini's and a member of his inner circle. His message was that Iran wanted a quick resolution of the hostage problem on terms more acceptable than before, and that Khomeini would confirm those terms in a public speech. The Ayatollah did so on September 12, narrowing Iranian demands: a promise that the United States would not interfere in Iranian affairs and settlement of three financial issues. There was no longer any quest for a humiliating investigation and an apology.

Why the Iranians decided to resolve the hostage issue is still a puzzle to me. Perhaps they had demonstrated the impotence of the United States to the rest of the world as much as they thought useful. Perhaps the hostages were losing their usefulness as a political litmus test. Since November 4, any politician who wanted to resolve the hostage problem was branded as favoring a secular, American form of government rather than a theocracy, a test that had displaced Prime Minister Bazargan two days after the hostages were taken and driven Bani Sadr into near powerlessness as President. But now, though the Khomeini revolution was far from consolidated, even the virulently anti-American leaders had to recognize that Iran was facing serious problems of internal disorder and economic decline. And our economic and political pressures were making it more difficult for the government to solve the problems. Cy Vance's concept of steady, if not spectacular, pressure seemed to be paying off in bringing some moderate Iranians to conclude that the time had come to release the hostages.

Then Foreign Minister Ghotbzadeh gave a different twist to the situation. He recommended publicly that all of the hostages be released by the end of September so that their continued detention would not "encourage the election of Ronald Reagan," whom he associated with the Shah's close friends Henry Kissinger and David Rockefeller.[3] The real deadline, though, was November 4, our Election Day. There seemed to be ample time to meet that, especially after the initial talks in Bonn between Warren Christopher and Sadegh Tabatabai went reasonably well. As Tabatabai was heading home on September 22 to carry back the results of the discussions, however, Iraq invaded Iran. Iranian air space was closed to all commercial traffic, and Tabatabai did not make it home until early October.

That was only the first delay. Despite Khomeini's establishing new terms for release of the hostages, hardliners in the Majlis wanted to extract more from us, including an apology. Twice these extremists brought the Majlis to a halt by preventing a quorum. By the time the Majlis passed a resolution endorsing terms for release, it was Sunday, November 2, just two days before the election. That was almost certainly too late, but President Carter interrupted campaigning when word reached him and returned to the White House. It did not take him long to see that the Majlis had thrown a monkey wrench into the works by adding amplifying conditions to Khomeini's terms. Some of these exceeded the President's authority; for example, he was supposed to "annul decrees by American courts" and "guarantee security and free transfer of assets regardless" of legal proceedings in U.S. courts.[4]

There was now no hope for an immediate release, and we had to explain this to the American public. What followed was an extraordinary drafting session by two separate groups working independently but side by side in the Vice President's office. Most of us from the SCC were on one side of the room; our primary concern was the speedy release of the hostages after the election. We hoped that if the President went on national TV and said we were on the verge of accepting the Iranians' terms, they would be willing to start negotiating again right after the election.

On the other side of the room, Ham, Jody, the pollster Pat Caddell, the media specialist Gerry Rafshoon, and a few others came and went. These campaign advisers believed the statement by the President would be the final determinant in the election, and they wanted the President's response to lay the blame squarely on the Iranians. The conflict of priorities was stark.

Each group prepared its statement. Only the President could resolve the differences in wording. His choice did not surprise me. He said that the conditions set by the Majlis "appear to offer a positive basis [for a resolution of the hostage crisis]."[5] By making the hostages his top priority, he did not help his chances for re-election. And by the end of election night, it was clear that the Iranian terrorists had had a heavy impact on a U.S. presidential election.

Earlier in the campaign, both candidates had shied away from the hostage issue. When Khomeini set out his terms for release of the hostages, Ronald Reagan took a statesmanlike position, recommending that the President accept without haggling and get the hostages back.[6] By late October Lou Cannon of the *Washington Post* wrote: "The anticipated release of the American hostages in Iran has left Ronald Reagan's campaign team perplexed and unsettled about how to deal with what is fast becoming the overshadowing event of the presidential race. While Reagan has sought to regain the political offensive with hard-edged speeches . . . the focus of the voters . . . has shifted to the hostage issue. Reagan's aides know this, but they don't know what to do about it."[7]

But on October 20, candidate Reagan went on the offensive. He charged, "I don't understand why 52 Americans have been held hostage for almost a year now,"[8] and pledged to "restore the ability of the CIA and other intelligence agencies to warn against terrorism."[9] Three of Reagan's advisers met in Washington with a representative of Khomeini to discuss the hostage issue.* Although this meeting certainly took place, the result remains in dispute. Some claim there were more meetings and that a deal was made according to which Iran would withhold release of the hostages until after the election. In exchange the Reagan administration, once in office, would surreptitiously deliver arms to Iran. The advisers who met with the Iranian claim they rejected any such suggestion and stopped all contact. I have not found evidence of such a deal, and it would have been so callous that I find the charge hard to believe.

The Reagan campaign team, however, must have repeatedly planted stories about Jimmy Carter's "October surprise." No amount of denial or lack of evidence suppressed these. The "surprise" was to be either a military invasion of Iran, which certainly was not contemplated, since there was no movement whatsoever of forces toward Iran, or a deal to supply arms to get the hostages home before November 4. In a televised debate with Ronald Reagan on October 28, Jimmy Carter fueled the arms-for-hostages rumors by saying, "When I made my decision to stop all trade with Iran as a result of the taking of our hostages, I announced then, and have consistently maintained since, that if the hostages are released safely we would make delivery on those items which Iran owns — which they have bought and paid for — also that the frozen Iranian assets would be released."[10] President Carter never had to decide whether he would actually release arms to an Iran that was now engaged in a war with Iraq, because in the negotiations going on behind the scenes, Warren Christopher was able to finesse the subject when Tabatabai raised it. It never came up again, perhaps because it was a controversial issue inside Iran too. In late October, on his return from a visit to the United Nations in New York, the Iranian Prime Minister found it necessary to deny having gone to the United

---

* They were Laurence H. Silberman, Richard V. Allen, and Robert C. McFarlane.

States in order to make a secret deal of hostages for arms to fight the war with Iraq.[11] To Iranians, making a deal with the United States for arms was just as repugnant as it was to Americans to make a deal with Iran for hostages.

Prophetically, a number of commentators warned Ronald Reagan after he won the election to avoid any deal for our hostages that involved arms. In the words of *The New Republic:*

> This is the situation which Ronald Reagan faces during his transition to power. It will surely come as no surprise to him that an arms-for-hostages trade . . . would be a disastrous signal to our allies who would see us humbled once more before the Iranian terrorists and once more switching course. Reagan, presumably, knows this, since two of his most prominent Republican supporters, Gerald Ford and Henry Kissinger, have come out strongly against supplying any arms to Iran, however noble-sounding the intention.[12]

The President-elect appeared not only to agree, but to be even more cautious. Two and a half weeks before his inauguration, he criticized even the deal, then shaping up, of returning Iran's frozen assets in exchange for the hostages. He said, "I don't think you pay ransom for people that have been kidnapped by barbarians."[13]

Following the election, the negotiations flagged and the Iranian hard-liners were able to make a second effort to thwart any agreement. It took the next American political milestone, the change of administrations on January 20, to set off another burst of feverish negotiations. Again, only two days before the deadline, the Iranians agreed to terms: release of the hostages for the return of a portion of their frozen assets, plus the putting in escrow of more of those assets against claims of Americans on Iran. A few minutes after Jimmy Carter left office, fifty-two Americans found freedom after 444 days of incarceration. Another American President had made a deal with terrorists.

The captors did not get what they originally demanded — the return of the Shah and his wealth and an investigation that would excoriate the United States for its past role in Iran. All the deal did was to release Iranian assets we had frozen in retaliation for the hostage taking. Was that a deal that would encourage more hostage taking? I think not. First, the hostage takers received only what was rightfully theirs, which they would have received in due course anyway. Second, this was not an inducement to more hostage taking; it was not clear that there were any more frozen assets.

This is not to say the Iranians went away empty-handed. Some had received domestic political benefits from holding the hostages; others had secured satisfaction from humiliating the United States. The administration's preoccupation with the problem played right to the Iranian objective of humiliating the United States. Jimmy Carter, though, did not have the option of moving the issue out of the spotlight once it was there. Lyndon Johnson had been able to avoid strong, sustained public attention to the *Pueblo* crisis, but Carter's crisis had more dramatic elements. The hostages were not primarily military people; they were civilians. And in the twelve years since the *Pueblo,* the American media had become far more investigative in nature and more critical of government. Those trends, plus the drama of live television shots outside our embassy in Tehran, made the full focus of the media unavoidable. How could Americans accept waiting it out? How could the President tell the public he was depending on a wild, irrational man like Khomeini to make us an offer? Yet waiting patiently probably would have done as much for the hostages as anything else, and it is the course we eventually followed.

Although the result is marred by the loss of the eight servicemen who died in the rescue attempt, the President's one success was the safe return of all of the seventy-two Americans who were taken hostage or were forced into hiding with the Canadians.

THE CHANGING
OF THE GUARD

Let terrorists be aware . . .

— Ronald Reagan[1]

SEVEN DAYS after his inauguration, Ronald Reagan greeted the hostages and their families on the south lawn of the White House in a highly emotional ceremony. The new President used the occasion to lay down a marker on terrorism: "Let terrorists be aware that . . . our policy will be one of *swift and effective retribution.*" Clearly referring to President Carter's handling of the crisis, he added, "We hear it said that we live in an era of limits to our powers. Well, let it also be understood there are limits to our patience."[2]

This attitude toward terrorists reflected the mood of the country — relieved to have the hostages back, but angry, frustrated, and confused that it had taken 444 days to solve the problem. This, then, was a time for reflection and for a thoroughgoing, thoughtful analysis of how to do better if and when there was another hostage crisis. It looked at first as though there would be such a review when the new Secretary of State, General Alexander M. Haig, Jr., elevated "international terrorism [to] the place of human rights" as the top priority of American foreign policy in the Reagan administration.[3] I applauded this attention to solving the long-term issues of terrorism, but wondered whether the administration could put terrorism that high on its agenda. I understood Al Haig's feelings about terrorists, remembering that just before he retired as Supreme Commander of NATO in 1978, he had narrowly escaped death when terrorists detonated a remote-controlled bomb almost under his automobile.

I understood this priority better when in Al's further remarks he equated countering terrorism with countering the Soviets. In the same press conference he pointedly said that the Soviets were involved in "training, funding, and equipping" international terrorists.[4] Having been one of his principal subordinate commanders in NATO, I knew his deep conviction that the Soviets would stoop to almost any level to undermine us. While I basically agreed with that, in this case I did not believe the facts supported his conclusion that the Soviets were the principal hand behind international terrorism, especially in light of Khomeini's violent dislike of them. When I had left the CIA just a few days before, our best intelligence estimate was that the Soviets were selling arms and giving military training to states like Libya, Syria, and South Yemen, which were among the nations practicing terrorism. There was no evidence, however, of their masterminding specific incidents. It was no surprise just a few weeks later when a newspaper reported, "The CIA 'strongly disagrees' with Reagan administration contentions that the Soviet Union is a key supporter of international terrorism." *

Whatever the Soviet role actually was, our most severe problem at that moment was with the Iranians. What might their violent hatred of the United States bring next? Unfortunately, the only high-level discussion of Iranian terrorism by the new administration appears to have been whether to honor President Carter's agreement with Khomeini's government. Recognizing the strong public disdain that had developed for Khomeini and Iran, two of the President's political advisers, James Baker and Michael Deaver, were inclined to scrap the agreement. They recalled President Reagan's remark, just before his inauguration, that the Carter agreement amounted to paying ransom to barbarians. On the other side, several of the President's key foreign policy advisers — Al Haig, William Casey, and Richard V. Allen, the Assistant to the President for National Security Affairs — argued that the United States could not abrogate a legally binding agreement it had just signed. Eventually, President Reagan opted to honor the agreement.[5]

---

* "CIA Said to Doubt Soviet Tie to Terrorism," *Washington Post,* March 29, 1981. In 1990, as Eastern European communist states unraveled, it became clear that some of their intelligence agencies had long given aid and shelter to international terrorists. It is difficult to believe the KGB was not aware of this, if not involved directly. Al Haig's intuitions may well have been closer to the mark than we in the CIA believed in 1980. Still, at that time the only evidence the CIA had, such as the selling of arms to Libya, was circumstantial.

I was reminded of how peremptory President Carter had been with me when I had suggested at Camp David that we should agree to almost anything to get the hostages out and then renege as far as we could. On February 18 the State Department issued a statement that the United States would observe the agreement, but added, "The present administration would not have negotiated with Iran for the release of the hostages."[6]

The administration's policy, then, more or less evolved. First, it was speech writers who coined "swift and effective retribution." Now, it was public relations people papering over the fundamental difference between the President's advisers who favored accepting Jimmy Carter's negotiated deal and those who insisted on claiming that we would never again do such a thing. The result was a two-pronged policy: no negotiations, and early resort to "swift and effective retribution," presumably by the use of military force.

Yet I doubted that this or any administration would allow American hostages to languish rather than negotiate if retribution did not bring them home reasonably promptly. And did they really believe resort to military force could solve most problems with terrorists, or was that just talk? When Al Haig was asked what the President had in mind as retribution, he responded that the President was being "consciously ambiguous" but that terrorists would understand.[7] It sounded to me as though Al was counting on deterring terrorists with threats of force — in the image of Teddy Roosevelt. The President seemed to confirm this a few days later when, asked whether he would exact retribution from Iran for its having held our hostages for 444 days, he responded, "Well, what good would just revenge do and what form would it take? I don't think revenge is worthy of us."[8] Implicitly he was saying that he was passing up his first opportunity to seek retribution because other factors, like our moral stature, seemed more important.

With all of this emphasis on the use of force, I found it impossible not to wonder whether President Carter could have better used our military power on behalf of the hostages. Certainly he could have set a different tone by immediately rushing *Midway* to the Persian Gulf as a show of force. He could have been even more threatening by ostentatiously bringing up additional forces. I believe he was unduly intimidated in the early days of the crisis by the students' threat of retaliation against the hostages if we moved forces toward Iran. When we did bring two aircraft carrier groups into the Arabian Sea after a few weeks, nothing happened.

Had we actually employed military force against Iran and killed Iranians, that would have been a different matter. I believe the students would then have felt justified in harming their captives. That thought must have been behind President Carter's statement at Camp David in March that he would consider military attacks only in the event that the hostages were harmed or placed on trial. Being cautious in the actual use of force, I believed then, as I believe now, was sensible. Punitive attacks would not have brought the hostages home any earlier.

Mining, on the other hand, would have cut off all of Iran's external trade. That, combined with our freezing the bulk of Iran's financial reserves, would have had a severe economic impact. I still think we should have mined Iran's ports very early. Then, while we tried to bring about serious negotiations, Iran would have grown progressively weaker under our economic squeeze. Whether the students would have retaliated against the hostages, we'll never know.

Also, President Carter should have considered a rescue mission from the very start. He might have ruled it out because of the risk to the hostages, but the best time to have struck was before the students dug in and became organized. Our military was not capable of executing a rescue in the early days, but serious discussions of the option might have speeded the military's preparations.

Finally, I remembered that we in the Carter administration vested control over countering terrorism in the NSC. The disadvantage of that approach was that the spotlight immediately focused on the White House and President Carter when the hostages were taken. The Reagan team set out to distance the President from such crises, or at the least to give him greater control over the appearance of involvement. The State Department was put in charge of managing terrorist crises overseas, and the FBI in the United States. Unfortunately, when the Reagan administration encountered its first instance of terrorism, the new mechanism did not work very well.

On December 17, 1981, Brigadier General James L. Dozier, U.S. Army, was kidnaped from his apartment in Verona, Italy. President Reagan called the kidnapers "cowardly bums,"[9] but he was at a loss in seeking "swift and effective retribution." Surely he could not bomb Italy, a close ally. The enemy, after all, was the Red Brigades, a domestic terrorist group the Italians were pursuing diligently for many crimes. Even the use of our rescue forces was out of the question, as the Italians were hardly likely to step aside on their own soil and admit they could not handle the problem themselves. In the Lufthansa hijacking, Italy, plus countries like Oman and Somalia, had resisted West German appeals to let GSG-9 operate on their soil.

Still, a small survey team was immediately dispatched to Europe to prepare the way for our rescue force. This advance team was to acquire as much information as possible about Dozier's plight and be available to advise the Italians if they consulted us before doing anything that might jeopardize Dozier's life. However, the team ran into a bureaucratic melee. The administration had never tested its plans for dealing with such a crisis and now found that too many cooks were stirring the soup.

The survey team necessarily landed in the territorial domain of the European theater commander, who already had his own exploratory team on the scene in Verona. The theater commander rightfully wondered who was going to oversee this additional unit, which could communicate by satellite directly with the Joint Chiefs. Would these people be hard-charging Charlie Beckwiths who might unilaterally attempt a daring rescue operation? If members of the rescue force got into trouble, the theater commander might have to extricate them. On top of this intramilitary rivalry, the American ambassador to Italy, Maxwell Rabb, also thought he was in charge. The incident was in his territory, and the State Department was responsible for directing responses to terrorism overseas. The State Department, however, proved no match for the Pentagon in asserting authority, especially when the victim was a senior military officer.

Back in Washington, the NSC staff was also working on the Dozier problem when someone came up with the idea of posting a reward for information on the general's whereabouts. It turned out there was no legal basis for using government funds as rewards. Oliver North, on the NSC staff, remembered that Ross Perot had spent his own time and money in attempting to get American prisoners of war out of Vietnamese prisons. He approached Perot, who immediately put up $500,000.[10] North had demonstrated that he could work around bureaucratic and legal obstacles. The reward, however, failed to elicit legitimate information.

For forty-two days, the Italians conducted a massive manhunt, with the Italian Prime Minister publicly ruling out negotiations with the terrorists and saying that our government agreed.[11] Finally, the Italian police located Dozier, stormed the hiding place, and rescued the general, unharmed.* I was at a national prayer breakfast in Washington nine days later when President Reagan introduced Dozier as a returning hero. This, plus the reception at the White House the previous January when the fifty-two hostages returned, sent a message that securing freedom for Americans held hostage was a matter of highest priority, a matter for presidential attention. Although these were steps toward identifying the President publicly with the plight of hostages, it was difficult for the administration to pass up the domestic political benefits of a successful conclusion to what had been two highly visible problems.

The following March the Italians convicted seventeen members of the Red Brigades, eight in absentia, and sentenced them to terms ranging from twenty-six months to twenty-seven years, breaking the back of the group.

The Reagan administration's first encounter with terrorism, then, appeared to have been handled quite adequately. There was no reason to question the new policy on toughness, nor did it seem there was an urgent need to iron out the matters of jurisdiction between the new joint rescue force command just created in line with the Holloway review group's report, the theater commanders, and the State Department. The administration's next crises with terrorism, though, would force to the surface differing views on whether to exact retribution, the bedrock of policy, and lead to a thorough reappraisal of policy.

---

* The success of the Italian police in ferreting out Dozier's kidnapers was, in my opinion, related to the kidnaping and murder of former Prime Minister Aldo Moro by Red Brigades in the spring of 1978. This egregious act pushed the Italians to become very serious about suppressing the Red Brigades. Three and a half years of tracking down individual members, convicting them and extracting information about the organization paid off for Dozier.

· 20 ·

RETRIBUTION — EASIER SAID
THAN DONE

WE WILL MAKE AMERICA FACE A SEVERE DEFEAT

> — Sign on the main gate of the
> former U.S. embassy in
> Tehran, 1984.[1]

IN JUNE 1982, Israel invaded Lebanon, a move designed by Israel's Defense Minister, Ariel Sharon, to drive the PLO out of that country. In July, George P. Shultz replaced Al Haig as Secretary of State and was forced by the Israeli military presence to concentrate attention on Lebanon. His idea was to use a multinational force (MNF) to provide internal security and stability to the weak Lebanese government, negotiate the withdrawal of both Syrian and Israeli military forces, and help the Lebanese government reassert its sovereignty. After that, a wider Middle East peace process would be possible. Shultz's proposal for a multinational peacekeeping force composed of U.S. Marines and Italian, French, and British troops was vigorously opposed by Secretary of Defense Caspar W. (Cap) Weinberger and the Joint Chiefs of Staff. Shultz, however, won out on the grounds that the MNF would remain in Lebanon only a few months.

For about six months, the MNF was welcomed as a stabilizing factor. Then, as was almost inevitable with a role of bolstering the government of Lebanon, it became identified less with peacekeeping and more with partisan support for that Christian-led government. Competing factions resented this, not only the Israelis and Syrians but Maronite Christians, Sunni and Shiite Muslims, Palestinians, Druze, and other religious and ethnic groups.

This began to tell in March 1983, when five Marines were slightly wounded by a grenade pitched from a window while they were on a routine patrol. On April 18, a suicide driver rammed a van with two hundred to five hundred pounds of TNT into the front wall of the U.S. embassy in west Beirut (see Map 9). Sixty-seven people were killed, seventeen of them Americans. It was a particularly hard blow for the CIA and for me personally, as one of the victims was the CIA's Robert C. Ames. Bob was my close adviser on the Middle East and was widely acknowledged as one of our country's most talented experts on that area. He had been visiting Lebanon; when the bomb exploded, he was in an office just above the front door of the embassy. He and most of the CIA people in Beirut were killed. Although I couldn't help wondering whether there had been a leak about Bob's visit and the attack had been timed to kill him, there has never been any evidence to support such a hypothesis. Three groups, including the Islamic Jihad, claimed responsibility.

This was a new faction in Lebanon, formed by Shiite fundamentalists emboldened by Khomeini's revolution. All around the Islamic world, extremists were taking the offensive. One approach to converting their less rigorous brethren was to demonstrate that fundamentalism could defeat and humiliate nonbelievers, like Americans. Khomeini had done that with hostage taking; they were ready to do it with whatever form of terror suited the circumstance. The Americans held hostage in Tehran had been pawns in the struggle for power between the more and the less fundamentalist factions. Now Americans in Lebanon were caught in a similar, internal power struggle.

Why Lebanon? Because the Israeli invasion gave Khomeini's mullahs an excuse to send help to their coreligionists there. Very quickly they moved more than a thousand Revolutionary Guards into the Bekaa Valley, just behind and to the east of Beirut. The Islamic Jihad moved in with them. Shortly after, David S. Dodge, Acting President of the American University in Beirut, was kidnaped as he left his office. Very likely this was in retaliation for the abduction of four Iranian diplomats by right-wing Christian forces associated in Muslim minds with the United States. During a year in captivity, Dodge spent a good bit of time in Tehran. Most people jumped to the conclusion that the Islamic Jihad was behind both the bombing and the kidnaping. President Reagan revealed, though, that evidence did not support that: "We don't know yet who bears responsibility for this terrible deed. What we do know is that the terrorists who planned and carried out this cynical and cowardly attack have failed in their purpose. They mistakenly believe . . . they will weaken American resolve. Well, if they think that, they don't know too much about America."[2]

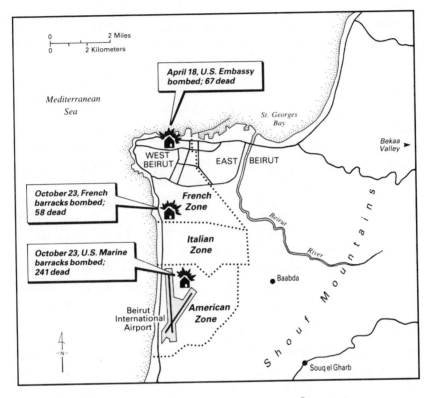

MAP 9. BEIRUT BOMBINGS, 1983

The President was indicating that he had no intention of withdrawing from Lebanon. But the administration did substantially reduce the size of the embassy staff. Those who remained were moved into temporary quarters behind barricades guarded by a large contingent of Marines. We began converting a building in east Beirut into a new embassy, because the eastern, Christian, sector of the city was thought to be less dangerous than the Muslim one, where the old embassy lay in shambles. There was no "swift and effective retribution."

The reasons were clear. Our intelligence could not be sure which group was responsible, and retaliation would probably kill people who had no connection to the bombing incident. When confronted with those terms, the administration once again set aside its policy of retaliation.

The fact that retribution had not been applicable to either of the administration's first two bouts with terrorism did not result in a re-evaluation of the policy. Then one of those little ironies occurred. Ronald Reagan became deeply moved by a story about someone else's problem with terrorism. On July 27, five Armenian terrorists seized the residence of the Turkish ambassador in Lisbon, venting a long-standing grievance about the alleged Turkish genocide of Armenians in 1915. The terrorists blew up the building, killing themselves, a Portuguese policeman, and a Turkish woman, whose young son jumped to safety despite a wounded leg. There were no Americans involved, the incident did not take place on our soil, and Armenian terrorism had never been a major concern of ours. Nonetheless, the President chose to speak out. He did so without any scripting from his staff, who preferred that he not get any more involved in incidents of terrorism than necessary. His principal point became a third leg of the administration's policy on terrorism, and the one that would be the most effective: improved cooperation with other nations against terrorists. "I will be speaking to other heads of state in the days ahead regarding urgent and more effective cooperative measures to eliminate from the civilized community such barbaric and inhuman acts."[3] This emotional, direct presidential concern encouraged his staff to review where it stood on organization and procedures for dealing with terrorism.

But before anything was done, the situation in Lebanon went from bad to worse. The Marine component of the MNF was hunkered down at the airport in south Beirut on the lowest and least defensible terrain in the area, squeezed between rival Sunnis and Shiites on the north and south, against the Mediterranean Sea to the west and the Shouf Mountains to the east (see Map 9). The position was obviously vulnerable, but the commander's mission was to restore a sense of order to

Beirut, and keeping the airport under firm control was part of that.

On August 29 mortar fire from Druze batteries in the hills to the east killed two Marines at the airport. For the first time, the Marines fired back in self-defense. It is possible the Druze thought the Marines had fired at them first, although that actually was done by the Christian-dominated Lebanese Army, deployed adjacent to the Marines. Within a week, two more Marines were killed by mortar attacks, and the Marines were joined by Navy ships in returning fire. Then, on September 19, the President made a seminal decision to use Navy guns, not in defense of the Marines, but to help the Lebanese Army. A Lebanese unit was under siege at Souq el Gharb in the hills above the airport. Despite the strenuous objections of the commander on the scene, Marine Colonel Timothy J. Geraghty, the President acted on the advice of his special envoy to the Middle East, Robert C. (Bud) McFarlane, who was in Beirut. The Marines were no longer in a peacekeeping role. They had become one of the factions firing on others.

On Sunday morning, October 23, at six-twenty, a yellow truck, much like the trucks that made regular runs to and from the airport, crashed past a guard post and drove at full speed directly into the Marine barracks, a four-story, reinforced-concrete building. A sophisticated, gas-boosted bomb detonated, killing the driver and 241 American military men, most of whom were asleep. The FBI estimated the explosion at the equivalent of twelve thousand pounds of TNT, the largest conventional explosive they had ever confronted.

Again the President declared that we would not retreat. Again he did not retaliate. And again the Islamic Jihad claimed responsibility, though a new pro-Iranian Islamic group, the Hezbollah, was also suspect. The Hezbollah's spiritual leader, Sheik Mohammed Hussein Fadlallah, was rumored to have blessed the driver of the yellow truck before his suicide mission. Were the Islamic Jihad and Hezbollah perhaps one and the same? We did not know. Other factions may also have been interested in causing trouble at that moment, because a conference on Lebanese national reconciliation was scheduled to begin in a week in Switzerland. As the Prime Minister of Lebanon commented, "Every time we make some headway [toward peace], evil elements act to set us back by killing and destruction."[4]

Once again U.S. intelligence failed to warn of the impending attack or to identify the terrorists afterward. In the *Mayaguez* incident, because of faulty intelligence we lost eighteen Marines in a fruitless rescue effort. And because of the CIA's inability during my tenure to pin down where the students were holding our hostages in Iran, President

Carter had fewer options than he might have had. Now, because his intelligence had twice failed to identify and locate the terrorists who bombed our facilities, President Reagan had lost the opportunity to retaliate, as he had promised he would do.

This was not the whole story. The barracks in which the French element of the MNF was housed had been bombed almost simultaneously with ours, with fifty-eight deaths. Three and a half weeks later the French, using aircraft from the carrier *Clemenceau*, bombed the Sheik Abdullah Barracks in the Bekaa Valley, supposedly the training base for those who bombed both the French and American barracks. Why didn't we join the French in this retaliation? Surely we had as good information as they, or they would have shared what they had with us. The President explained our failure to participate as a crisis of conscience. Our intelligence was still checking the facts to ensure that innocent people would not be killed when "someone else [presumably the French] evidently knew more than we did or was not as careful as we were and took that target out before we could get to it. It was as simple as that."[5]

But it was not as simple as that. There had been an intense debate within the administration. Some thought that while it would be unfortunate if we hit innocents as well as terrorists, it was important to make known our firm resolve. Others thought any attack would incite more violence against the Marines. The President is reported to have sided with the former and ordered his first act of retribution.[6] Cap Weinberger, however, the man with his finger on the trigger, was one of those who urged caution. Somehow the orders from the Pentagon to the Navy's carriers off Beirut did not arrive in time for our aircraft to join those from *Clemenceau*. As one of Weinberger's predecessors put it, "The Secretary of Defense can always find a reason not to do something. There's always bad weather."* Whether Weinberger was worried about involving our military in the morass of Lebanon or about killing innocents, President Reagan was constrained by one or both of these concerns.†

---

* Comment by Melvin R. Laird, Secretary of Defense from 1969 to 1973, when asked whether he had similarly failed to carry out an order of President Nixon to bomb the Palestinian camps in Jordan during the crisis at Dawson Field in 1970. From Seymour Hersh, *The Price of Power,* (New York: Summit Books, 1983), p. 235.

† Secretary Weinberger strongly denies any recollection that the President authorized a joint air attack on the Sheik Abdullah Barracks. See Martin and Walcott, p. 139.

When the dust settled after the catastrophe at the airport, Weinberger appointed retired Admiral Robert L. J. Long to head a five-member commission to see what had gone wrong. The charge was to "examine the rules of engagement in force and the security measures in place at the time of the attack . . . and to report findings of facts, opinions, and recommendations as to any changes or future actions."[7] This directive gave Bob Long the authority to levy criticism if warranted, something the instructions to the Holloway review group had not. Knowing Bob well, I was confident he would call a spade a spade. He did.

The commission's report recommended "that the Secretary of Defense take whatever administrative or disciplinary action he deems appropriate, citing the failure of the [theater commander's] operational chain of command."[8] This could mean accountability as high up as the European theater commander and as far down as just below the commander on the scene, Colonel Geraghty. The suggestion that very senior commanders be held responsible was reminiscent of Voltaire's comment: "In this country it is thought well to kill an admiral from time to time to encourage the others."[9] In this case, I hoped that, whether or not any admirals or generals deserved to lose their heads, the tone of the report would cause the administration to examine carefully its preparedness for lower levels of military endeavor, like terrorism.

One of the most damning conclusions of the Long report concerned preparedness. "The Commission concludes that the U.S. Multi-National Force was not trained, organized, staffed or supported to deal effectively with the terrorist threat in Lebanon [and] . . . that much needs to be done to prepare U.S. military forces to defend against and counter terrorism."[10] This was three and a half years after our failure at Desert One. We had still not given sufficient attention to this level of ambiguous warfare nor appreciated the way in which political objectives dominate how we employ our military in peacekeeping or rescue missions.

Again, though, no one was held responsible. On December 27, President Reagan blunted the impact of the Commission's report by saying, "I do not believe that the local commanders on the ground, men who have already suffered quite enough, should be punished for not fully comprehending the nature of today's terrorist threat. If there is to be blame, it properly rests here in this Office and with this President. And I accept responsibility for the bad as well as the good."[11] The country was on the eve of a presidential election year and Ronald Reagan was not going to risk having the disaster at Beirut in the forefront of the news while military investigations, and possibly courts-martial, dragged on. Much the same reason, of course, was behind Jimmy Carter's decision not to launch a full-scale investigation of Desert One.

While the administration could avoid casting blame for the bombing of the Marine barracks, it could not avoid facing the question of why its stated policy of retribution had not been applied to any of the three cases of terrorism it had faced: the Dozier kidnaping, the bombing of the embassy in Beirut, and the destruction of the Marine barracks. The debate over terrorism policy had already begun as a result of the President's remarks about Armenian terrorism in Portugal. Now it became more urgent.

A new buzz word emerged: "pro-active." In part this meant being more than just reactive, that is, getting out in front and disrupting terrorists before they strike. In part it meant being rigorous in meting out punishment after terrorist strikes, thus deterring further acts of terrorism.

In both cases, it could mean aggressive military or covert action, like bombing terrorist training camps or killing terrorists themselves. Because such a shift was bound to be controversial, the administration chose to brief the media in mid-April 1984 on the new policy, one hammered out in a secret directive, National Security Decision Directive 138 (NSDD 138). Some public commentators questioned whether taking the offensive against individual terrorists would amount to assassination, which was ruled out by a presidential Executive Order. Others worried about how we would decide who was a terrorist and what was a training camp. For instance, were the French right in bombing the Sheik Abdullah Barracks? Or were we in questioning whether we had adequate information? The more arbitrary our pre-emptive actions, the more they are the equivalent of terrorism.

George Shultz made a speech supporting the pro-active policy almost as soon as NSDD 138 was signed. Cap Weinberger was quiet for the moment, having expressed concern within the administration that military force employed in a pro-active role might drag us into never-ending commitments. DCI Bill Casey was in favor of pro-action, but did not carry much of his agency with him, because the CIA professionals remembered being pilloried by Congress for past efforts at assassination and wanted no more of that. But in the wake of the shocking loss of life in Beirut, there were no strong media or public objections to a more active policy, though the *Wall Street Journal* cautioned, "It remains to be seen whether the Reagan administration will be as tough in carrying out the policy as officials are in explaining it."[12]

Even while this new, tough policy was still being discussed, on February 6, 1984, the administration announced that the Marines were pulling out of Beirut.[13] The withdrawal to ships offshore began the next day. The 16-inch guns of the battleship *New Jersey* provided what was called "protective fire," though 288 rounds of 2000-pound projectiles seems more like revenge.

The President called the retreat of the Marines a "redeployment," but the world understood. Terrorists, or the combination of terrorists and public opinion, had driven the United States military out of Lebanon.

Ronald Reagan had been under public pressure since August 1983, when the first Marines were killed and members of Congress began asking why the Marines were in Beirut at all. After the October 23 bombing, many in Congress and across the country favored moving out the Marines. The nebulous "presence" mission they had been given was not worth the loss of more lives. Despite his own determination and strong rhetoric, Ronald Reagan could not stand up to that kind of pressure in a democratic society, any more than Jimmy Carter had been able to ignore American impatience with the delays in getting the hostages back.

Our record in Lebanon was poor: 262 Americans dead and no retribution. Moreover, by withdrawing most of our diplomatic and military presence, we had given the terrorists much of what they were demanding. The President had, though, adhered to his policy of no negotiations.

Still, the Islamic Jihad and Hezbollah wanted more. They wanted all Americans out — now.

HOSTAGES AGAIN —

INTELLIGENCE "FAILURE" AGAIN

We're feeling the effects today of the near destruction of our intelligence capability in recent years, before we came here.

— Ronald Reagan,
September 26, 1984[1]

NSDD 138, signed on April 3, 1984, was a reaffirmation of administration resolve to exact retribution from terrorists. But the terrorists in Beirut were making retribution more difficult by shifting from bombings to hostage taking. In Beirut, over a period of four months starting in January 1984, one American was murdered and four were kidnaped. Retribution could endanger the lives of hostages.

Malcolm Kerr, President of the American University at Beirut, was shot outside his office by two gunmen on January 18. The first kidnaping victim in this wave also came from the American University: Frank Regier, Chairman of the Department of Electrical Engineering. He and Kerr were probably selected because of their ties to an institution that symbolized the American presence in the Middle East. The next three kidnaping victims also had ties to organizations with strong American identification: the CNN television network, the CIA, and the Presbyterian ministry. The kidnapers demanded both that the United States get out of Lebanon completely and that seventeen convicted and jailed Shiite terrorists be released from jail in nearby Kuwait.

The latter demand went back to December 12, 1983, when six bombs were detonated in Kuwait City within a ninety-minute period. One killed five Kuwaiti employees of the American embassy and injured thirty-seven others, including Americans. The terrorists appeared to have ties to the ones giving us problems in Beirut. They used gas-enhanced bombs like the one detonated at the Marine barracks in Beirut the previous October, and one of the seventeen arrested and convicted in Kuwait was the brother-in-law of the reputed head of the Islamic Jihad.

The Reagan administration was split on whether to ask the Kuwaitis to make a deal on behalf of our hostages. Bill Casey was ready to do almost anything to get back William Buckley, the CIA's Chief of Station in Lebanon. Besides his deep personal concern for Buckley, there was the inescapable fact that if Buckley were to be tortured into revealing what he knew, it would not only set back our intelligence efforts inside Lebanon but also do damage in much of the remainder of the Middle East. Beyond Casey's intense interest in Buckley, though, there was little pressure to do something for these hostages. The media could not find much of a story in their situation, as there was little to televise beyond distraught families. With this lack of pressure, and with many in the administration believing their own rhetoric about our never dealing with terrorists, the decision was not to press the Kuwaitis.

There was talk about being bold and bombing Iran, but it was only talk. The evidence that Iran was behind the murder and kidnapings was circumstantial, and the most likely result of any bombing would be the death of hostages. Once again, a terrorist situation left little scope for the administration's threat of retribution.

One option, however, was a rescue operation. When the Israeli rescue force set out for Entebbe in 1976, their hostages were over two thousand miles away. When the West Germans started toward Mogadishu in 1977, they had to pursue the hijacked aircraft more than five thousand miles across the Mediterranean and around the Middle East. When we sent Delta Force toward Tehran in 1980, the fateful flight was launched from about a thousand miles away. In comparison, getting a rescue force into position in Beirut would be simple. It could assault directly from helicopters based on Navy ships just offshore, move clandestinely into the city over land from Israel, or infiltrate by small boats from the sea. The problem, as with the planned rescue in Tehran, would be getting the hostages back out of a crowded city with its numerous, well-armed militiamen. We might have to use helicopters, but, again, they were readily available on the ships just offshore.

There was no rescue effort. Why? Ronald Reagan acknowledged some years later how difficult it was to learn where the hostages were in Beirut, despite his campaign pledge to improve our intelligence against terrorism.[2] Finding hostages in Beirut in 1984 should have been downright simple compared with determining the precise location of the hostages inside our embassy in Tehran in 1979 and 1980. In Beirut, we still had an embassy and full access to the country, and foreigners were commonplace rather than automatically suspect. Moreover, Beirut is a center of intrigue, with numerous competing factions to play off against one another. In mid-April, for instance, a pro-Syrian faction of Shiites located Frank Regier and literally stole him from their rivals, the pro-Iranian Shiites of the Islamic Jihad; then they released him. And with Lebanon having been a focus of policy in the Middle East since 1982, there had been time to concentrate intelligence efforts. There had also, of course, been setbacks: the death of Bob Ames and of most of the CIA personnel assigned to the embassy, and the recent abduction of Buckley. But intelligence operatives, like military men, are measured more often than not by their ability to adapt to setbacks and the unexpected. It was clear there had been little improvement in intelligence against terrorism. Ronald Reagan acknowledged that in September, when he blamed the next disaster in Beirut on a failure of intelligence.

On September 20, for the third time, a truck loaded with explosives crashed through U.S. defenses, exploding just a few feet from a new embassy annex in east Beirut (see Map 10). Fourteen people were killed, two of them Americans. Again, the Islamic Jihad claimed responsibility. The reason we were caught flat-footed was soon obvious: the defenses around the new building had not been completed when we moved in. The steel gate that would have forced the Chevrolet van to stop was lying beside the road, awaiting installation. On top of that, most of the Marines who had been guarding the embassy premises had recently been replaced with hired Lebanese. It was as though we were not listening. Just two weeks before, the Islamic Jihad had boasted that it would attack "one of the vital American installations in the Middle East."[3] Had we paid attention, we could easily have erected a temporary gate, perhaps using a truck sideways across the access road.

This neglect of elementary precautions galvanized George Shultz to increase the attention being paid to the physical security of State Department installations overseas. He appointed the Advisory Commission on Overseas Security, chaired by retired Admiral Bobby R. Inman. The commission's report, released the following June, contained 91 recommendations and evaluated 134 of the department's 263 posts as substantially below minimum security standards. The cost of a corrective program was in the neighborhood of $5 billion. Despite the report and despite George Shultz's personal concern, it was more than two

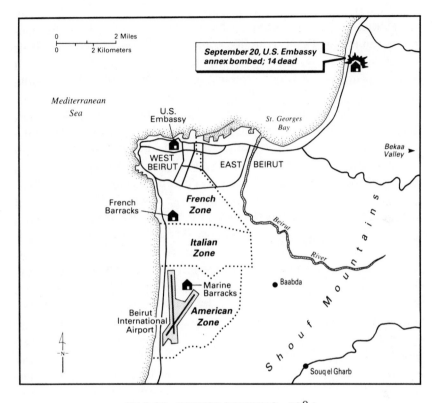

MAP 10. BEIRUT BOMBING, 1984

years after the bombing before Congress appropriated any monies toward this sum. Surprisingly, a good part of the delay resulted from the failure of the administration to submit a legislative proposal. Then, a year and a half after money was in hand, Secretary Shultz stated that "budget realities are forcing us to slow the program down."[4] The Congress, too, became more dollar-conscious, and was skeptical that the funds it had appropriated were being spent wisely. A similar cycle of high concern followed by waning interest had begun in 1980 after attacks on our embassies in Tehran, Islamabad, and Tripoli.

Rather than accept that the defensive preparations at the annex in Beirut were faulty, the President attempted to deflect the blame for this third bombing on "the near destruction of our intelligence capability in recent years." He contended that the public attitude during those years was that "spying is somehow dishonest and let's get rid of our intelligence agents . . . and we did that to a large extent."[5] This was either an uninformed or disingenuous reference to the trimming, by President Carter and me, of a bloated bureaucracy at CIA headquarters. We had not eliminated a single position overseas. A few days later, President Reagan telephoned President Carter to tell him, "I was not suggesting that you or your administration were responsible for the declining intelligence capability and I certainly did not suggest that your administration was the cause of that happening at the embassy in Beirut." A spokesman made it clear that this was not to be interpreted as an apology.[6]

President Reagan had been in office almost a full term and could have increased his intelligence agents in Lebanon if he had wanted to. His problem was not numbers; it was an unrealistic expectation of what could be accomplished by having more agents. All recent Presidents had found their intelligence on terrorism to be deficient. Lyndon Johnson had no warning about North Korea's intent to capture *Pueblo*. Richard Nixon's intelligence people could not tell him where the hostages had been taken when the three aircraft hijacked to Dawson Field were evacuated. Gerald Ford's attempt to rescue the crew of the *Mayaguez* was based on faulty intelligence about the location of the hostages. I had been unable to give Jimmy Carter information about the whereabouts of our hostages when they were scattered across Iran. Now Ronald Reagan was encountering repeated intelligence shortcomings in Beirut, despite his obvious conviction that improving intelligence was a simple matter.

There are lots of "experts" around to tell a President how easy it is to improve intelligence. Most commonly, they argue that more daring leadership at the top, more spies, a greater willingness to employ covert action, and less congressional interference will produce better intelligence. In selecting Bill Casey as his DCI, Ronald Reagan had a man tailored to those specifications. He loved risk taking, human spying, and covert action, and had some related, though outdated, experience with them from his service with the OSS in World War II. He was blatant in snubbing the Congress and circumventing congressional controls over his domain. Still, the Congress acceded to the President's requests to give Casey additional money and people. Casey then recalled veteran CIA clandestine officers to be sure he had enough agents who suited his style.

He also gave personal attention to the condition of human intelligence in Lebanon. When the Chief of Station was due to be replaced, Casey picked Buckley for the job, despite the risks, in that unstable environment, of exposing a veteran who was bound to be well known as a CIA officer. Lebanon became a testing ground for a Reagan-Casey effort to improve intelligence about terrorism through better human spying. That there was no perceptible improvement confirms how extraordinarily difficult it is to get inside terrorist organizations and learn of their plans; and it raises doubt that human intelligence will provide warning of terrorist attacks more than occasionally. Certainly there have been those occasions. As DCI, I witnessed a coup when CIA agents penetrated a terrorist organization and thwarted a heinous action. Yet I also saw one of our agents penetrate another terrorist group, only to have us withdraw him rather than permit his participation in an inhumane, illegal action he could not otherwise have avoided.

A big part of the problem is that terrorist alliances are difficult to penetrate because, more often than not, they are small, fanatical, suspicious, and constantly shifting in composition. And such groups often seize opportunities of the moment rather than scheduling operations in advance, which leaves little time, if any, for us to learn of their plans.

Still another limitation on our human spying stems from cultural inhibitions. When a CIA officer goes overseas to lead a spying effort, we must provide him or her with a cover for being there. If the cover is a U.S. government position, the person is entitled to the protection of a diplomat should he be apprehended while spying. That protects the individual but weakens his cover. It is almost inevitable that a CIA officer posing as a government official will be identified by a foreign intelligence service, and that substantially diminishes his usefulness.

The Soviets are more willing to accept the risks of nongovernmental cover. They are also more patient. They will have an agent and his family emigrate and establish themselves in another nation for years before he begins spying. We would find it very difficult to ask such a sacrifice of our people, especially considering the standards of living and culture they might have to endure.

Ronald Reagan was finding that retribution and a refusal to negotiate were not a sufficient policy against terrorism. Nor was improved intelligence the panacea he was seeking.

· 22 ·

STILL NO RETRIBUTION

As soon as men decide that all means are permitted to fight an evil, then their good becomes indistinguishable from the evil they set out to destroy.

— Christopher Dawson[1]

We can get so lost in humanitarian concerns as a nation, we could float off into oblivion.

— Nelson Rockefeller[2]

IT APPEARS the culprits in the third bombing in Beirut came from the Sheik Abdullah Barracks in the Bekaa Valley. After the fact, photo interpreters are reported to have studied again satellite photos of the barracks and found a mock-up of the obstacles that had been placed incompletely in front of the new embassy annex, plus track marks on the ground showing that drivers had made practice runs through them.[3] There could have been other explanations of these activities, but the photo interpreters should have noted that something new and unusual was going on at a location that must have been under close observation. Why had they not called attention to these telltale signs? Either the DCI had not set Lebanon high enough on the list of priorities in targeting our satellites, or had failed to have the interpreters alerted to the continuing threats to U.S. facilities there, or both. This was an intelligence problem that could have been corrected, though not by flooding Lebanon with more human agents.

The photographic evidence opened once more a sore point within the administration. Six months earlier, when debating NSDD 138, the President's advisers more or less agreed on the pro-active policy, but they had not been able to settle on what circumstances would justify resorting to pre-emptive or retaliatory attacks. Now they had to decide whether to retaliate in this specific instance.

Cap Weinberger argued that the photographic evidence was not sufficient justification for military strikes. The culprits might have moved on, leaving occupants in the barracks who had not been involved in the bombings, even our own hostages. His stand reflected a conviction of our military rooted in the trauma of Vietnam: never commit military force without broad and clear support of the American people. Weinberger must have believed the support was not there.

George Shultz, angry that Weinberger would want up-to-the-minute evidence before responding to such an egregious act, was convinced that our lack of action would invite further terrorism. President Reagan disliked taking sides when his advisers disagreed, and without his express support for Shultz, Weinberger won again; the administration once more retreated. With a presidential election coming up in a matter of weeks, it hastily withdrew all but a handful of our diplomats from Lebanon lest there be another mishap. A few returned later for a short while, but the bombing on September 20 effectively ended our embassy's operations in that country.

Shultz and Weinberger now went public with their differences. Shultz was forceful:

> We may never have the kind of evidence that can stand up in an American court of law. But we cannot allow ourselves to become the Hamlet of nations, worrying endlessly over whether and how to respond . . . Fighting terrorism will not be a clean or pleasant contest, but we have no choice but to play it . . . The public must understand before the fact that there is a potential for loss of life of some of our fighting men and the loss of life of some innocent people.[4]

Weinberger responded, "You don't want to shoot a gun into the crowded theater in the hope that somebody's there who might have done something."[5]

This strong disagreement between two Cabinet officers revealed how deeply divided the Reagan administration was on this issue. The President tried to waffle when first asked whether he agreed with Shultz on the occasional necessity for killing innocents, but ended up directly contradicting his Secretary of State. During a campaign debate with Walter Mondale he said, "We want to retaliate, but only if we can put our finger on the people responsible and not endanger the lives of innocent civilians."[6]

George Bush was even more direct: "I don't agree with [Shultz]. I think you have got to pinpoint the source of that attack. We are not going to go out and bomb innocent civilians or something of that nature. I don't think we ever get to the point where you kill 100 innocent women and children just to kill one terrorist."[7]

What drove George Shultz to his position? Was it a sense of guilt that the loss of life in Beirut was in some way due to his insistence on having the Marines stay there? Was he saying that none of the bombings need have happened if we had been more willing to use force in response to earlier terrorist attacks? He contended that *"experience* has taught us over the years that one of the best deterrents to terrorism is the certainty that *swift and sure measures* will be taken against those who engage in it."[8]

This was indeed the philosophy underlying the administration's approach to terrorism, but whose "experience" was Shultz talking about? It was not that of Lyndon Johnson, Richard Nixon, Jimmy Carter, or Ronald Reagan, none of whom had attempted "swift and sure measures" against terrorists. Even Gerald Ford's bombing of Cambodia did not support Shultz's point, since the terrorists released the hostages before we bombed, not after. The only democratic nation that has consistently pursued a policy of assured retribution is Israel.

Since late 1968, Israeli policy has called for reprisals against terrorists for every act of terrorism. Carrying out this policy has frequently meant bombing terrorist bases in Lebanon. What constitutes a terrorist base is, of course, a subjective judgment, and in the course of most such attacks innocents as well as terrorists are killed. The Israelis are also willing to bypass the law by conducting assassinations as a means of retaliation. Following the massacre of Israeli athletes at the 1972 Munich Olympics, they tracked down and killed the perpetrators, but in the process also killed an innocent Moroccan waiter in a Norwegian hotel.

A policy of determined retribution certainly sends a message to terrorists, but how much it achieves is debatable. Terrorist attacks on Israelis have not ceased. Some people even believe the terrorists may have continued attacking as a matter of counter-retaliation. On the other hand, the situation might well have been worse without the retaliatory attacks; neither Syria nor Jordan any longer permits attacks on Israel from its territory. And the Israeli case must be placed in the perspective of Israel's being at war with a number of its neighbors. Most democracies that are not in similar peril are less willing to violate their normal respect for human life and the process of law.

Great Britain, for instance, suffers a continuing and grievous problem with the terrorism of the Irish Republican Army (IRA). It has driven their police into breaking the law in dealing with the IRA; even the courts have been less than even-handed toward accused terrorists.[9] Although the British public tolerates this, there are voices of protest. And the public's respect for law checks the government from straying too far. For instance, when Parliament passed the Prevention of Terrorism Act of 1974, weakening habeas corpus by permitting police to detain suspects longer than is normal, it made the law effective for only one year. The government has had to justify the need for it annually. The British model, then, is one of reluctant resort to the use of extraordinary means in the fight against terrorism.

George Shultz appeared to be advocating a position somewhere between the British and Israeli models. Like the Israelis, he was willing to risk the lives of innocents in fighting terrorists. Like the British, he was reluctant to do so, as reflected in the fact that his counsel, Abraham D. Sofaer, felt it necessary to develop a legal argument that retaliatory attacks were justified as self-defense under Article 51 of the Charter of the United Nations. But how do we define "self-defense"? For policemen, self-defense is permitted only when they are under imminent threat. Sofaer was saying that self-defense for our nation can include an attack on anyone we *think* is going to sponsor terrorism against us. As he put it, democracies have the "moral right [to] . . . preventive or pre-emptive actions against terrorist groups before they strike."[10] When, though, does self-defense become aggression?

From 1979 to 1981, the students holding our hostages in Tehran seemed to be aggressors but asserted that they were acting in self-defense. They claimed that the United States had injured Iran by supporting the Shah over many years and would continue to do so unless forced to stop. Since taking the hostages was a form of defense, the rule of international law on the immunity of diplomats was a secondary matter to them.

The Islamic Jihad in Beirut also believed it was exercising self-defense against efforts by the United States to perpetuate a Christian-dominated government in Lebanon against the will of the majority. The sentiments of Sheik Fadlallah, expressed in an interview with an American journalist, were not far from those stated by George Shultz:

We do not support or encourage attacks against purely American cultural institutions, or against American individuals doing normal business in the world. But in the meantime, we feel that when America pressures the Islamic world and Muslims, especially through Israel, it is very natural that the war being waged by those opposed to the policy of the American Administration take the form of attacks on strictly political U.S. interests . . . When it is necessary, I approve of violence. Also, every person needs to defend himself. If a man needs to use violent ways, he must use it.[11]

What the students, Fadlallah, and Secretary Shultz were all saying was that if one's purposes were important enough, the use of violence — self-defense — to preserve them is warranted. As Americans we feel we are defending the rights of the individual to a safe, humane, and unmolested life. The Shiite fundamentalists in Tehran and Lebanon feel they are awakening individuals to the spiritual values in life. Differences in outlook as to what justifies the use of violence has for years hindered debates in the United Nations on the definition of terrorism. There are those who insist that what we call terrorism is not that when it is carried out to liberate people from cruel domination — the African National Congress's struggle against apartheid; the Romanians' overthrow and killing of Ceaucescu.

Such flexibility in defining terrorism has led to the cliché "One man's terrorist is another man's freedom fighter." In a speech in June 1984, George Shultz used the word "insidious" to describe this formula. He claimed that "Freedom Fighters or revolutionaries don't blow up buses containing noncombatants; terrorist murderers do."[12] Who, though, could deny that the contras whom Shultz supported in Nicaragua committed atrocities against the civil population? Certainly they fought against the Sandinista army as well, but the contra leadership itself on numerous occasions investigated abuses of civilians by its soldiers, even purging some as a result. Shultz was saying the contras were freedom fighters because we shared their political aims, but the Shiite fundamentalists were terrorists because we did not.

We can only hope to reach agreements with other nations on dealing with terrorism if we remove political considerations from the definition. That means defining it by actions, not purposes:

Terrorism: The threat or use of violence for political purposes by individuals or groups . . . when such actions are intended to shock, stun, or intimidate a target group wider than the immediate victims.[13]

· 23 ·

THE FADLALLAH FOLLY

The CIA did not believe that deaths caused by U.S.–trained counterterrorists would violate the ban on assassinations imposed on U.S. intelligence agencies in 1976. Its officials contended that if there is proof that a terrorist intends to kill, then killing him first is self-defense rather than assassination.

— Robert C. Toth[1]

AS PRESIDENT REAGAN approached his second term in office, his counterterrorism program was proving to be all threat and no action, so he turned to the CIA and covert action. Also, covert·action would give the activists — Shultz, Casey, and McFarlane — a means of bypassing Weinberger and the bureaucrats in both the State Department and the CIA who had been resisting a broad interpretation of the proactive policy. It would be Casey's finger on the trigger, not Cap's. And the CIA's extreme compartmentation of information about covert actions would help Casey control opponents within the Agency. He would need to persuade only a handful of people to carry out a covert action.

Casey later indirectly confirmed that his first move was to get a presidential finding for a covert action in which the CIA would train the Lebanese to counter terrorists. He said, "All Americans are at risk in Lebanon. We have lost better than 300 people there in terrorist attacks. We told the Lebanese it's up to them to protect our people and our installations, but we offered to help them. We've worked to strengthen their capabilities, train them, give them technical support. But they do any operations themselves."[2] Training Lebanese to collect information would be a routine matter of collaboration on intelligence. Training them to "do operations" is, by law, a covert action and requires a presidential finding.

What kind of operation did the finding authorize? It has never been released, but there is no question that it was somehow related to a massive car-bomb explosion near the home of Sheik Fadlallah in Beirut on March 8, 1985. The Sheik was not there and survived, but eighty people in an apartment building next door were killed and over two hundred wounded. Casey vehemently denied the CIA was involved in planning the bombing or was in contact with the people who did it. Then, commenting on how the CIA's training of the Lebanese under the finding related to the explosion, he said, "Before the bombing, we were ready to consider helping them with planning that sort of action if they did it in a surgical, careful, well-targeted way — if they really knew what they were doing." In short, car bombings were included in Casey's plan for training the Lebanese, though he intended any actual bombings to be "surgical." In his view it was "the fault of the Lebanese that the Fadlallah event was not surgical." However, he added one item that raised a question as to whether the CIA's role was as distant as he implied: "Well, we didn't like the way that situation was handled. So we pulled back from any involvement in the planning or preparation of operations."[3] That meant canceling the presidential finding, but doing so clearly showed that the CIA was uncomfortable with its proximity to the attempted assassination. However little involved the CIA had been, Casey had realized there was at least the appearance, if not the fact, of a connection between the finding and the bombing. I was dumfounded to think Casey had considered dealing this way with the Lebanese intelligence organization. In the best of times its standards were far from ours.

I find it impossible to believe that CIA people would have condoned a Lebanese operation that risked the lives of hundreds of innocents in the attempt to kill one terrorist. When the intelligence committee of the House of Representatives immediately investigated the CIA's relationship to the bombing, it reported that "the committee's review has uncovered no evidence that any U.S. intelligence agency has encouraged or participated in any terrorist activity in Lebanon." And "the committee states that its review of relevant documents and files and its interviews of appropriate government officials leads to the conclusion that no U.S. Government complicity, direct or indirect, can be established with respect to the March 8 bombing in Beirut."[4]

While the committee's statements are categoric, some troubling questions remain. How objective could an oversight committee be on a covert action it knew about in advance?* Even though the intelligence committees do not have authority to stop a covert action, the fact that they were informed of this one made them a party to it. They might well have been embarrassed at how it turned out or at their not recognizing that the finding was so broadly worded as to permit an assassination attempt. It is also possible the committee's investigators were misled by Casey, who was notorious for withholding information from Congress. But I think we can accept the committee's report that the CIA was not directly involved in or aware of this specific operation. The report does not, however, answer the question of whether the CIA in some way encouraged the assassination attempt.†

Whatever training the CIA did, or discussions it had, with the Lebanese could have been interpreted by them as a sign that the United States looked favorably on their getting rid of Fadlallah. The Lebanese did not need to be convinced of the virtues of a pro-active strategy of assassination. In Beirut, bombing one's enemy is a way of life. But what seemed to be the United States' endorsement of that practice with respect to Fadlallah may well have started the Lebanese on their way to his door. The Christian-dominated government may even have wanted to settle some scores with this Shiite.

Bob Woodward, who broke the Fadlallah story in the *Washington Post* on May 12, 1985, seemed at the time to agree with this thesis. Later, in his book *Veil,* he changed his mind, claiming Casey had not

---

*I presume the committees were informed, since no one said otherwise. Had the committees not been informed, there would have been vocal complaints, as in 1984 when there was a question as to whether Casey had informed the committees about the CIA's role in the mining of Nicaraguan harbors.

†I believe there is an untold story here. The prohibition on assassination is straightforward, saying, in effect, that no one will carry out an assassination or plot to have someone else do so. That does not prohibit the CIA's participation in an operation in which someone may be killed, unless the intent is to kill a particular person. During the Iran-contra revelations in 1986–1987, the intelligence committees were embarrassed at not having been informed of the CIA's role. They sought ways to ensure that there would be no repetition and made demands on a weakened administration. The administration sent the committees a letter expanding the interpretation of the ban on assassination. I can understand that the committees would attempt to extract a promise of prior notification of covert actions, but I have difficulty understanding why they wanted a clarification of what constitutes an assassination unless, during the investigation of Iran-Contra in 1987, they learned that the CIA or Casey himself was more involved in the Fadlallah affair than had been revealed. If that was the case, they would have wanted assurances for the future.

been able to get the professionals in the CIA, most especially his deputy, John McMahon, to go along with the covert action.[5] That came as no surprise to me. John McMahon is a very moral man, who would do his best to protect the CIA from being involved in, and made the scapegoat for, shaky operations concocted by outsiders. In *Veil,* Woodward contended that Casey went behind John's back and worked with Saudi Arabia's ambassador to Washington to persuade the Saudis (Sunnis) to arrange the attempt on Fadlallah (a Shiite).* It is conceivable, but we may never know for sure whether the Saudis did it at Casey's urging, or the Lebanese did it on their own with the CIA's indirect encouragement.

In any case, there were two reasons for the fiasco. The first was Casey's willingness to train the Lebanese, apparently even in truck bombing. For years the CIA had withheld advice, training, and equipment from foreign intelligence services with poor records on human rights, just so that we would not become an indirect party to practices such as torture or assassination. In reversing that practice, Casey opened a Pandora's box. Moreover, we did not have evidence that Fadlallah was behind the bombings of our facilities. Much of the evidence pointed to pro-Iranian Shiites, but not to Fadlallah personally. He insisted that he was not involved in such day-to-day secular activities, and up to now, no evidence has been made public to prove otherwise.

The second reason was that the administration's pro-activists let themselves be stampeded into believing conditions in Beirut warranted such drastic action as assassination. They had reportedly inserted into NSDD 138 the sentence "The U.S. Government considers the practice of terrorism by any person or group in any cause a threat to our national security."[6] We certainly had serious problems in Lebanon, but none that threatened our national security.

If the Reagan administration had stampeded in its response to terrorism, it was not, of course, the first to do so. Jimmy Carter had let his administration become wholly preoccupied with its hostage problem; Richard Nixon's press secretary had reported that the President was deeply concerned with the Dawson Field incident; Lyndon Johnson had agonized over the *Pueblo* hostages. The Reagan administration's pro-active strategy, though, sprang from a sense of urgency that justified more radical solutions than those resorted to by any previous

---

* He further alleges that when that assassination did not work, Casey arranged for the Saudis to bribe Fadlallah into stopping the truck bombings. There were no more.

administration. Casey made it abundantly clear that he had assassination in mind:

> If the Lebanese discharge their duty to protect the lives and property of their citizens as well as other nationals, and if in the course of doing that someone gets killed, are we assassinating that guy? No. We're helping the Lebanese perform a security function. If someone gets killed or hurt, well, it's a rough game. If you don't resist and take protective action against terrorists because you worry that there's going to be somebody who might say, "Ah, that's assassination," then terrorists can own the world, because nobody's going to do anything against them.[7]

Casey was implicitly arguing against a provision of the first presidential Executive Order on Intelligence issued by Gerald Ford when George Bush was his DCI. Jimmy Carter had modified it slightly to: "No person employed by or acting on behalf of the United States Government shall engage in, or conspire to engage in, assassination." Ronald Reagan had retained the same wording in his Executive Order.* Only once before had a question arisen about a possible violation of this order. In 1983 a CIA adviser to the contras in Nicaragua drafted a manual employing a phrase about "neutralizing" government officials which patently condoned assassination. When this hit the press, the President quickly disavowed it, but that did not raise many cautionary flags with the pro-active advocates within his administration. For instance, even if the subsequent finding on training the Lebanese was not deliberately pointed at assassination, there certainly was a high risk that it would go in that direction. And, just weeks after the Fadlallah fiasco, McFarlane and Casey contended, in speeches with almost identical language, that "we cannot and will not abstain from forcible action to prevent, pre-empt or respond to terrorist acts where conditions warrant. We need not insist on absolute evidence."[8]

This was about as close as anyone in the government could go in arguing publicly for assassination, since it was banned by the President's Executive Order. A debate, though, did go on behind the scenes and in the media — and it still does. Almost every time there is a serious

---

* Carter's wording placed added emphasis on no indirect support of assassinations, that is, no conspiring to engage in assassination, but that was clearly implicit in the Ford wording.

terrorist incident, a columnist or commentator comes out in favor of rescinding the presidential prohibition.[9] There are three recurring arguments in favor of assassination. The first is that most everyone would agree to shooting a man who was in the act of throwing a switch to detonate a bomb that might kill many people. But detonating a bomb is a criminal act, and our laws permit shooting a person when a criminal act is imminent. It is the definition of "imminent" that creates the distinction between prevention of a crime and unwarranted killing. Who sets out that definition? What if an intelligence report tells us a certain individual will detonate the bomb tomorrow? Who determines the reliability of the report? If the situation is not imminent, there are usually other recourses, like evacuating the area or detecting and defusing the bomb.

The second argument is part and parcel of the pro-active theory that we must respond with force or become increasingly vulnerable. It says that resorting to assassination is less likely to kill innocents than almost any military attack and is more humane. The argument is logical, but it rests on the assumption that we *must* retaliate with military force if we don't turn to assassination.

A third is the "Hitler argument": if someone had killed Hitler early in his rise to power, it would have saved millions of lives. This has a. facile appeal, but it rests on questionable assumptions: that we would have identified Hitler early enough so that assassinating him would not have started a war; that we would not have killed other would-be but ultimately unsuccessful tyrants; that Hitler's successor would have been better than he; that, as a people, we would be comfortable with exercising the right to determine which world leaders should live or die.

The last is the primary counterargument. That is, our national ethic will not accept the responsibility of assassination. Our record since World War II seems to confirm this. For its first twenty-nine years, the CIA was not barred from assassination; it plotted a number of them, but never carried them out. When those plots were exposed in the 1976 hearings of the Church Committee, the reaction was strong. "The Committee does not believe that the acts which it has examined represent the real American character. They do not reflect the ideals which have given the people of this country and of the world hope for a better, fuller, fairer life. We regard the assassination plots as aberrations. The United States must not adopt the tactics of the enemy."[10] There were no dissenting votes.

A MEDIA HIJACKING

I only know that none of us, any country, can afford to pay off
terrorists . . . because that will only lead to more crimes.

— Ronald Reagan [1]

DAY 1 was Friday, June 14, 1985, when TWA's Flight 847 lifted off
from Hellenikon Airport in Athens at 10:10 A.M., bound for Rome
with 153 passengers, 122 of them Americans, plus a crew of eight.
Before the pilot had turned off the seat-belt sign, two Arab men in
their late teens or early twenties bounded out of seats at the very rear
and ran down the aisle, brandishing grenades and pistols. Forcing their
way into the cockpit, they demanded that the pilot, John L. Testrake,
divert the plane to Algiers. Captain Testrake managed to convince the
frantic hijackers that he did not have enough fuel to reach Algiers.
They opted for Beirut (see Map 11).

About an hour after TWA 847 reversed course, at 4:30 A.M. Washington time, shrill phones awakened members of the Reagan crisis
management team. It was only six months since the team had faced
the administration's first hijacking, when terrorists had seized a Kuwaiti airliner and taken it to Tehran. There, they killed two American
passengers while demanding the release of the seventeen Shiites imprisoned in Kuwait. Although the aircraft was on the ground in Tehran
for six days, there was no attempt to launch a rescue operation. After
the Iranians stormed the aircraft and released the surviving hostages,*
the administration settled for a promise by the Iranian government that

---

* A number of witnesses believed it was a staged affair, since none of the hijackers
was killed or wounded.

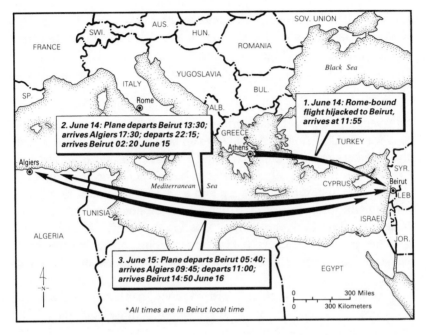

In the map:

FRANCE

SWI. AUS. HUN.

ROMANIA

YUGOSLAVIA

ITALY

SP.

Rome

ALB.

BUL.

SOV. UNION

Black Sea

GREECE

Athens

TURKEY

1. June 14: Rome-bound flight hijacked to Beirut, arrives at 11:55

2. June 14: Plane departs Beirut 13:30; arrives Algiers 17:30; departs 22:15; arrives Beirut 02:20 June 15

Algiers

Mediterranean Sea

CYPRUS

SYR.

Beirut

LEB

TUNISIA

ISRAEL

ALGERIA

JOR.

3. June 15: Plane departs Beirut 05:40; arrives Algiers 09:45; departs 11:00; arrives Beirut 14:50 June 16

EGYPT

-N-

0   300 Miles

0   300 Kilometers

*All times are in Beirut local time

MAP 11. FLIGHT OF TWA 847, JUNE 1985

the hijackers would be brought to justice in the Iranian courts. In the intervening months, however, there had been no sign that the hijackers ever went to trial or that our government pressed the Iranians to keep their promise. Once again, the United States appeared helpless before terrorism. The impression was reinforced by a new wave of kidnapings of Americans in Beirut. Between December 1984 and June 1985, five more were taken hostage, one escaped, and another, CIA Chief of Station William Buckley, died.* This left six Americans being held hostage; apparently nothing was being done for them.

Now, the administration once again seemed helpless as TWA Flight 847 began flying back and forth across the Mediterranean. The first stop was the diversion to Beirut. After an hour and a half on the ground, the hijackers ordered Captain Testrake to take off and head for their original destination, Algiers. After only five hours on the ground in Algiers, the hijackers ordered a return to Beirut, then back to Algiers, and, finally, back to Beirut. After fifty-three hours and eighty-three hundred miles, Captain Testrake was close to physical exhaustion. Overhearing the hijackers talking about going on to Tehran next, he staged an engine failure, and the peregrinations of TWA 847 ended.

Why the shuttling back and forth? It could be that, in the wake of the successful rescue operations at Entebbe and Mogadishu, the hijackers knew it was risky to remain in one place very long. And they had probably heard news reports from the United States that Delta Force was being assembled to fly across the Atlantic and get "close enough to the hijacking so they can be used if the country where the plane is wants help."[2] I surmise the hijackers were intent on going to Algiers because of the Algerians' reputation for brokering deals over hostages. What these hijackers wanted to negotiate was the release of some 766 Lebanese prisoners, mainly Shiites, from the Atlit jail in Israel. Ini-

---

* The hostages taken were Peter Kilburn, librarian at the American University at Beirut, December 3, 1984; the Reverend Martin L. Jenco, head of Catholic Relief Services in Beirut, January 8, 1985; Terry A. Anderson, correspondent for the Associated Press, March 16, 1985; David P. Jacobsen, director of the hospital at the American University, May 28, 1985; and Thomas M. Sutherland, professor at the American University, June 9, 1985.

Jeremy Levin, correspondent for CNN, escaped or was released on February 14, 1985. The Islamic Jihad claimed they killed Buckley on October 5, 1985. It has since been found that he was subjected to prolonged torture and died on June 3 from the torture and the lack of medical treatment.

tially they also called for freedom for the Shiites in jail in Kuwait, an admission by the United States that it was behind the Fadlallah affair, and a general condemnation of the role of the United States in Lebanon, especially the shellings by U.S.S. *New Jersey* in late 1983 and early 1984. Apparently to give evidence of their seriousness, they brutally murdered Robert D. Stethem, a U.S. Navy petty officer, and dumped his body onto the tarmac at the Beirut airport during the second stop there.

As expected, the Algerians started negotiations and managed to persuade the terrorists to release all but forty male American passengers and the three cockpit crew. The Algerians had to make one concession. One of the terrorists, while listening to a passenger's portable radio, heard that an accomplice, trying unsuccessfully to board TWA 847, had been apprehended by the Greek police. The terrorist threatened to kill all eight Greek passengers on board if Ali Atweh was not permitted to join them within nine hours. The Greek government caved in and sent Atweh to Algiers on a special Olympic Airways flight. He joined his comrades on board TWA 847 and began stealing valuables from the passengers' persons and baggage.

The concession by Greece was no surprise. The government had often accommodated terrorists in the expectation that there would be no acts of terror against Greeks. In this case, though, the release of Atweh left us without a bargaining chip. On the other hand, it did lead to freedom for more than fifty hostages, eight of whom were Greek.

After TWA 847's final stop in Beirut, all but the three cockpit crew were taken off the aircraft and dispersed to several makeshift prisons. The first phase of the TWA 847 crisis had ended and with it any prospect of rescuing the hostages by an assault on the aircraft while it was on the ground. A rescue from the prisons was impossible because of a lack of intelligence. There were no other options. Economic or political pressures could not be applied to a terrorist group, and a military attack was out of the question while the hostages were still in custody.

Remembering that Jimmy Carter had made his problems more difficult by isolating himself in the Rose Garden during his hostage crisis, Ronald Reagan's advisers did their best to distance the President from this crisis. The hijacking took place on a Friday, and the President stuck to his plans for a weekend at Camp David. By Sunday afternoon, though, he returned to chair a meeting of the National Security Council. On Day 6 he acknowledged, "I've pounded a few walls myself when I'm alone about this."[3] On Day 11, for the first time in his administration, he canceled a vacation in California.

A telling report from a presidential press conference helps explain his inability to stay away from visible involvement in this crisis: "It was a different President Reagan than most reporters had known. In the past he has exuded confidence and assurance. Now, he was clearly hesitant and cautious, admitting that he had no easy solution. 'I have to wait it out as long as those people are there and threatened and alive and we have a possibility of bringing them home.' "[4]

But waiting it out was not easy. Instead, Ronald Reagan, like George Washington, Thomas Jefferson, Teddy Roosevelt, Lyndon Johnson, Richard Nixon, and Jimmy Carter before him, started down the road of making a deal with terrorists. President Reagan followed the Roosevelt model in having someone do it for him. In Roosevelt's case it was the Sultan of Morocco; in this, the Israelis. The shape of a deal had been there from the very beginning, since the Israelis were already in the process of releasing these prisoners because they were being held under questionable circumstances anyway. Some three hundred had been sent home before the hijacking, and it was only a matter of time until others were freed.

But now the Israelis did not want the next release to be seen as part of a deal. If it appeared they were exchanging prisoners for hostages, they would be at a disadvantage whenever they took prisoners. Fortunately for them, the President, who continued to state that the United States would never countenance a deal with terrorists, was reluctant to ask the Israelis openly for help.

Instead, an elaborate non-negotiation took place, resulting in a deal that was supposedly not a deal. Secretary Shultz still contends that all he did was relay information back and forth between the Israelis and Nabih Berri,* the chief negotiator for the hijackers.[5] Using French and Swiss diplomats as intermediaries to help maintain the illusion, Shultz asked the Israelis their intentions with regard to the prisoners. Then he passed that information to Berri, got Berri's plans for the hostages, passed that back to the Israelis, and so on. Eventually each side was satisfied that it could proceed without any formal arrangement and do only what it claimed to have planned all along.

---

* Berri is the leader of the Amal faction of Shiites in Lebanon, from which the fundamentalists like Fadlallah had broken away to form the Islamic Jihad. Because Amal was less virulently anti-American, Berri was in a better position to act as a broker between the hijackers and the Americans.

It is difficult to believe there was no arm twisting. For instance, it is clear we turned to Syria and Iran to put pressure on Berri and the recalcitrant members of the Islamic Jihad. In addition, the Speaker of the Majlis, Hashemi Rafsanjani, happened to be in Damascus and, though his exact role remains murky, it seemed to the administration that he helped to bring this affair to a conclusion. That, whether fact or perception, later had an important bearing on the arms-for-hostages deals during the Iran-contra affair. In the end, Berri certainly believed a deal had been made by which Israel would release the prisoners immediately after the hostages were freed, on Day 17, June 30. He was incensed when he found that Israel was going to stretch the release of the prisoners over several months so as to make it look less like a deal.*

Why did both the United States and Israel insist on going through with the charade? It was hardly a secret that both countries would make deals with terrorists. Only a month before, Israel had baldly swapped 1154 prisoners for three Israeli soldiers who had been captured in Lebanon.† At home, with three out of four of the last American Presidents having made deals over hostages, most observers assumed Ronald Reagan was making a deal. We were too pleased to have the crisis behind us to quibble over the inconsistency between the President's talk and his actions. Personally, I thought the charade an astute maneuver. Despite the administration's having backed itself into a corner with repeated assertions about not making deals, Secretary Shultz was able to create enough ambiguity to deny any contradiction. On June 23, Shultz explained the desirability of the thin subterfuge:

Just remember, there are problems all over the world in countries that are friendly to us. Some genuine problems, some imagined problems that people have. Do we want to get ourselves in a position where we invite people who have a grievance somewhere to grab some Americans and then assert a connection and cause us to try to put pressure on somebody to do something about it? We certainly do not want to invite that pattern of behavior.[6]

---

* Thirty-one prisoners had been released on June 23 as an enticement that, it was hoped, would lead to the release of the hostages. It did not, and there were more negotiations or exchanges of information before the hostages were released. Then, three days later, on July 3, three hundred more prisoners were freed. The remainder were sent home, in small groups, through September 9.

† The 1154 included Kozo Okomoto, one of the crazed killers in a brutal massacre at Lod Airport in 1972, in which twenty-six were killed and seventy-six wounded.

Whatever George Shultz and Ronald Reagan chose to call the swap, it amounted to their first accommodation with terrorists. They did not bomb, did not rescue, did not use political or economic pressures, and did not hold firm. Nor did the Jihad release the prisoners out of kindness of heart. It was a deal, and as deals go it must be judged as only marginally successful. That is, the terrorists obtained a big piece of what they originally demanded, the release of their compatriots from jail, and that was bound to encourage them to strike again. Nor were the terrorists any more deceived by Ronald Reagan's professions that he had not made a deal than was the bandit Raisuli by Teddy Roosevelt's bombast. Less than four months later, Palestinian terrorists took over an entire cruise ship and demanded that Israel release still more prisoners. From the beginning, one part of the Reagan strategy against terrorism had been no deals. That was now being ignored.

The other part of the original strategy, "swift and effective retribution," had not been used in response to any of the numerous bombings and kidnapings of the previous four and a half years. Now, as soon as the TWA 847 hostages were released, retaliation was hotly debated. This time the excuse that we could not identify the culprits was pretty weak. We knew exactly who Ali Atweh was from the Athens police file. A number of the passengers and crew of TWA 847 had observed the two original hijackers for better than two days, as well as others who joined them during the second stop in Beirut. The hostages sent to prisons in Beirut saw a good bit of the people who guarded them for fourteen days. And there were fingerprints all over the aircraft.

But how do you carry out retribution on a group, as opposed to a state, even if you know exactly who the hijackers are? One choice is to track them down and attempt to get them into a country where they can be arrested. That, it turns out, is just what the Reagan administration did. It took close cooperation with the West Germans and a year and a half of their patient surveillance of the brother of Mohammed Ali Hamadei, the leader of this operation. When Hamadei finally showed up in West Germany, he was arrested, tried, convicted, and sent to jail.

Assassination was another option, but as far as we in the public know, it was not attempted or even considered in this case. The administration should have been wary of hired killers, after the disastrous Fadlallah affair.

Then there was the option of a military attack. The problem in a densely packed civilian population was that any bombing aimed at the terrorist group would almost certainly have killed innocent bystanders. Some advocates of tough responses contended that with "smart" bombs we could hit only the terrorists and their facilities. That there was no attack in this instance argues that an attack was not considered likely to be surgical enough. Whatever his reasons for failing to retaliate, the President was taken to task from both the right and the left.* He had, though, forecast his decision in an interview during the crisis: "If you just aim in the general direction and kill some people, well, then you're a terrorist, too."[7]

Why did the administration get into such a position that it had to abandon both parts of its strategy and, instead, rely on slow, patient police work to apprehend Hamadei? The only other choice was to wait out the terrorists, and the pressures of public opinion were too great for that. The media gave this incident big play, and the public responded. The travelers were seen as having been caught up in the conflict between the Palestinians and Israelis; it was only because they were Americans that they were useful as pawns. There had not been a similar concern for the six Americans already held hostage in Beirut, one of whom had been there for 401 days when this hijacking occurred. One difference was that the six were missionaries, educators, and journalists, who had gone to Beirut voluntarily. The public did not relate to them in the same way as it did to ordinary travelers, which they themselves might be one day.

The American media covered the story from everywhere — on the scene in Beirut, Cyprus, Athens, Jerusalem, and Amman, and at the homes of the hostages' families in the United States. In addition to the newspapers, magazines, and national TV networks, over fifty local or regional TV stations sent correspondents to Beirut for live shots of the aircraft at the airport and whatever snippets the terrorists fed them. And when more than a hundred people were released from the plane during the first two days, there were all sorts of opportunities for interviews. The hijackers soon realized they could use the media and even demanded to see reruns of the previous day's American TV coverage to learn what kind of a splash they were making.

On Day 6, June 19, there was a dramatic moment when an ABC cameraman was allowed to interview Captain Testrake, who was lean-

---

* From the left, editorial, "Unfinished Business," *New Republic*, July 29, 1985. From the right, George F. Will, "With a 'Genteel' Touch," *Washington Post*, July 2, 1985.

ing out a window in the cockpit while a hijacker held a gun to his head. Testrake's shouted message was that the United States should not attempt a rescue effort: "I think we'd all be dead men if they did, because we are continuously surrounded by many, many guards." [8] The United States was checkmated by a handful of hijackers.

This kind of manipulation of the media continued the next day when the hijackers brought five hostages before a horde of reporters, who, with incredibly undignified behavior, turned the event into a circus. With dozens of microphones thrust forward and questions repeatedly shouted at him, the spokesman for the hostages had difficulty just making his statement. When he finally did, he dramatically increased the pressure on the President by pleading that the United States persuade Israel to release the 766 Lebanese prisoners. He cited the President's earlier rebuke of Israel for holding these prisoners against the Fourth Geneva Convention on prisoners of war; and even endorsed the claim of the hijackers that holding passengers and crew from TWA 847 was no more illegal than what Israel was doing. [9] The wisdom of the spokesman can be questioned, but it was a good example of how terrorists can benefit by playing to the media.

In addition, the networks allowed Berri to become a regular on American TV. He put pressure on Ronald Reagan by telling Americans that if their President would only arrange for Israel to release the Lebanese prisoners, the hostages would be freed. One anchorman even turned to Berri at the end of an interview and asked, "Any final words to President Reagan this morning?" [10]

Thus, the media became participants, not just reporters, and were accused of making the negotiations more difficult for the President by broadcasting interviews with hostages whom the terrorists selected. The State Department's legal adviser, Abraham Sofaer, characterized the media's performance as an "extravaganza that gave irresponsibility and tastelessness a new meaning." [11]

In some ways the media's role was only part of a broader trend toward involvement of individuals and corporations in foreign affairs. For instance, at Christmas 1979 three American clergymen who had visited the hostages in Tehran commented, "Private citizens cannot negotiate for governments. But when a government is having a hard time talking, it's up to private people to try to discuss the situation." [12] In late 1983 Jesse Jackson went to Syria and negotiated the release of a U.S. Navy flier who had been shot down over Lebanon. In 1984 the sister of the hostage Jeremy Levin in Beirut went to Syria and Lebanon to talk with government officials on behalf of her brother. Ross Perot and his corporation conducted a rescue operation in Iran in early 1979. Numerous other corporations have paid ransom for executives kidnaped abroad. It would be futile to inveigh against all such intrusion into foreign relations, for the government at times can be slow and cumbersome. Private citizens, corporations, and the media, though, should be acutely aware that there may be wider implications to rescuing an individual or assisting a group. This is especially true for the media, which must not let their involvement in a crisis jeopardize their responsibility to report that crisis objectively.

In the case of TWA 847, some of the media were embarrassed afterward by what appeared to be excessive zeal in reporting, but almost all of the senior executives defended their performance. They argued that it was their job to inform the American public and they had done that well and thoroughly. They also pointed out that they had rendered useful service by advancing the pace of the negotiations when they acted as a channel of communication with Berri. And they had given reassurance to families that hostages who appeared on TV were alive. They cited the government's having subpoenaed TV tapes which had not been broadcast as evidence that they were also providing useful intelligence.

Should the media have been more responsible in their reporting? The answer from Attorney General Edwin Meese III was an implicit yes. He suggested that the government discuss with media representatives whether their coverage had been "helpful or hurtful from the standpoint of getting the crisis ended in a satisfactory manner." He further suggested the government negotiate a written agreement with the media that would provide for delays in "the release of information which would be inimicable to the peaceful or rapid solution of a particular operation, or perhaps temporarily withhold information or interviews that might be dangerous or endanger captives if they're hostages."[13] At the same time, Meese made it clear that he was not suggesting legislation to control the media, recognizing that such a move would arouse strenuous opposition on the grounds of infringement of freedom of speech.

Still, there are democracies where there are controls over the media, or where the media themselves display considerable restraint. In September 1977, for instance, a West German businessman, Hans-Martin Schleyer, was captured by terrorists who pressured the government to release other terrorists from jail. The German media remained virtually silent until the case ended with Schleyer's death. In Great Britain in 1980 the media agreed to withhold sensitive information during a siege at the Iranian embassy in London.[14] In 1988 the British government, in addition, established restrictions on TV interviews with members of terrorist organizations.[15]

That government interference, or even voluntary restraint, is unacceptable to the American media was reflected in comments on the TWA 847 crisis by a thoughtful journalist once president of CBS News, Fred W. Friendly. He made short shrift of Meese's suggestions for voluntary restraints:

> The *third* worst outcome of the Lebanon tragedy would be if the government imposed restrictions on reporting during a terrorist crisis. The *second* worst outcome would be to require a blue-ribbon panel of network executives and government officials to come up with a long list of agreed-upon pledges and guidelines. They would be impossible to write because every crisis is a no man's land, and even if you could write them they would be impossible to enforce.

He went on, though, to recognize that the status quo was not entirely satisfactory:

> But the *most* tragic course of action would be for American journalism to continue their defensive posture over those 17 days [TWA 847] and to learn nothing and to do nothing . . . The danger is that if we don't critique ourselves, the government may step in to fill the void.[16]

Fred Friendly had a very good point, but it is difficult to suggest how the media could jointly decide on rules for reporting on terrorism. Friendly himself noted that the government and the media would have an impossible task doing so together; so, too, would the media among themselves. What highlights this dilemma is that nothing specific came from Meese's or Friendly's suggestions, though there was a good deal of soul searching within the media.

· 25 ·

STILL NO RESCUES

A message to terrorists everywhere . . . "You can run, but you can't hide."

— Ronald Reagan[1]

DURING LUNCHEON on October 7, 1985, a steward on the Italian cruise liner *Achille Lauro,* steaming off the Egyptian coast, entered Cabin 82 and stumbled on four Palestinians cleaning an assortment of guns and grenades. Discovered, the four proceeded to seize control of the ship and announce their demand — the release of fifty more Palestinians from jail in Israel. President Reagan's deal three months earlier for the TWA 847 hostages had come back to bite.

The hijackers, not having intended to make their move until the ship docked in Israel a few days later, had no plan of action. Searching for what to do with the ship they now controlled, they moved it about the eastern Mediterranean for two days (see Map 12). As part of pressure on the Syrian government to let them dock at a Syrian port, they killed a helpless American in a wheelchair and dumped his body into the sea.* Finally, their superior in the Palestinian Liberation Front (PLF) ordered them by radiotelephone to have the ship proceed to Port Said, Egypt. At this point, American and Egyptian interests clashed. We wanted the hijackers brought to justice. The Egyptians wanted to avoid potential problems with fellow Arabs of the PLO and the risk of terrorism against Egyptians. They promised the hijackers safe passage to Tunis, where they would supposedly be brought to trial at the headquarters of the PLO, and pretended that the hijackers had already left Egypt when we raised objections.

---

* Leon Klinghoffer, age sixty-nine, of New York.

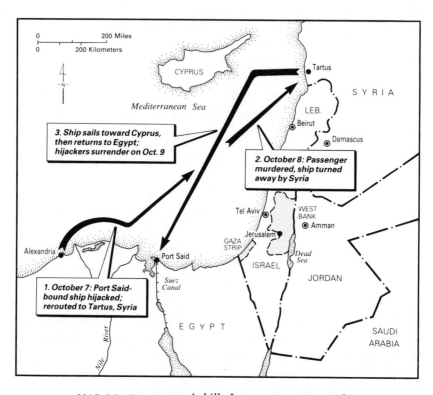

3. Ship sails toward Cyprus, then returns to Egypt; hijackers surrender on Oct. 9

2. October 8: Passenger murdered, ship turned away by Syria

1. October 7: Port Said-bound ship hijacked; rerouted to Tartus, Syria

MAP 12. TRACK OF *Achille Lauro*, OCTOBER 1985

A Navy captain, James R. Stark, working on the NSC staff in the White House, had a brilliant idea. He recalled the incident in World War II when an intelligence breakthrough told us that Admiral Isoroku Yamamoto, architect of the Japanese attack on Pearl Harbor, would be flying around the Upper Solomons Islands in the South Pacific. We sent P-38 fighters to intercept Yamamoto's aircraft, and they shot it down. Stark, deducing the odds were high that the Egyptians would send the hijackers to Tunis by air and over the Mediterranean Sea, where our Sixth Fleet has one or more aircraft carriers, flashed the idea to another staff member, Oliver North. North rapidly moved it to his superior, Vice Admiral John M. Poindexter, and on to the Joint Chiefs of Staff. Vice Admiral Arthur S. Moreau and the new Chairman of the Joint Chiefs, Admiral William J. Crowe, Jr., drew up a plan and sent it to the President. President Reagan was traveling, and the proposal reached him when he was touring the headquarters of the Sara Lee company near Chicago. Using one of the bakery's offices as a makeshift command center, the President gave his approval to move forces into position. Later that day, while returning to Washington on *Air Force One*, he gave his final approval to put the plan into action.

Rear Admiral David E. Jeremiah received his orders on the carrier U.S.S. *Saratoga* in the Ionian Sea and quickly dispatched fighter aircraft to search for the Egyptian airliner carrying the hijackers to Tunisia. Intelligence reporting on the aircraft's takeoff and identification number had to be excellent. Late that night over the Mediterranean near Crete, Navy F-14 fighters converged on the plane. When the fighters suddenly turned on their lights, the Egyptian pilot saw a fighter just a few feet off each of his wingtips. Stunned, he complied with orders to follow the fighters to a NATO airbase at Sigonella, Sicily (see Map 13). The Army's Delta Force had just arrived there, and it quickly surrounded the Egyptian aircraft, expecting to seize the hijackers and send them off to the United States for trial. Italian troops from the base, though, surrounded Delta and asserted their jurisdiction. We did not have full control, but soon learned we had hit the jackpot. Not only were the four hijackers on board, but also the mastermind of the operation, Abu Abbas, a member of the PLO's executive council.

Now, Italian and American interests clashed. The Italians refused to extradite the four hijackers to the United States and fell over themselves to let Abu Abbas leave their country, claiming that the legal case against him was weak. The Italians have a commendable track

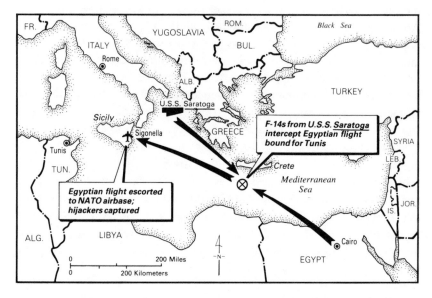

Black Sea

FR.

YUGOSLAVIA
ROM.
BUL.

ITALY
Rome

TURKEY

ALB.

U.S.S. Saratoga

Sicily

Sigonella
GREECE

SYRIA

Tunis
LEB.

TUN.

Crete

F-14s from U.S.S. Saratoga
intercept Egyptian flight
bound for Tunis

Mediterranean
Sea

JOR.

Egyptian flight escorted
to NATO airbase;
hijackers captured

IS.

ALG.
LIBYA

Cairo

0   200 Miles
–N–

0   200 Kilometers
EGYPT

MAP 13. INTERCEPT OF EGYPTIAN AIR FLIGHT, OCTOBER 1985

record fighting domestic terrorism, but like the Greeks, they had been accommodating international terrorists in the hope of avoiding attacks on their nationals. In time, however, the Italians did put on trial fifteen members of the PLF. Eleven of them were convicted, including Abu Abbas, who was tried in absentia.

The policies of self-protection pursued by the Egyptians and Italians — and the Yugoslavs, who also refused to extradite Abu Abbas when he passed through their country — made the Reagan administration fume. "State Department officials said they were furious at the speed with which the Italians and the Egyptians, working with the Palestine Liberation Organization, agreed to let the hijackers go free."[2] If the Egyptians had not made a deal, though, the hostages would have continued under the capricious control of the hijackers, at additional risk. And despite our protests on the extradition policies of the Italians and Yugoslavs, our record on extradition was far from unblemished. When the Soviets, surprisingly, condemned the *Achille Lauro* hijacking, they pointedly noted that a Soviet father and son who had hijacked an Aeroflot flight in 1970, and eventually taken refuge in New York, had not been extradited. Then, when George Shultz roundly chastised Yugoslavia in public, that government pointed out that it had been waiting many years for us to extradite a Yugoslav indicted as a war criminal. That extradition was arranged quickly. And at this same moment, while we were complaining about other governments taking selfish actions to protect their citizens from terrorists, we were violating our own embargo on selling arms to Iran in the hope of securing the release of American hostages in Beirut.

At home there was euphoria at our having snatched the hijackers out of the air in a brilliantly executed, if illegal, maneuver. We had finally struck back at terrorists, and this helped erase the unhappy memory of the failure at Desert One. The difference in military performance was that Desert One was an unusual, low-intensity operation for which there was little precedent, whereas forcing down an airliner was a maneuver closely akin to the standard, wartime operation of intercepting, identifying, and shooting down enemy aircraft. That is something fighter pilots rehearse over and over. What went unnoticed in the *Achille Lauro* situation was that our rescue forces were again not ready. There was no rescue attempt although the ship was at sea under control of the hijackers for more than forty hours.

Why? Because it took about twenty hours to get the rescue forces moving from the United States. The commander didn't leave until he had filled four giant C-5A transport aircraft with equipment and men.[3] It took another ten hours to reach the Mediterranean from the United States. Concern over not having enough equipment added another handicap: the commander tried to load up for every contingency. By the time the forces arrived on the second night, it was too late to assault the ship during the remaining darkness. Plans were made for the third night, using Navy ships just over the horizon from the *Achille Lauro* as the jumping-off point. By that third night, though, the ship was in Port Said and the hostages were free.

Nor had much attention been paid to the fact that there had been no rescue effort during the TWA 847 incident. That aircraft had made five stops, ranging from an hour and a half to twenty-five hours at Beirut and Algiers. At neither airport were conditions favorable for an assault: in Beirut the airport was virtually under the control of the hijackers, and in Algiers the government was loath to give permission for even the exploratory team from our rescue forces to survey conditions. The relevant point, though, is that even if conditions had been favorable, the President did not have a rescue option available to him. By the time the rescue forces arrived in the Mediterranean area, there was yet one more impediment. The hijackers had brought aboard additional weapons and people during the second stop in Beirut, and the hostages would have been at grave risk if we had attempted a rescue.

The rescue forces were not responsive in this case because the military was reluctant to send them to the Mediterranean until the grasshopping aircraft settled down and plans for a rescue could be made. Otherwise they would be sending forces into the field with virtually no plan at all. And when it was finally decided to dispatch the forces across the Atlantic, there was a delay in finding aircraft to transport them! With some three hundred long-range transport aircraft in our military airlift fleet, that seems an almost unbelievable neglect of an urgent operational requirement. Even though there was a new central commander who was supposed to have most of what he needed under his command, he was just as dependent for transport on outside resources as Major General Vaught had been.

Rescue force responsiveness had improved in one important respect, however. About nine hours after the TWA 847 hijacking, an emergency support team (EST) left Washington for Algiers. Composed of representatives of the State and Defense Departments, the various rescue forces and the CIA, it was designed to advise our ambassadors in the area, offer assistance to foreign governments in dealing with the terrorists, and prepare the way for the rescue forces. This was the idea the West Germans had employed when Minister Wischnewski had followed the hijacked *Landshut* all the way around the Middle East to Mogadishu in 1977.

Unfortunately, this helpful step was offset by the fact that the rescue forces were so far away that transit time was a problem, even though all manner of U.S. forces were near the scene of both of these incidents. There were two reasons. First, the military had created a central, multiservice command for low-intensity conflict, in line with a recommendation of the Holloway review group. It was located in the United States lest it be within the domain of one of the theater commanders. Second, recognizing how politically sensitive rescue operations could be, the JCS wanted to retain close control. Neither excuse is adequate.

We must position rescue forces forward, which means the theater commander would normally control them during operations. That was the arrangement when forces were dispatched in the TWA 847 incident and has the advantage of engaging the theater commanders at this level of war. The commanders have powerful influence in shaping and training our military forces, and since the collapse of communism in 1989, the focus of our military will inevitably shift toward lower-intensity conflict, including rescue missions. The central commander could be charged with developing the doctrine, equipment, and training routines for rescue operations.

Rescue missions can be politically sensitive, though; witness Helmut Schmidt's feeling that he would have resigned if the Mogadishu operation failed, and Jimmy Carter's electoral defeat after the debacle at Desert One. But Washington authorities have options. One is for the JCS to bypass the theater commander in a specific instance and exercise control through the central commander in the United States, just as they did in the Desert One operation and the attempt to seize the *Achille Lauro*.

A second, more controversial, alternative would be for the President to appoint an on-site political commander, much as Minister Wischnewski was for Helmut Schmidt. This will sound heretical to our military, but need not be antithetical to their interests. Decisions on the scene of a rescue effort can have such a high political content as to be beyond the scope of a military officer and yet may have to be made instantly. Having the President's Chief of Staff or another person from his political entourage on the scene could lift the political burden from the military commander. Like Minister Wischnewski, this person would have to have the sense not to tell the military commander how to do his job, only whether and when.

We have not yet solved the problems of rescue forces and must continue to pay attention to them lest we be caught short again.

WE WILL MAKE DEALS

We are especially not going to tolerate these acts [of terrorism] from outlaw states run by the strangest collection of misfits, Looney Tunes, and squalid criminals since the advent of the Third Reich.

— Ronald Reagan,
July 8, 1985 [1]

UNLIKE the TWA 847 incident, which had a strong effect on Ronald Reagan's attitude toward Americans being held hostage, the fate of the seven Americans who had been kidnaped in Beirut over the previous fifteen months had received little attention from him or the public. But they came to the fore during the media's intense coverage of the TWA affair. When it became apparent that a deal was being made for the airliner's hostages, relatives of the seven began lobbying to have them included. At the last minute George Shultz added them, but he received no response. Nonetheless, the Forgotten Seven became a media item.*

The family of the Reverend Martin L. Jenco, one of the early hostages, managed to attend a meeting the President held in Chicago on June 28, 1985, with the relatives of the TWA hostages. The Jencos forcefully pointed out to the President that he was making a swap of 766 prisoners from an Israeli jail for thirty-nine Americans hijacked on the TWA flight, whereas he had steadfastly declined to support an exchange of seventeen prisoners from a Kuwaiti jail for seven Ameri-

---

* There were actually six hostages alive in Beirut, but none of us knew at the time that William Buckley had died.

cans locked up in Beirut. The President's feeling for these seven and their families began to grow. From then on, he found it difficult to say no to any of the schemes presented to him for securing their release. A report by the Senate Select Committee on Intelligence later noted, "Documents and testimony reflect deep personal concern on the part of the president for the welfare of U.S. hostages both in the early stages of the initiative [arms sales to Iran] and throughout the program." [2] The Iran portion of what came to be known as the Iran-Contra affair had gained its own momentum.

The President soon began asking about the hostages at most of his daily briefings. [3] Most of the presidential pressure fell on the NSC, where Oliver North was already deeply involved in the hostage problem. At DCI Casey's behest, North had been working to ransom hostages, again using funds provided by Ross Perot. Ransom had not worked, and now, with the President wanting results, the NSC staff turned to selling arms to Iran.

There were six separate sales, beginning in late August 1985. When the final score was toted up fourteen months later, it showed that:

- The Iranians had purchased antitank and antiair missiles and spare parts to help offset the advantages in heavy armor and bomber aircraft held by Iraq in the war between them.
- The United States had won back three hostages.*
- Three new hostages were captured.† There is no evidence that the Iranians prompted these three kidnapings, but the two Lebanese groups claiming responsibility were both pro-Iranian, and one was the same group that had acceded to Iranian pressure to release the three hostages in exchange for arms. That is, Iran did have some influence over these hostage takers.

---

* Three hostages were released in the course of the six deals of arms for hostages; the Reverend Thomas Weir, September 15, 1985; the Reverend Martin Jenco, July 24, 1986; and David Jacobsen, November 2, 1986, the day before the operation became public.

† The three new hostages were Frank H. Reed, Headmaster of the Lebanese International School in South Beirut, September 9, 1986; Joseph J. Cicippio, Acting Comptroller of the American University, September 11, 1986; and Edward Austin Tracy, a writer, October 31, 1986.

- One hostage was killed.*
- A total of five Americans remained in incarceration.†

This is a simplification of a complex series of maneuvers, but it is not a distortion. The United States was completely outmaneuvered, and achieved no improvement in its position. Normally, before so many mistakes could be made, someone at a high level would blow a whistle and get the President's attention; or the bureaucracy, with its accumulated experience, would manage to halt the slide. In this case, neither happened, because the President's men on the NSC staff, operating with exceptional freedom under the Reagan management style of maximum delegation and minimal supervision, were able to circumvent the bureaucracy. For example, as one of the investigations noted, "Poindexter ensured that . . . McFarlane would fly to Iran for an expected high-level meeting with the Iranians without any consultation with the Secretary of State,"[4] and "North admitted that he and other officials lied repeatedly to Congress and to the American people about the Contra covert action and the Iran arms sales, and that he altered and destroyed official documents. North's testimony demonstrates that he also lied to members of the Executive Branch, including the Attorney General and officials of the State Department, CIA, and NSC."[5]

Because of their distrust of the bureaucracy, the NSC staff turned to other sources of advice and information. They ended up relying on a motley mixture of outsiders, mainly American, Iranian, and Israeli arms dealers. Unbelievably, most of the so-called intelligence about the Iranians' willingness to help with our hostages if we sold them arms came from an Iranian arms dealer who stood to profit from the sales. When Bud McFarlane of the NSC first met this man, he quickly evaluated him as one of the most "despicable" characters he had ever met.[6] Despite that, and despite the man's having failed two CIA polygraph tests, he remained at the center of the sales for another eight months.

No corporation could stay in business if its vice presidents operated in the style of the NSC staff: depending on unproved and untrustwor-

---

* Peter Kilburn, librarian of the American University, was killed in April 1986, apparently in retaliation for an American bombing of Libya. The Libyans are reported to have purchased Kilburn for this purpose.

† Terry Anderson, captured on March 16, 1985, and Thomas Sutherland, captured on June 9, 1985, were still in captivity when the arms swaps ended, as were Reed, Cicippio, and Tracy, captured during the arms deals.

thy sources of information, lying to one another, destroying documentary evidence of what they had done, and taking kickbacks from suppliers. Many Americans condoned all this when it was first revealed in November 1986, but the majority were indignant, and the Reagan administration almost came to a halt for months while the facts were sorted out. In March 1987, five months after the initial disclosures, a reporter commented, "Until last week, the question was whether Reagan would be able to put the Iran-Contra arms scandal behind him. Now thoughtful people ask whether he can survive politically." [7] This was a high price for any President to pay for seven hostages, especially when his only successes in obtaining their freedom were offset by more kidnapings.

The public's reaction, in my opinion, sprang from a justified fear that fundamental national values, especially the intent of the Constitution, had been threatened. The most basic strength of that document is that it entrusts the people to make the ultimate decisions for the country — but they cannot do that if the government lies to them about what it is doing. Nor can the system of checks and balances among the three branches of government work properly if one branch withholds information that the others are entitled to have. What these violations of procedures inherent in the Constitution signify is that because terrorism is such a difficult problem, we are tempted to compromise our basic values and standards when combating it. Ronald Reagan and his people, however, were not the first to face this temptation.

- Teddy Roosevelt failed to inform the public, in the midst of his hostage crisis, that he had learned the man he was attempting to rescue was probably not an American citizen. In 1862 Perdicaris, the American-born son of a native Greek, had registered as a Greek citizen in Athens as a way of deterring the Confederacy from confiscating property that he, a Northerner, owned in the South. By the time Roosevelt learned of this, the fleet was already in Tangier and the country aroused. He buried the information. It was twenty-nine years before a historian uncovered it. [8]
- Jimmy Carter came close to breaching a number of our constitutional freedoms by tapping the Shah's telephone, denying the right of assembly for pro-Khomeini demonstrators in Lafayette Park, and requiring that Iranian students be singled out for inspection of their visas.

The incursions of Roosevelt and Carter into our constitutional privileges were minor compared with those committed during the Iran-

Contra affair, but they alert us to the harm that may be done if future Presidents become too emotionally involved with hostages. Ironically, President Reagan was quite aware of the price Jimmy Carter had paid. "In hindsight," said a White House aide, "one of the things everyone learned from [Carter's] experience was that by becoming so engrossed in Iran, Carter just unwittingly fed into the terrorists [sic]. Now, the President's time and energy and activities are not solely involved in the Beirut situation. A conscious decision was made. We don't abdicate. We run the government."[9] That wisdom did not deter Ronald Reagan from deep personal involvement. What could have?

Some observers suggest it would help if Presidents did not meet the families of hostages. In our society, such a prohibition would be difficult to effect. Perhaps a President could limit the contacts, but it would not be wise to try to eliminate them; an integral part of our democratic system is the pressure individual citizens bring on their government. In this very instance, the administration neglected the Forgotten Seven until their relatives' voices became louder.

Another precaution against too intense a personal involvement is the avoidance of exaggerated rhetoric. Ronald Reagan's calling the terrorists "Looney Tunes" was bound to create public impatience; Americans thought of their fellow citizens as being held by totally capricious captors. And advertising "swift and effective retribution," when it was highly improbable, reinforced the impression that terrorist situations can be corrected quickly if only we are sufficiently firm. The claim in NSDD 138 that terrorism is a threat to our national security aroused unnecessary concern. Terrorism alone has never yet threatened the basic security of any society, even though it has raised severe personal and political problems. Each of these was a small factor, but each increased the pressure on the President.

It was this kind of exaggeration that opened the door, almost inevitably, to the use of covert action. The President in January 1986 signed an intelligence finding directing the CIA to:

> establish contact with *moderate* elements within and outside the Government of Iran by providing these elements with arms, equipment and related material in order to enhance the credibility of these elements in their effort *to achieve a more pro–U.S. government in Iran* by demonstrating their ability to obtain requisite resources to defend their country against Iraq and intervention by the Soviet Union.[10]

· Intelligence findings are usually worded with considerable ambiguity, but the italics supplied above make clear that replacing Khomeini and his government with one composed of "moderates," or people "more pro–U.S.," was what was intended. It is difficult to imagine the government of Iran turning moderate or even slightly pro–U.S. with Khomeini still at the helm. It is difficult to estimate how many in the administration believed it was possible to topple Khomeini as distinct from laying the groundwork for a post-Khomeini regime. (There were constant rumors that the eighty-five-year-old man was dying.) But even the hope that the next regime would be different had to be wishful thinking; the grip of the Ayatollah and his close followers was tight and rigid.

For instance, Bud McFarlane, after leading a delegation to Tehran in May 1986, noted that he was not able to meet with the three principal Iranian leaders below Khomeini, including Rafsanjani, because they were "traumatized by the recollection that after Bazargan, Khomeini's first Prime Minister, met with Brzezinski [at a conference in Algiers in October 1980], he was deposed, so strong was popular sentiment against doing business with the Great Satan." [11] Only the biased intelligence reporting of the NSC staff's outside sources could conjure up a prospect of successful negotiations with virtually the same Iranians the Carter administration had dealt with in vain.

Besides getting carried away with a poorly devised covert action built on a shaky premise, the Reagan administration hurt itself by protesting too much that it did not make deals with terrorists. It had to pretend the six swaps of arms for hostages were not deals after all. For instance, because the first was done through the Israelis, the argument was made that *we* were not selling arms. Later, when arms were flowing directly from U.S. arsenals to the Iranians, the rationalization was that the United States was dealing with the Iranian government, not with the terrorists in Beirut. On occasion sophistry may harmlessly salve the conscience, but in this case it had the deleterious effect of precluding such questions as "How does this deal compare with Jimmy Carter's? Or Richard Nixon's? Or Lyndon Johnson's? Or the one on TWA 847?" And "Does it stack up well enough for us to consider it?"

How, though, should an administration distinguish between different deals with terrorists? Some must be less undesirable than others. There are four useful questions:

- Were the terrorists encouraged to believe that terrorism pays off because they got what they demanded?
- Was their demand for something they might easily ask for again?

- Did the deal damage our national honor by making us look weak?
- Did we get what we sought?

By answering these questions, we can compare the seven Presidents whose deals we have studied.

George Washington's deal merited poor marks except that it did get the hostages back, but only after some had been held for ten years. It certainly damaged our young nation's honor, but our first President's only alternative was to let the hostages stay where they were.

Thomas Jefferson did better. He forced down the asking price, and he did less damage to the national honor because he was able to stop the payment of annual tribute that Washington had started.

Teddy Roosevelt did poorly on all counts, except that he obscured the damage to national honor by making it look as though the Sultan of Morocco was making the concessions.

Lyndon Johnson did pretty well, even though after eleven months of bickering he gave the North Koreans what they had originally demanded. He protected our honor and reduced the likelihood of repetition by baldly denying the truth of the confession he had signed.

Richard Nixon's deal was very questionable, like Roosevelt's, except that it was more apparent to the world that we were condoning the deal. Hence, there was some damage to our honor.

Jimmy Carter's returning $8 billion to Iran did not give the hostage takers what they had demanded and did not encourage them to do it again because there was no more money available if they seized more hostages. Our national reputation was damaged considerably by the failed rescue mission and by the fact that it took 444 days to make this deal, but not by the terms of the deal itself.

The Reagan TWA 847 deal raised the probability of repetition, but damage to national honor was mitigated somewhat by the thin fiction that it was an Israeli deal.

The six Reagan arms-for-hostages deals did badly in all categories; they did not even succeed in a net release of hostages, and they clearly invited the terrorists to come back for more.

Why are intelligent people so obstinate as not to realize that Presidents do make deals with terrorists and that, though none is desirable, some can be less objectionable than others? In part because the reasoning that concessions breed more terrorism is compelling, and there is evidence to support the thesis. George Washington's deal led directly to added demands from the Barbary pirates; Ronald Reagan's swap for the TWA hostages very likely contributed to the *Achille Lauro* hijacking; and the West Germans are convinced that their exchange of some Baader Meinhof prisoners for a hostage in 1975 set off a rash of terrorist incidents, all with demands for the release of more prisoners.

But that is not the entire story. Some deals have not had adverse repercussions. Raisuli was satisfied with what he obtained from Roosevelt and did not come back again; the North Koreans did not take another ship, because another false confession would not have been much of a prize; and the Iranians did not seize more diplomats because it was useless to demand more frozen assets. Another deal that produced more good than bad involved an airliner the Palestinians hijacked to Algiers in 1985, demanding the release of the seventeen Shiite prisoners in Kuwait. The Algerians negotiated a deal that assured the hijackers safe passage in exchange for release of the hostages. No one liked seeing the criminals go free, especially since they had killed two passengers. The alternative was to leave the hostages at risk. Some would argue that sacrificing a relatively few people today is sometimes necessary to deter terrorists from endangering many more tomorrow. That is not likely to be accepted in our democracy. When present suffering is almost certain and future suffering only problematical, present concerns almost always win out.

A President, understandably, will be reluctant to acknowledge that he is willing to make deals, lest he seems to be sending an invitation to terrorists. Condemning all deals, though, may force him to choose between letting Americans suffer as hostages and appearing to violate his pledge. What that means is that a President may have to contrive some artifice to claim a deal he made was not a deal.

We have seen that George Shultz was handily able to obfuscate the deal through the Israelis for 766 prisoners. But as the administration made repeated arms sales to Iran, its reasoning grew more and more tortured. We may have hoped the Reagan experience would lead the next administration to temper its rhetoric on deals, but that was not to be. When George Bush became President, he was saddled with the exhortation "no concessions to terrorists" from the report of a task force on terrorism he had chaired for President Reagan.[12] His administration started by affirming this position over and over.

AN UNEXPECTED IMPACT OF
"SWIFT AND EFFECTIVE RETRIBUTION"

If necessary, we shall do it again.

— Ronald Reagan [1]

EARLY in the Reagan administration there was boasting that not a single country would go communist during Reagan's presidency. I find it difficult to believe the ambition was that modest. Bill Casey undoubtedly gave its actual dimensions when he said, "I'm looking for a place to start rolling back the communist empire."[2] There were two likely candidates: Nicaragua and Libya. Lucky Libya came up first.

Three months after taking office, Ronald Reagan closed the Libyan embassy in Washington and sent its diplomats home, saying, "From the first days of the Administration, both the President and Secretary of State Alexander M. Haig, Jr., have made known their very real concern about a wide range of Libyan provocations and misconduct, including support for international terrorism."[3] Over the next year the administration methodically challenged Muammar Qaddafi: sending Navy fighter aircraft over the Gulf of Sidra to defy his claim that this international airspace belonged to Libya and, in the process, shooting down two Libyan aircraft that fired at them first; urging Americans to leave Libya and invalidating U.S. passports for any others to travel there; banning imports of oil from Libya; accusing Qaddafi of sending "hit" teams to the United States to assassinate the President; and reportedly charging the CIA through an intelligence finding to destabilize Qaddafi. The administration may have hoped these moves would unseat Qaddafi. They did not.

In the summer of 1982, the administration's focus in foreign affairs shifted to Lebanon, and Libya dropped off center stage. Then, on December 27, 1985, Qaddafi's fingerprints turned up on the edges of two gruesome and senseless acts of terrorism. Palestinians simultaneously sprayed bullets at the El Al ticket counters in the Rome and Vienna airports, killing twenty people, five of them Americans, including an eleven-year-old girl. The mastermind of this operation was Abu Nidal, an outcast from the PLO. He probably was sponsored by Libya or Syria. One surviving terrorist confessed that he had been trained by Syrians in the Bekaa Valley. Two of the passports used by the terrorists in Vienna were among a number that had been confiscated the previous summer by Libyan authorities from Tunisian workers being expelled from Libya. A third had been reported lost by a Tunisian worker in Libya.

Although the evidence against Libya was no more incriminating than that against Syria, Syria was not as suitable a target for military retaliation. Libya was not linked as closely to the Soviet Union, and its air defenses appeared to be less effective — the Syrians had earlier shot down two U.S. aircraft over the Bekaa Valley. A few days after the Rome and Vienna attacks, the American press began speculating about military air strikes against Libya.[4] The media were right that plans were being shaped, but the administration wanted a stronger case before unleashing a military attack. Also, there were still some fifteen hundred Americans in Libya, down from about eight thousand in December 1981, when the administration first advised Americans to leave. The President now ordered those fifteen hundred out, threatening penalties if they did not depart immediately, and he instituted stringent economic sanctions against Libya, including the freezing of Libyan assets in the United States.

George Shultz dispatched his deputy to Europe in an attempt to persuade our allies to follow suit. It was futile. A number, like Italy, had substantial economic interests and a large number of citizens in Libya. When the responses were flaccid, the President obliquely condemned these friends by saying, "There is a moral issue involved here with regard to a sovereign state that is so obviously resorting to terrorism literally against the world."[5] As it happened, the President assumed this moral stance against terrorism in Libya at the very moment he was working on his third sale of arms to Iran, despite the U.S. embargo against that country because of its involvement in terrorism.

I doubt that President Reagan and his advisers expected sanctions to have much effect on Qaddafi, but imposing them was one more step they felt they had to take before resorting to force. They also sent the Navy to tweak Qaddafi again with carefully staged intrusions into the Gulf of Sidra from January through March 1986.[6] Again, Qaddafi walked right into the trap when, on March 21, Libyan shore batteries fired antiaircraft missiles unsuccessfully at two Navy planes. The aircraft retaliated by knocking out the missile installations plus two patrol boats.

Qaddafi then made matters worse for himself. Perhaps because of his several humiliations on the battlefield, he decided to strike back at the United States through terrorism. The very next day, the National Security Agency (NSA) intercepted a message from the Libyan intelligence service to seven embassies in Europe, directing them to develop plans for terrorist attacks on Americans.[7] Despite this warning, and another intercepted message pointing to Berlin as the first target, we failed to head off a bombing in a West Berlin discothèque on the night of April 5, 1986. Two U.S. Army sergeants were killed. For the next ten days the probability that we would strike at Libya dominated the news. NBC News even chartered an aircraft and located an aircraft carrier of the Sixth Fleet moving into position.[8]

I happened to be in London at the time. During an interview on a Sunday morning TV show I predicted confidently that the United States would not attack Libya. With so much publicity about the possibility, we had forsaken any chance of surprise, and besides, I believed the longer the debate went on, the more likely that cooler heads would prevail. I did not appreciate that, because the debate within the administration on the use of force against terrorists had dragged on for over two years, the pro-active voices were loudly and insistently urging an attack on Libya, and because our humiliation at the hands of terrorists had continued, the voices of the more cautious were becoming muted. I also did not discern at the time how assiduously the administration had been preparing for the use of force.

Two mornings later, on April 15, I was back on British television, trying to explain why we had bombed both Tripoli and Benghazi and what the consequences might be. The most immediate result at home was an almost audible sigh of relief that at last we had done something (see Map 14). Two weeks later, 76 percent of those polled supported the attacks, and the pollsters said this "shows the public strongly behind aggressive action against terrorism"[9] Basking in this long-awaited success, the President declared, "I warned that there should be no place on earth where terrorists can rest and train and practice their deadly skills. I mean it. I said that we should act with others, if possible, and

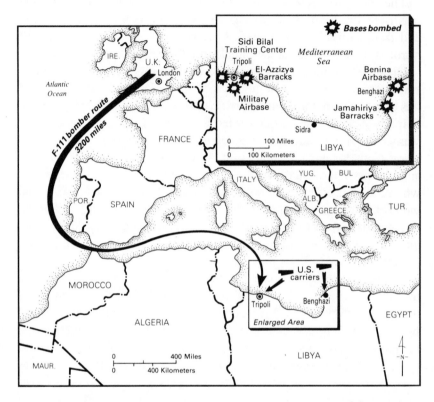

Within the enlarged area map:

Bases bombed

Sidi Bilal
Training Center
Tripoli
El-Azzizya
Barracks

*Mediterranean
Sea*

Benina
Airbase

Benghazi

Military
Airbase

Jamahiriya
Barracks

Sidra

LIBYA

0   100 Miles
0   100 Kilometers

Within the main map:

*Atlantic
Ocean*

IRE.

U.K.
London

F-111 bomber route

3200 miles

FRANCE

POR.   SPAIN

ITALY

YUG.   BUL.

ALB.

GREECE

TUR.

MOROCCO

U.S.
carriers

Tripoli   Benghazi

Enlarged Area

ALGERIA

EGYPT

LIBYA

MAUR.

0   400 Miles
0   400 Kilometers

N

MAP 14. U.S. ATTACK ON LIBYA, APRIL 14, 1986

alone if necessary, to insure that terrorists have no sanctuary anywhere." [10]

The public's euphoria bothered me. Justification for the use of force was not much greater than in the TWA 847 case, yet Ronald Reagan had demurred then because, he said, he did not want to be like the terrorists. There was only one significant difference. Libya was a state, whereas the culprits in the TWA 847 case were the Hamadei group. It was easier to select targets in Libya so as to minimize civilian casualties than to attack individual terrorists somewhere in Beirut. We could aim at government facilities, especially military ones, even though it was difficult to be certain that all had a role in supporting terrorism. The key target was El-Azzizya Barracks — Qaddafi's residence and supposedly a national command center. This raised the question of whether the attack was an attempt at assassination by bombing, which would be a violation of the Executive Order on Intelligence. Spokesmen for the administration claimed it was not, though they acknowledged they would not have been unhappy had Qaddafi been killed. The best evidence that it was is the effort expended on striking the residence, which seemed greater than that warranted by a command center. Whatever the intent, the bombs failed to hit Qaddafi.

This illustrates the fundamental dilemma of a democracy in using force against terrorists: if we strike too broadly, we kill innocents, and are just like the terrorists; if we aim too narrowly, we appear to be targeting a person, and violate our policy against assassination. The margin is slender; if we use force, we will almost always transgress one boundary or the other.

I believe Ronald Reagan saw as acceptable the encroachment in both directions. He countenanced an assassination attempt that was ambiguous; he accepted a modest amount of harm to innocents. (Thirty-seven were reported killed and ninety injured, though we are dependent on the Libyans for these numbers.) Polls showed that the American people viewed the attacks as a reasonable response to the provocation, because they were frustrated with our previous impotence. I heard no expressions of remorse at the killings and injuries, some of them almost certainly of innocent civilians. Whether or not the decision to unleash the bombers was justified by the effect on terrorism, the action undermined our nation's values because we failed even to regret the killing of innocents. That moved us a step toward the terrorists' moral standards — or lack of them.

Interestingly, those opinion polls showed that about the same percentage of the public said they thought the attacks would do little to curtail Libyan terrorism. For a time, these skeptics seemed to be right; there were several immediate bursts of what looked very much like Libyan-backed terrorism. Among them was the killing of Peter Kilburn, one of the hostages in Beirut, reportedly at Libya's behest. But after a few weeks, Libyan terrorism against Americans did abate. That created a popular impression that the bombing successfully deterred Qaddafi from further terrorism. I do not doubt the bombing had some such effect, but I believe we overestimated it. In part, that is because we exaggerated how much Libyan terrorism there was before the bombings; it always came and went in cycles. For example, during the first months of the Carter administration, we uncovered a Libyan plot to assassinate our ambassador to Egypt. President Carter let Qaddafi know how serious the consequences of such an act would be, and that was the last we heard of Libyan terrorism against Americans for the remaining years of the Carter administration. In part, it is because we cannot positively identify Libya's hand behind some anonymous terrorist attacks against Americans after the bombing. The columnist Jack Anderson thinks he can: "There has been more Libyan-sponsored terrorism since the raid than before it." [11] His calculation, however, attributed a number of incidents to Libya for which the evidence was not conclusive.

Qaddafi survived the Reagan administration's effort to unseat him. Unfortunately, he is likely to be back at us when it next suits him. We may well find it expedient to strike at him again, but we should be careful not to interpret any success of the April 1986 bombing as proof of the efficacy of combating all terrorism by bombing. First, it took a long time and much deliberate provocation for the administration to push Qaddafi into a position where it could justify an attack. And even then the circumstances were very special: we had reasonably good evidence of complicity; Libya was a pariah state without sponsors or friends; its military capabilities were modest, though we did lose one aircraft in the attack on Tripoli (it is unclear whether this resulted from Libyan antiaircraft fire or an accident); and most of all, Libya did not hold any American hostages, though we did not take into account Libya's being able to arrange the killing of Peter Kilburn in Beirut.

It is the last factor, the presence of hostages, that has been the primary restraint on the use of force against state-sponsored terrorism. Thomas Jefferson confronted it in two respects: risks to hostages from our own attacks; and risks from retaliation by the hostage holders.

While Lieutenant Bainbridge and 306 of his sailors from the brig *Philadelphia* were prisoners in Tripoli in 1803, our Mediterranean fleet bombarded Tripoli to pressure the Bashaw into releasing them. A shot from *Constitution*, however, entered Bainbridge's prison chamber and slightly injured him — a risk that must have inhibited Jefferson's combativeness. Then, in 1805, when Jefferson sent William Eaton marching toward Tripoli to obtain the release of Bainbridge and his men, the Bashaw of Tripoli threatened to kill them if Eaton continued. Jefferson settled for a negotiated deal.

Teddy Roosevelt was similarly constrained by the fear of what Raisuli would do if he sent Marines to search for Ion Perdicaris in the mountains behind Tangier.

Lyndon Johnson did not lash out militarily at the North Koreans for fear that they were sufficiently vicious to kill *Pueblo* sailors in retaliation. He also felt an even broader concern. "There's a lot you don't know about this," he told his brother, who had suggested the use of force to get the crew back. "My first impulse may have been the same as yours, but I can't go around giving in to the first impulse that hits me. I'm the President of my country and my responsibilities are to the whole world on something like this. I've got to hold back on a lot of things that could lead to a third world war — or maybe the last one." [12]

Richard Nixon, who had excoriated Lyndon Johnson for not using force to defeat a fourth-rate military power, [13] was hamstrung when the PFLP hijacked the three airliners to Dawson Field in 1970 because they threatened to blow up the aircraft with the hostages on board if we attacked. In addition, because the PFLP was only a group, not a nation, military attacks would have been on the territory of Jordan, a friendly country already under siege.

Jimmy Carter certainly believed the students in the embassy might harm our hostages if we moved against Iran with military force.

Not only were there special conditions that made force an acceptable response to Libya's evident involvement in the terrorism in Berlin, but the resulting benefit was unusual also. It is difficult to measure the impact on Qaddafi's readiness to terrorize Americans, but the bombing surely had a salutary effect on the Europeans. Ironically, they were the last to think bombing could be beneficial. Their experience with terrorism convinced them that violence incites more violence. Prime Minister Bettino Craxi commented that "Italy settled accounts with internal terrorism" using "patience, firmness, and moral force before military force." [14] The Italian experience, though, was largely with their own nationals, the Red Brigades, on their own soil. Similarly, the West Germans with the Baader Meinhof, the British with the IRA, and the French and Spanish, each with the Basque ETA, were dealing with domestic terrorism. Our American experience has been largely on other people's soil, that is, with international terrorism. We have not been in a position to try the European technique of patient, solid police work to close in on terrorists on our own. We have needed the collaboration of other responsible nations to track them down. Until the bombing of Libya, we had not got much of that.

After the bombing, the Europeans began to appreciate that greater cooperation with us was essential if they wanted to avoid more American military strikes against terrorists. They remembered the President's words: "If necessary we shall do it again."[15] They worried that more bombing would induce more terrorism, and even if it was against Americans, it would most likely be on European soil. A perceptive European commentator, Christoph Bertram, diplomatic correspondent for the German weekly *Die Zeit,* captured the essence of a changing European attitude when he wrote, shortly after the bombing raids:

> On most of these occasions, as in the recent crisis over Libya, the main common denominator of European politics has been to criticize the United States. It is true that European criticism has often been justified. But the credibility of Europe's objections has all too often been undermined by the fact that these have served as a convenient cover for European unwillingness or inability to do anything about the problems themselves.[16]

In early May 1986, at another economic summit of the Big Seven, in Tokyo, the other six nations were willing to discuss collaborative efforts against terrorism, something they normally resisted as inappropriate to these meetings on economics. Out of the summit came a communiqué on terrorism containing all the bland generalities one would expect about standing firm and united against terrorism. But it also included a list of seven kinds of actions that the seven nations pledged to take jointly to clamp down on terrorists.

The first group was pointed at apprehending individual terrorists. Most effective have been exchanges of intelligence about terrorists and closer cooperation between police and security organizations. Collaboration has led to the arrest and imprisonment of a number of terrorists, among them Mohammed Hamadei, the key hijacker of TWA 847. When Hamadei was arrested, he was carrying a list of telephone numbers that put the French police on the trail of other terrorists in Paris, demonstrating how a little cooperation on one event can help with others.

A second group of actions was designed to isolate states that support terrorists. The most effective results here were from tightened controls over Libyans and other suspected terrorists throughout Europe. This resulted in over a hundred Libyan diplomats being sent home, and Libyan embassies and national airline offices, which had provided cover for Libyan agents, being pared down in size.

The communiqué of the summit failed to mention deals with terrorists. All the heads of state would almost surely have taken a public position that they would not countenance deals, but they were too wise to be pinned down. Nonetheless, individual nations became more self-conscious about making separate deals or placating terrorists in the hope of being exempted from attacks. For instance, in the spring of 1988, when the Kuwaiti airliner was hijacked and eventually flown to Algiers, no nation but Iran gave support to the hijackers.

It was particularly significant that the communiqué also did not address either economic sanctions or punitive military actions. Cutting off trade could, of course, seriously affect some domestic economies, and military action could be highly controversial with electorates. None of the heads of state could be expected to agree to anything that would force him to undertake an action that might adversely affect domestic politics.

Despite these reservations on how far politicians will commit themselves in advance, what they will seek in a given instance is a balance between domestic interests and the pressure they feel from the international community. That is why the Reagan administration's arms sales to Iran were particularly damaging, not only to the domestic political standing of the President, but to our nation's ability to fight terrorism. The administration had repeatedly entreated our allies not to sell arms to Iran on the grounds that Iran was supporting terrorism, and on four occasions since 1983 had urged these allies to tighten their controls on exports to Iran, as we were doing. When it was revealed that we had violated our own rules, we lost our credibility in seeking cooperation against terrorism. And we need that cooperation more than most, since terrorism against us is largely international.

No Silver Bullets

but Room for Hope

Terrorism has had the unanticipated consequence of facilitating interdependence between nations.

— Irving Louis Horowitz [1]

WHEN RONALD REAGAN left office in January 1989 his eight-year record against terrorism looked dismal. Over 550 Americans had been killed in terrorist incidents; fifty-seven Americans had been held hostage in Beirut; six were still being held, one having been there almost fourteen hundred days; and the arms-for-hostages deals had abused our constitutional system of government and damaged America's international reputation. Yet largely because of his aggressiveness against Qaddafi in 1986, Reagan's reputation against terrorism was good.

The impression that Reagan's antiterrorism stand had been a success added credibility to those advocating the following pro-active responses to terrorism:

Assassination — repeal of the presidential prohibition against it.
Punitive military attacks — making terrorists pay for what they do.
Covert action — using dirty tricks to counter terrorists.
Rescue operations — moving in quickly with military force to extricate hostages.
Improved intelligence — penetrating terrorist organizations and taking the offensive against them.
Media restraint — curtailing reports that play into the hands of terrorists.

One indication of the growing support for pro-activism was the report of the President's Commission on Aviation Security and Terrorism, appointed by President George Bush in August 1989. The genesis of the commission was the last terrorist incident Ronald Reagan encountered. On December 21, 1988, just weeks before Reagan left office, Pan Am Flight 103 exploded over Lockerbie, Scotland, and all 259 people on board, plus eleven on the ground, died. Families of victims demanded that George Bush determine what had happened and how such incidents could be avoided in the future.

The commission recommended specific improvements for in-flight and airport security procedures, but, more to the point here, also recommended that we take the offensive against terrorists with "active measures"— pre-emptive or retaliatory, direct or covert, even urging that we not refrain from acting against terrorists just because we cannot meet the standards of proof required for law enforcement;[2] and improving "human intelligence-gathering on terrorism, in cooperation with other nations" because "the first line of defense [against terrorists] is the collection of accurate and timely intelligence."[3]

The fact that support for a pro-active strategy is a legacy of the Reagan administration's struggle with terrorism is ironic. While Ronald Reagan preached the strategy, he was able to get only one of the preceding six pro-active measures off the ground, the single punitive military attack against Libya. The rest of the time he employed actions from what I term a "pro-legal" strategy, that is, actions less likely to be illegal or at variance with our democratic values:

Economic and political pressures — applying economic sanctions, such as Reagan instituted against Libya and made more stringent against Iran; or issuing political condemnations, as Reagan frequently did with respect to Libya, Syria, and the terrorists in Lebanon.

Defensive security — implementing defensive procedures and constructing physical defenses at overseas government installations, as Reagan did, to the tune of hundreds of millions of dollars, in the wake of the three truck bombings in Beirut.

Deals — making deals with terrorists for hostages, as Reagan did a total of seven times in the TWA 847 and Beirut hostage situations.

Legal recourse — apprehending individual terrorists, as when Reagan made use of the Germans' capture of Mohammed Hamadei of TWA 847; or ostracizing states that sponsor terrorism, as Reagan attempted by encouraging our European allies to reduce the Libyan presence in their countries.

Jimmy Carter and Cy Vance preferred these pro-legal options, though Zbig Brzezinski was pushing Carter in the pro-active direction. Carter's four-year record against terrorism when he left office was good. Fewer than fifty Americans had been killed by terrorism, including the eight servicemen lost at Desert One in the hostage rescue attempt. And though fifty-two Americans had been held hostage for 444 days, none was still hostage when the President left office. Jimmy Carter's reputation against terrorism, though, was terrible as a result of the dismal failure at Desert One. It was when Carter abandoned his strong preference for a pro-legal strategy and adopted the pro-active rescue operation that he came a cropper. There is surely some correlation between the lateness of his attention to the rescue attempt and its failure. For instance, three weeks after the hostages were taken, Carter called a halt to rescue planning and then did not hear a full briefing on the plans for another two and a half months, when he declined to authorize the CIA's exploratory flight to Desert One. He made his decision on that probe so late that the military had only three weeks to reshape their plans. While the Joint Chiefs of Staff should not require motivating, they might have responded to a sense of presidential urgency by sending an aircraft carrier into the Persian Gulf to launch the helicopters on an unrefueled mission.* Perhaps, too, more enthusiasm would have been felt by the helicopter pilots, who manifestly lacked motivation.

Carter found it necessary to shift to a pro-active option because the pro-legal ones simply were not producing results; and he could not wait out Khomeini because the public, urged on by the drumbeat of the media, was impatient with what it perceived as our national impotence.

Interestingly, Ronald Reagan found himself in exactly the same kind of bind, though with the strategies reversed. Reagan shifted from attempting pro-active options to embracing the pro-legal one of making deals with terrorists. In that process he too came a cropper. Reagan not only lacked enthusiasm for shifting strategies, he railed against the very idea of dealing with terrorists. As a result, he and his advisers never sought to differentiate between acceptable and unacceptable deals, and ended up making bad ones. Reagan shifted strategies because pro-active moves were not solving his hostage problems and he was too

---

*The Joint Chiefs did send carriers into the Persian Gulf when we were at war with Iraq in 1991.

emotionally involved to wait it out. Also, his loose style of management permitted some of his subordinates to persist far too long in making deals.

There is a lesson here. Presidents and their advisers cannot afford to focus on only one strategy against terrorism. Because we are a democracy and the public voice counts, Presidents can be driven far from their preferred paths. Between them, the Presidents we have reviewed attempted all ten of the pro-legal and pro-active options. That means that they, and we the public, must understand the strengths and the pitfalls of each one. My views on these are:

1. Assassinations are neither an appropriate nor an effective counter-terrorist tactic.

The lure of assassination is that it seems surgical and final. It is neither. If we attempted to kill a foreign leader, we would logically turn to foreigners to do the deed or to help our people get away safely; thus, we would lose control, as we did in the Fadlallah affair.

There is seldom a guarantee that the assassinated leader's successor will be better than he was. Because an assassination would be a major foreign policy choice, it would require an order by the President, who would then be embarked on a game of dirty tricks in which our opponents are likely to be far more ruthless and persistent than we.

Even more germane is the record showing that during the twenty-nine years when assassination was not formally prohibited, the United States did not resort to it. The reasons are not likely to change. Assassination is morally repugnant to the majority of Americans. Judging from the report of the Church Committee, a leak that our government was planning or had conducted an assassination would arouse an adverse public reaction that would force an end to such practices anyway. It is always dangerous to counter terrorism with terrorism. We can lose what we are defending in the process of defending it.

Still, most administrations, when frustrated beyond measure by a Khomeini or a Qaddafi, will be tempted to consider assassination. I believe we need a law, not just the present presidential Executive Order, prohibiting assassination. The rationalization that the deliberate killing of an individual can be classed as "justifiable homicide," not assassination, would be more difficult to maintain against a law than against an Executive Order.[4] I believe, though, that such a law should be limited to peacetime. Targeting specific leaders in wartime, when the country has determined openly that widespread killing is justified, is quite different from a President's making a secret political decision to take someone's life.

2. Punitive military attacks are a remedy we should use, but sparingly.

It is futile, even irresponsible, to advocate consistent use of force against terrorists. The record shows our people will not accept it. For instance, Ronald Reagan unleashed only one attack, despite repeated provocations; Gerald Ford, one; Lyndon Johnson, Richard Nixon, and Jimmy Carter none.

A principal inhibition on Reagan was the reluctance to take human life outside the due process of law or war. Even the advocates of punitive force tacitly acknowledge concern about the killing of innocents when they talk of employing "surgical attacks." But surgical attacks can go astray. In Libya in 1986, though we employed F-111 aircraft because of their accurate laser bombing system, some bombs hit the French embassy.

Nonetheless, it would be equally irresponsible to rule out punitive responses. There are times when our society will condone some level of killing, even if it is to vent our accumulated frustrations with terrorists, as was the case with the Libyan bombing, which the public overwhelmingly supported.

Perhaps the best argument for exercising the punitive option is that doing so reinforces all other options. Allies, for instance, are more likely to be cooperative if they believe we really will turn to the use of force. Terrorists are more likely to come to terms for the same reason.

In short, between "never" and "always" there is some ground for the occasional use of punitive force.

3. Covert actions should be undertaken, but judiciously, because the probability of success is low.

There are a number of covert techniques that can be effective against terrorists, such as infiltrating an organization and making its plans go awry, feeding disinformation to groups to mislead them and perhaps cause them to terrorize one another, and toppling governments that sponsor or provide support to terrorists. Maneuvers like these present formidable challenges: Carter's efforts to change the complexion of the Khomeini government never made headway; Reagan's attempt to use arms to advance the position of moderates in that same government ended in a giant con game.

In assessing the potential benefit of covert activities, we must take into account that these actions come under even less scrutiny than other secret government operations. Who, for instance, will make the judgment that the people we support to overthrow a government will do so within our bounds? Who will determine the cost if our disinformation feeds back into our own media? We should not ignore covert actions just because there are such risks, but we must weigh the prospects for success against the threat to our values.

4. Rescue operations have a role but will continue to be highly risky for the United States.

Any government would like to maintain a capability for rescuing its citizens if they are taken hostage. And a rescue operation will be tempting because if it is successful, it will solve the problem instantly.

But rescue operations carry high risks. They endanger the lives of the hostages. Many former hostages say they were afraid of being killed during a rescue attempt, either deliberately by their captors or accidentally by the rescue forces.

Because such operations are complex and often demand feats approaching the heroic, they can fail through poor execution, as with the assault on Koh Tang Island and the staging operation at Desert One, or bad timing, as with TWA 847 and the *Achille Lauro*.

Maintaining competent rescue forces will always be difficult for the U.S. military, because it is expected to have such a wide range of capabilities. At one end it must deter thermonuclear war, and at the other outwit a handful of twenty-year-olds who have seized an airliner. Naturally, attention is concentrated on the greater threat, on the assumption that if our military is prepared to answer the most formidable challenge, it surely possesses the skills and equipment needed to subdue terrorists. Unfortunately, this has not been the case, and that leaves our military in a dilemma. Do the requirements for rescue operations demand a corps of specialists dedicated to that very task, or with extra training can regular forces do the job? Neither arrangement will work unless the Joint Chiefs of Staff and the theater commanders focus adequate attention on the lower level of warfare. After forty-five years of concentrating on major, sophisticated warfare, they will not make such a shift with ease. Presidents and Secretaries of Defense would do well to make periodic inquiries about the readiness of rescue forces and order unannounced tests of them, as a modest amount of such high-level attention to low-level operations will advance the day of readiness.

5. Improved intelligence, especially human, is always desirable but difficult to achieve.

Without good intelligence, rescue operations are impossible, as has been the case with the Beirut hostages since 1982. Good intelligence can enable us to take defensive steps against acts of terrorism, or, alternatively, to track down terrorists and arrest them, both desirable ways to handle terrorism. Penetrating terrorist organizations, though, is difficult, as evidenced by the failure of the Reagan-Casey efforts. Even more, American intelligence operatives also work under the handicap of being easily identified. Most are unwilling to accept the privations associated with living their cover — actually working at their cover job as well as their spying. And since the criticisms of the CIA in the 1970s, it is difficult for them to obtain the cooperation of other government agencies and private organizations in providing cover jobs.

There is a danger that overemphasis on improving human intelligence as an antidote to terrorism could lead to the neglect of technical intelligence systems. Satellite photos revealed who was probably behind the third terrorist bombing in Beirut. NSA electronic intercepts produced the clinching evidence about the terrorist bombing in Berlin that sent our bombers over Libya in 1986. When President Bush's Commission on Aviation Security and Terrorism recommended more attention to human intelligence, just what did it expect the President to do? He could have called in his DCI, Judge William H. Webster, and told him to put more agents into the field, but Webster was almost certainly doing all he could in that respect. And the commission's calling intelligence the "first line of defense" was misleading. The number of times our intelligence has given operationally useful warning of impending acts of international terrorism is so low that it can hardly be termed a line of defense. At most it is a soldier in the battle. That is not to say we should not sustain a major intelligence effort against terrorism, but if a President counts too heavily on it, he will be disappointed and may ignore important alternatives.

We must also be careful that our intelligence agencies, in their zeal to track down terrorists, do not intrude unlawfully on the privacy of Americans.

6. Restraint of the media could be helpful, but modest self-restraint is the most we can expect.

Publicity for their cause is usually one objective of terrorists. Consequently, there is no question that almost any media coverage plays into their hands.

There are also situations when our counterterrorist efforts are hurt by media reporting, as when the hijackers of TWA 847 were tipped off that Delta Force was on the way to the Mediterranean; or when too many details are printed about hostages. Brian Keenan, an Irishman held hostage in Beirut for four and a half years, made this point eloquently when he was released:

> To all members of the press and the media, I would ask you to use all your judgment and exercise restraint in your reports, remembering the lives and the physical and psychological well-being of those who remain in captivity. Some members of the American media issued reports after the release of [a hostage] which suggested the tapes their kidnapers had given them to bring out had been coded by the hostages. Such unfounded remarks came within a hair's breadth of having some of the remaining hostages executed.[5]

On the other hand, the First Amendment is integral to the character of our society, and while the media have come to interpret that amendment very broadly, erring on the side of the openness that keeps our government accountable is preferable to governmental control of our sources of information. In any event, as a practical matter, there is little prospect of our government's establishing controls over the media. This was evident in the poor response given Attorney General Meese's mild suggestion for voluntary restraint following the TWA 847 incident.

There is, though, occasional evidence of media self-restraint. In late 1979 and early 1980, when some Canadian and American media deduced that a few American diplomats were hiding in Tehran, they did not publish that conclusion. In exercising such self-restraint, the media face difficult decisions. Would publication of the information harm the national interest? Or is the administration attempting to bury a political embarrassment or to use secrecy to do something the public might reject? Administrations that appreciate the media's dilemma will think carefully before attempting to manipulate them in terrorist incidents. (It is not only terrorists who attempt manipulation of the media.) In building credibility and understanding about terrorism, administrations would do well to conduct simulations of terrorist incidents with media participation. Each side could learn to appreciate the other's considerations.

Over the long run, it is the public that exercises the most suitable outside control over our media. What the public demands of the media and what it tolerates are the major determinants of how the media will balance their obligations to the First Amendment and to the nation's security. For instance, in 1986 NBC News interviewed Abu Abbas, mastermind of the *Achille Lauro* hijacking, after agreeing not to disclose where the interview took place. Giving a platform to an outlaw who refuses to disclose his location was seen as a questionable act by many, including other media, which claimed they had declined the interview.[6] The best way to deter such acts is for the public to express its disapproval, as it did in this instance. The alternative is the one Mrs. Thatcher employed in 1988, when her government used its powers to forbid such interviews, with all the opportunity for abuse such action involves.

7. Economic sanctions should be used against state sponsors of terrorism, even if they take a long time to be effective.

Unilateral economic sanctions can have only limited effect. Jimmy Carter's freezing of Iranian assets in American banks was an exception because Iran had placed so much money in those banks. Someone else will usually fill whatever gap we create and take the business away from us besides. The Congress in 1985 strengthened the hand of Presidents by authorizing them to bar imports from or aid to countries that harbor or otherwise support international terrorism. Those are useful tools.

Presidents Jefferson, Johnson, Carter, and Reagan all found how difficult it is to obtain the international cooperation needed to impose multinational economic sanctions. Despite these hurdles, Presidents will regularly turn to economic sanctions when there are few other choices. Americans tend to believe there must be something we can do to solve any problem, and just forcing other nations to decide whether to honor or reject our requests for sanctions can help. These countries must evaluate what they believe to be their responsibilities; over time, their assessment can help make them more reliable.

8. Defensive security is unlikely to receive sufficient attention or money.

Our recent history in Beirut shows how difficult it is to persuade Americans to take security overseas seriously. Within seventeen months we were struck by three bombings, largely because of our lack of physical preparedness. Once the Congress and the administration became committed to the construction of better physical defenses in Beirut and elsewhere, they both lost interest. We refuse to barricade ourselves inside fortresses, chafing at both the inconvenience and the symbolism of fear and vulnerability. And too much security can make it impossible for an embassy, for instance, to do its job of dealing with a foreign public. The record also shows that Americans are lax in personal security procedures. Even a professional like CIA Chief of Station William Buckley in Beirut reportedly, and with tragic results, failed to vary his route and timing to and from his office.[7]

But there are new forms of physical defense that are easier to accommodate, and we should encourage their development to warn of impending attacks, improve perimeter defenses, and provide greater security against hijackers or bombs on commercial aircraft. In 1985, in the wake of TWA 847, Congress passed the Foreign Airport Security Act, directing the Secretary of Transportation to assess periodically the security of 247 foreign airports. President Bush's Commission on Aviation Security and Terrorism noted, though, that "severe FAA personnel shortages generally limit the depth of these assessments to interviews and observations . . . Inspectors do not substantively test the operational effectiveness of security procedures."[8] A modest increase in resources would allow for rigorous inspections and make useful a provision of the 1985 act that permits the suspension of air services to any airport where conditions threaten the security of aircraft, crews, or passengers.

9. Deals are an option we cannot rule out.

The platitude that we should never make deals with terrorists because doing so inevitably leads to more terrorism is factually incorrect. We have seen deals like Lyndon Johnson's and Jimmy Carter's, which did not lead to repetition. More important, the record shows it would be futile to attempt to follow a policy of no deals. Except for Gerald Ford, every President since Lyndon Johnson has been involved in at least one deal with terrorists. The odds are high that any President will seriously consider a deal when other possibilities have been exhausted and Americans are in trouble.

In the wake of the political explosion that followed the exposure of Reagan's arms-for-hostages deals with Iran, politicians have become leery of any talk of deals. However, since the reality is that we will make them, we had better learn to differentiate between a deal that is acceptable and one that is not. Since our political leaders find it difficult to address such a distinction publicly, we citizens must encourage thorough and forthright discussion rather than be silenced by the superficial argument that all deals are unacceptable. And Presidents would do well to mute their rhetoric about not making deals, lest they box themselves in. Instead of stating categorically that they will never cut a deal with terrorists, they should stimulate discussion of all possible alternatives. Then, if a deal provides clear advantages for the United States, they would be in a better position to accept it without appearing weak.

10. Legal recourse is the option most compatible with American values.

Legal recourse against terrorists falls into two categories: apprehending terrorists, and isolating states that support terrorism.

Apprehending the terrorists themselves serves as a warning to would-be terrorists that they are likely to be caught. Despite the examples of suicide-bomb truck drivers, most terrorists prefer not to be killed or jailed.

Isolating a nation by means of political condemnation can be telling over the long run, though it seldom has an immediate impact. For instance, in October 1980, when the Iranian Prime Minister visited the United Nations to seek that body's denunciation of Iraq's invasion of his country, he found a total lack of sympathy, because for eleven months we had been reminding the world that Iran was holding our diplomats hostage. That must have given impetus to the pragmatists in Iran who wanted to put the hostage issue behind them.

Legal means are by far the preferable way of dealing with terrorism. They do least violence to our basic values, even if some of our efforts to arrest suspected terrorists violate our legal principles. When we forced down the aircraft carrying away the hijackers of *Achille Lauro,* we broke international law. In my view that was reasonable, as the rights of the culprits would have been only slightly abused had they been innocent. But just a few months later, after conducting a similar act of piracy against people who turned out to be innocent, Israel cited our action as precedent. Then, in 1987 the FBI lured a suspected terrorist, Fawaz Younis, into international waters in the Mediterranean and arrested him under a 1984 law allowing U.S. courts to try foreign nationals who take Americans hostage anywhere in the world. I believe this effort was justifiable and imaginatively conceived, but it almost failed in court because Younis was manhandled badly and a confession was extracted from him under questionable circumstances.

As desirable as it would be to rely only on arresting terrorists or diplomatically isolating nations that support them, that is impractical.

Such means frequently take too long; they try our patience. It took a year and a half before Mohammed Hamadei was apprehended for the hijacking of TWA 847. And the legal process can be frustrating, as when a culprit goes free because of a legal technicality, as Younis almost did. It also took almost a year for the diplomatic pressures applied by Jimmy Carter to have their effect on the Iranian Prime Minister during his trip to the UN.

It is because we are a democracy that the public's impatience in situations like these can rule out our waiting for legal recourses to work. The secret of dealing with terrorism, then, lies in selecting the option or mixture of options, both pro-legal and pro-active, that will have the greatest impact on the terrorists while minimizing the intrusions into our values. My appraisal of the effectiveness and the risks associated with each of the ten options will certainly not be shared by everyone. No individual's judgment in these situations is necessarily right and another's wrong; it depends on one's view of the seriousness of the particular terrorist threat.

It is all too easy to be misled by an immediate threat. Jimmy Carter's fear for the American hostages in Tehran led to unwarranted optimism about the rescue mission. Ronald Reagan's concern over the American hostages in Beirut led to a flouting of the Constitution. In each instance, the responses of the President damaged our national interests. A former Pentagon official involved with terrorism, Noel Koch, stated, "Most of the damage to U.S. interests done by terrorism has been self-inflicted."[9]

But there may be times when we choose to pay a high price. We might do so in response to two forms of terrorism we have not had to face: widespread terrorism at home, as the West Germans and the Italians experienced with the 1970s and 1980s with the Baader Meinhof gang and the Red Brigades, and nuclear terrorism.

Fortunately, international terrorists have hardly come to our soil because of the excellence of the FBI and our law enforcement system, and because they find it easier to attack Americans abroad. Foreign terrorists may move to the United States out of desperation if we and our allies close in on them. We would then have to rely on more difficult measures. One would be stringent inspections at international airports and other points of entry, with all the inconvenience that involves for Americans who travel abroad. Another would be intrusion into our private lives by law enforcement officials ferreting out terrorists who had slipped by.

Much the same would be the case with nuclear terrorism. Thus far, terrorist groups have not shown great interest in acquiring nuclear weapons or materials. We must be concerned, though, with states that support terrorism, like Libya and Iraq, and also aspire to nuclear capabilities. Again, tightening entry inspections at airports, ports, and border crossings would be one recourse. Military defenses against delivery by aircraft or missiles would be another. Our major effort, though, should be directed toward preventing the acquisition of nuclear capabilities by such nations. This will require worldwide, highly intrusive controls and inspection procedures, something possible only with the wholehearted support of all responsible nations, large and small.

That brings us to the importance of our government's working for heightened international cooperation against all forms of terrorism. With more cooperation we would not have had to lure Fawaz Younis out to sea but could have relied on local police forces to apprehend and extradite him. But in the case of the *Achille Lauro*, the Italians and Yugoslavs refused to extradite Abu Abbas in the hope that they would save their own citizens from terrorism, and the Egyptians gave the hijackers safe passage so as not to upset the PLO. Of course, our own record on extradition is not good, as we have seen with respect to Yugoslavia and the Soviet Union, nor have we readily sent members of the IRA back to Ireland. Our courts have broadly interpreted the Political Offense Exception clause in our extradition treaties, providing that "extradition shall not be granted if the offense in respect of which it is requested is regarded by the Requested State as a political offense."[10] We have only recently begun to negotiate extradition treaties that narrow this exception by making it inapplicable to crimes of violence. Some object that this will stifle revolutionary activity against governments that suppress liberty and human rights (even though we have limited such treaty revisions to "democratic" countries like the United Kingdom and the Republic of Germany). Here, then, is the question of what price we are willing to pay in order to promote the cooperation we need to obtain the extradition of terrorists.

If we are willing to pay some high prices to win international cooperation, we have special reason to be hopeful. The tenor of debate on how to handle terrorism has changed since the bombing of Libya in the spring of 1986. Back in 1978 at the economic summit, President Carter found it necessary to argue for sanctions against countries that harbored hijackers. Although the agreement that emerged did not result in much action — not one other country placed the Beirut airport off limits during and after the TWA 847 incident — nations that make self-serving deals with terrorists today at least feel constrained to justify their actions. The British and French, for instance, in 1989 and 1990 obtained the release of nationals being held hostage in Beirut and Tehran, but felt obliged to offer detailed explanations of why these were not deals after all.

In addition, since the summit of 1978 there has been one major change on the world scene that makes international cooperation against terrorism more achievable — the end of the Cold War. In the fall of 1990 I had the opportunity to explore this in Moscow when I called on the Chairman of the KGB, Vladimir A. Kryuchkov.

I asked Chairman Kryuchkov whether there were any prospects for cooperation between the KGB and the CIA against terrorists. He responded that the Soviet Union was willing to go to great lengths to cooperate with the United States. He was interested not only in exchanging intelligence, but in undertaking joint operations against terrorism. While Chairman Kryuchkov made no acknowledgment of any Soviet involvement with terrorists, he was forthright in saying that the reason he wanted to work with us was that terrorism has become a serious problem inside the Soviet Union. He noted that today's terrorists are well organized, professional, and adept at new technologies. He was worried about the possibility of nuclear terrorism. I believe he was saying the Soviets realize that if they hope to control domestic terrorism, they cannot ignore terrorism abroad. For instance, in December 1988, Soviet terrorists, using thirty schoolchildren as hostages, commandeered an Aeroflot aircraft and had themselves flown to Israel. With the United States facilitating communications, the Israelis disarmed and arrested the hijackers when they arrived in Tel Aviv. The price for continued assistance of this sort will be reciprocity and cooperation.

Kryuchkov also suggested that our countries promote a consensus within the UN on standard punishments for terrorism. I pointed out that the UN had never been able to agree on a definition of terrorism, and suggested that perhaps at least the United States and Soviet Union could do that, now that we no longer were competing in the Third World. He agreed.

The breakup of communist Eastern Europe has meant the disintegration of many intelligence services that supported terrorism; states like Syria and Iraq, which previously felt protected by the Soviet Union, no longer can rely on that relationship. Perhaps as important is that the responsible nations of the world are increasingly aware that terrorism affects them all. Historically, each wave of terrorism has been met and suppressed by civilized peoples largely through the military or police forces of one nation. Today we face the prospect of being able to meet the threat by selecting options weighted more toward the nonmilitary side, but that means being dependent on cooperation among several countries. As an expert on terrorism has put it, "Terrorism has had the unanticipated consequence of facilitating interdependence between nations. We find they can set aside differences in political orientations in order to preserve and protect the world community of nations."[11]

We should set our sights high in the hope that the burden of terrorism we are presently carrying will be a blessing in disguise by helping usher in a new era of world cooperation that will reach well beyond the suppression of terrorism itself.

ACKNOWLEDGMENTS

ACRONYMS AND INITIALS

NOTES

INDEX

ACKNOWLEDGMENTS

BILL ADLER provided the initial inspiration for this book. Because I failed to meet his suggested deadline of early 1986, I have had the benefit of advice and counsel from a large number of people at many stages in the course of this work.

As with almost everything I have written over the past eighteen years, I am indebted to George Thibault, principally for his substantive suggestions but additionally for his many, many hours of editorial work.

A number of friends have been kind enough to read parts or all of the manuscript and provide invaluable comments on substance and accuracy: Ned Beach, Rod McDaniel, Ken Taylor, Jeanette Morrison, Robin Wright, Felix Moos, and Chuck Cogan. I have benefited greatly from the considerable time each one gave.

Brian Thompson, Elisabeth Skowronnek, Parker Brophy, Russ Howard, and Shayna Steinger all provided valuable research assistance during some period of the production of the book. Justin Castillo, after being subjected to a course on terrorism that I taught at Davenport College, Yale University, became a principal research assistant. Much more, he was an adviser on the shape and direction of the book itself.

I taught a similar class on terrorism at the United States Military Academy at West Point. My students at Yale and West Point offered important stimuli to the development of my thinking on the subject.

Sherman Teichman of Tufts University was an important and helpful collaborator in the early stages.

My daughter-in-law Sheri Gilbert, Murrow Morris, and Pat Moynihan all suffered through the typing and retyping as the book evolved, and were understanding, patient, and effective.

Tom Patterson was meticulous and imaginative in creating the maps.

Hal Miller, then chairman of Houghton Mifflin Company, was wonderfully supportive of this undertaking, as were Nan A. Talese, who was the original editor, and Joe Kanon, the final one. As with my previous book, Frances Apt did a splendid job of manuscript editing.

I was required to submit my manuscript to the CIA for security review. As contrasted with a painful and time-consuming struggle over my previous book, the process this time was cooperative and speedy.

I am particularly grateful to Carnegie Corporation of New York for a generous grant that helped substantially, though the book is entirely my product and does not reflect the views of the corporation.

Acronyms and Initials

A-7 — Corsair II, attack bomber
B-52 — Stratofortress, Air Force long-range strategic bomber
BIM — Blade inspection method
C-130 — Hercules, Air Force transport aircraft
CH-53 — Stallion, Navy and Air Force troop transport helicopter
CIA — Central Intelligence Agency
CincPac — Commander-in-Chief, Pacific
CNN — Cable News Network
DCI — Director of Central Intelligence
DIA — Defense Intelligence Agency
DOD — Department of Defense
El Al — Israeli national airline
EST — Emergency support team
ETA — Euzkadi ta Azkazatuna (Basque Fatherland and Liberty), Basque terrorist group
FAA — Federal Aviation Administration
FISA — Foreign Intelligence Surveillance Act of 1978
GIGN — Groupe d'Intervention de la Gendarmerie National, French antiterrorist unit
GSG-9 — Grenzschutzgruppe 9, West German antiterrorist unit
INS — Immigration and Naturalization Service
IRA — Irish Republican Army
JCS — Joint Chiefs of Staff
KGB — Komitet Gosudarvsvenoz Bezopasnosti, Soviet intelligence and internal security organization
MNF — Multinational military force employed in Lebanon, 1982–1984
NATO — North Atlantic Treaty Organization
NSC — National Security Council
NSDD — National Security Decision Directive
OSS — Office of Special Services, U.S. World War II intelligence and covert operations organization

PFLP — Popular Front for the Liberation of Palestine
PLF — Palestinian Liberation Front
PLO — Palestine Liberation Organization
RH-53 — Sea Stallion, Navy minesweeping helicopter
SALT II — Strategic Arms Limitation Talks II
SAS — Special Air Squadron, British antiterrorist unit
SAVAK — Iranian intelligence organization under the Shah
SCC — Special Coordinating Committee of the National Security Council

NOTES

CHAPTER 1: THE FATEFUL DECISION

1. Charles A. Beckwith and Donald Knox, *Delta Force* (New York: Harcourt Brace Jovanovich, 1983), p. 95.
2. Hamilton Jordan, *Crisis* (New York: G. P. Putnam's Sons, 1982), p. 257.
3. Beckwith and Knox, p. 277.

CHAPTER 2: THE HOSTAGE-TAKING HABIT

1. Report to the Congress by President George Washington, February 28, 1795. *A Compilation of the Messages and Papers of the Presidents,* Vol. 1 (New York: Bureau of National Literature, Inc., 1897), p. 169.
2. Ray W. Irwin, *The Diplomatic Relations of the United States with the Barbary Powers, 1776–1816* (Chapel Hill: University of North Carolina Press, 1931), p. 74. Only one ship was delivered.
3. K. Jack Baver, ed., *The New American State Papers, Naval Affairs,* Vol. 2, *Diplomatic Activities* (Wilmington, Del.: Scholarly Resources, 1981), pp. 304–305.
4. Telegram from American consulate general, Tangier, June 10, 1904, *Foreign Relations* (Washington, D.C.: Department of State, 1904), p. 499.
5. Statement by Representative Durwood G. Hall of Missouri, *Congressional Record,* 90th Congress, 2nd Session, Vol. 114, Part I, January 23, 1968, pp. 685–686. Senator Hugh Scott of Pennsylvania also employed the quotation "Perdicaris alive or Raisuli dead." See *Congressional Record,* 90th Congress, 2nd Session, Vol. 114, Part I, January 25, 1968, pp. 1001–1002.
6. Included in statement by Secretary of State Dean Rusk, December 22, 1968, quoted in *New York Times,* December 23, 1968.

7. "Airlines Ask Tough Hijacking Laws," *Washington Post,* September 8, 1970.

8. "Israel and Arabs Stiffen Positions on Hostage Deal," *New York Times,* September 16, 1970.

9. *Public Papers of the Presidents of the United States, Richard Nixon, 1973* (Washington, D.C.: U.S. Government Printing Office), p. 157.

10. Gerald Ford, *A Time to Heal* (New York: Harper & Row and Reader's Digest Association, 1979), p. 277.

11. Thomas P. Ronan, "Carter and Sanford Support President on Mayaguez Step," *New York Times,* May 18, 1975.

CHAPTER 3: WARNING UNHERALDED

1. Jimmy Carter, *Keeping Faith* (New York: Bantam Books, 1982), p. 456.

2. Ken Follett, *On Wings of Eagles* (New York: New American Library, 1983), p. 365.

CHAPTER 4: OUR EMBASSY IS TAKEN

1. Speech by Khomeini, leader of the Islamic Revolution in Iran, to a group of workers from Islamshahr,·formerly Shani, in Qum on October 24, 1979, read by an announcer. Tehran Domestic Service in Persian, October 25, 1979; Foreign Broadcast Information Service, Middle East and Africa, Vol. 5, No. 209, October 26, 1979.

2. Representative Samuel Durne (R.-Ohio), in *Newsweek,* November 19, 1979, p. 64.

3. "Problems of War Victims in Indochina: Part III, North Vietnam," *Congressional Record,* Wednesday, August 16, 1972, Library of Congress Microfilm Records, S521–565, p. 9.

CHAPTER 5: OUR MILITARY FOUND WANTING

1. George S. Patton, Jr., *War As I Knew It* (Boston: Houghton Mifflin Co., 1947), p. 354.

CHAPTER 6: SEARCH FOR A STRATEGY

1. In a discussion with the author in the Oval Office.
2. Bob Woodward, "Casey Found to Have 'Misrepresented' Facts to Win Aid for Contras," *Washington Post,* November 19, 1987.
3. *The Papers of Thomas Jefferson,* ed., Julian P. Boyd, Vol. 17 (Princeton, N.J.: Princeton University Press, 1965), p. 435.
4. Dean Rusk, *As I Saw It* (New York: W. W. Norton, 1990), p. 391.
5. "How Not to Free the Pueblo," *New York Times,* November 30, 1968.

CHAPTER 7: HOIST ON OUR OWN LEGAL PETARD

1. Amendment to Section 662 of the Foreign Assistance Act of 1961 (22 U.S.C. 2422, enacted December 30, 1974).
2. The Foreign Intelligence Surveillance Act of 1978, S. 1586, H. 7308, which amended Title 18 of the United States Code.
3. Under the War Powers Act he would have to inform Congress within forty-eight hours of sending forces into hostilities or situations of imminent hostility, or sending forces equipped for combat into foreign territory, air space, or waters.

CHAPTER 9: STRATEGY BY DEFAULT

1. Passed by the United Nations Security Council on December 31, 1979, by a vote of 11 to 0, with four abstentions. The Soviet Union was one of those abstaining.
2. "The Iran Hostage Crisis — A Chronology of Daily Developments," Report prepared for the Committee on Foreign Affairs, U.S. House of Representatives (Washington, D.C.: 1981), p. 64.
3. Ibid., p. 67.

CHAPTER 10: TAKING STOCK

1. Hamilton Jordan, *Crisis* (New York: G. P. Putnam's Sons, 1982), p. 54.
2. Lyndon B. Johnson, *The Vantage Point: Perspectives of the Presidency* (New York: Holt, Rinehart & Winston, 1971), p. 532.

3. Comment of Ronald L. Ziegler, reported by Chalmers M. Roberts, *Washington Post,* September 11, 1970.
4. James Reston, "A Second Rescue Mission," *New York Times,* April 27, 1980.
5. Kathy Sawyer, "Haig Castigates Administration on Iranian Crisis," *Washington Post,* November 22, 1979.
6. Lou Cannon, "Reagan Finding It Hard to Restrain Himself," *Washington Post,* December 1, 1979.

CHAPTER 11: ON TO THE NEGOTIATING TRACK

1. "The Iran Hostage Crisis — A Chronology of Daily Developments," Report prepared for the Committee on Foreign Affairs, U.S. House of Representatives (Washington, D.C.: U.S. Government Printing Office, 1981), p. 77.
2. Hamilton Jordan, *Crisis* (New York: G. P. Putnam's Sons, 1982), p. 131.

CHAPTER 12: THE CANADIAN SIX

1. Jimmy Carter, *Keeping Faith* (New York: Bantam Books, 1982), p. 4.

CHAPTER 13: A FLING WITH IRANIAN MODERATES

1. Hamilton Jordan, *Crisis* (New York: G. P. Putnam's Sons, 1982), p. 103.
2. Ibid., p. 158.
3. "The Iran Hostage Crisis — A Chronology of Daily Developments," Report prepared for the Committee on Foreign Affairs, U.S. House of Representatives (Washington, D.C.: U.S. Government Printing Office, 1981), p. 104.
4. Ibid., p. 109.
5. Jordan, p. 165.
6. Ibid., p. 167.
7. "The Iran Hostage Crisis," p. 111.
8. Jordan, p. 103.

CHAPTER 14: THE DIE IS CAST

1. Jimmy Carter, *Keeping Faith* (New York: Bantam Books, 1982), p. 507.

2. Hamilton Jordan, *Crisis* (New York: G. P. Putnam's Sons, 1982), p. 249.
3. Carter, p. 507.
4. Jordan, p. 254.
5. Ibid., p. 263.
6. Memo of April 17, 1980 from Frank Carlucci to me.
7. Jordan, p. 263.
8. Ibid.
9. Carlucci memo.

CHAPTER 15: FAILURE IN THE DESERT

1. Charles A. Beckwith and Donald Knox, *Delta Force* (New York: Harcourt Brace Jovanovich, 1983), p. 277.
2. David C. Martin and John Walcott, *Best Laid Plans* (New York: Harper & Row, 1988), p. 8.
3. Miles Copeland, "The Hostages Can Be Freed," *Washington Star,* April 20, 1980. Copeland had been part of the CIA covert operations that helped overthrow Prime Minister Mossadegh in Iran in 1953. Copeland's plan called for a rescue force composed of Iranians recruited from dissident tribes and three Americans with special skills. Some of these people were to mingle with the crowds outside the embassy until a diversionary explosion signaled the moment to storm the embassy. Another group, having infiltrated the embassy compound, would then release an anesthetizing agent that would make groggy both the guards for the hostages and the hostages. (Allegedly the CIA possessed such an agent, but if it did, I never heard of it.) Three helicopters were then to arrive from a staging area on the outskirts of Tehran and carry the Americans and their guards away, with the latter becoming our hostages. They all would go to a safe haven inside Iran and somehow make their way out of the country.
4. From author's personal files.

CHAPTER 16: WHAT HAPPENED IN THE DESERT

1. Rescue Mission Report, Special Operations Review Group, August 1980, p. v.
2. Charles A. Beckwith and Donald Knox, *Delta Force* (New York: Harcourt Brace Jovanovich, 1983), p. 265.

3. Jimmy Carter, *Keeping Faith* (New York: Bantam Books, 1982), p. 519.

1. Rescue Mission Report, Special Operations Review Group, August 1980, p. vi.
2. Jimmy Carter, *Keeping Faith* (New York: Bantam Books, 1982), p. 518.
3. The importance of military accountability hit home a few months later when I received the report of the Navy's investigation of the death of my former aide and friend Commander Williams, killed in an aviation accident at sea the previous December. There was no question that the cause of Butch Williams's death was a personnel error, yet the report did not even address the question of accountability of the individuals involved. I knew nothing could be done for Butch by punishing those responsible, but how could we ask other pilots to accept the same risks if they knew no one would be held to account for a negligent act that might kill them? Because no one in the Navy seemed to believe anything needed to be done, I personally filed court-martial charges against those involved in Butch's case. The Navy conducted a second investigation, which did address the issue of culpability, but unconscionably exonerated everyone, despite clear evidence warranting action. Over time, that kind of indifference is bound to undermine the willingness of military men and women to put their lives on the line.
4. About a month later the British SAS conducted a superb rescue operation in London, where terrorists had seized the Iranian embassy and twenty hostages, killing one of them. The SAS stormed the building and rescued all of the remaining hostages. We, of course, cheered this, but it made Desert One look even more inept in comparison, though the British operation on home territory was a much simpler affair.
5. The Special Operations Review Group comprised Admiral James L. Holloway III, U.S. Navy (ret.); Lieutenant General Samuel V. Wilson, U.S. Army (ret.); Lieutenant General Leroy J. Manor, U.S. Air Force (ret.); Major General James C. Smith, U.S. Army; Major General John L. Piotrowski, U.S. Air Force; and Major General Alfred M. Gray, Jr., U.S. Marine Corps.

6. Rescue Mission Report, p. 11.
7. "Turbulence Factor Cited in RH-53 Iran Mission," *Aviation Week and Space Technology,* May 12, 1980.
8. "Washington Roundup," *Aviation Week and Space Technology,* May 5, 1980; and "Copter Failure Tied to Plugged Vent," *New York Times,* May 3, 1980.
9. Rescue Mission Report, p. 30.
10. Ibid., p. 16.
11. Conversation between the author and Colonel Kyle, July 2, 1989.
12. Charles A. Beckwith and Donald Knox, *Delta Force* (New York: Harcourt Brace Jovanovich, 1983), p. 277.
13. Zbigniew Brzezinski, *Power and Principle* (New York: Farrar, Straus & Giroux, 1983), p. 498.
14. Rick Atkinson, *The Long Gray Line* (Boston: Houghton Mifflin Co., 1989), p. 163.
15. Rescue Mission Report, p. 16.
16. Ibid.
17. Interview with author, July 2, 1989.
18. Rescue Mission Report, p. 50.
19. Ibid., p. vi.
20. Ibid.
21. Ibid., pp. 38–40.
22. Lou Cannon, "Reagan: Action to Rescue Hostages 'Long Overdue'," *Washington Post,* May 1, 1980.

CHAPTER 18: CARTER'S DEAL — TOO LATE

1. Jimmy Carter, *Keeping Faith* (New York: Bantam Books, 1982), p. 566.
2. Ray W. Irwin, *The Diplomatic Relations of the United States with the Barbary Powers, 1776–1816* (Chapel Hill: University of North Carolina Press, 1931), p. 11.
3. "The Iran Hostage Crisis — A Chronology of Daily Developments," Report prepared for the Committee on Foreign Affairs, U.S. House of Representatives (Washington, D.C.: U.S. Government Printing Office, 1981), p. 292.
4. Ibid., pp. 367–368.
5. Ibid., p. 369.
6. Editorial, "Governor Reagan on the Hostages," *Washington Post,* September 15, 1980.

7. Lou Cannon, "Reagan's Team Perplexed by Uncontrollable Events," *Washington Post,* October 21, 1980.
8. Lou Cannon, "Reagan Raises Hostage Issue in Campaign," *Washington Post,* October 21, 1980.
9. Don Oberdorfer and George C. Wilson, "An Information Gap," *Washington Post,* October 21, 1980.
10. *Public Papers of the Presidents of the United States, Jimmy Carter, 1980* (Washington, D.C.: U.S. Government Printing Office), p. 2487.
11. "The Iran Hostage Crisis," p. 341.
12. "Endgame," *The New Republic,* November 15, 1980.
13. Steven R. Weisman, "Reagan Calls Iran's New Demands a 'Ransom' Sought by 'Barbarians'," *New York Times,* December 29, 1980.

CHAPTER 19: THE CHANGING OF THE GUARD

1. Transcript of Remarks by President Reagan and Bruce Laingen at White House, *New York Times,* January 28, 1981. (Italics added.)
2. Ibid. (Italics added.)
3. Don Oberdorfer, "Haig Calls Terrorism Top Priority," *Washington Post,* January 29, 1981.
4. Ibid.
5. Alexander M. Haig, Jr., *Caveat* (New York: Macmillan, 1984), pp. 77–79.
6. Bernard Gwertzman, "Administration Assails Making of Hostage Deal," *New York Times,* February 19, 1981.
7. Excerpts from Haig's Remarks at First News Conference, *New York Times,* January 29, 1981.
8. Lee Lacaze, "Reagan Denounces Soviets but Speaks Gently of Iran," *Washington Post,* January 30, 1981.
9. *New York Times,* the Associated Press, December 18, 1981.
10. David C. Martin and John Walcott, *Best Laid Plans* (New York: Harper & Row, 1988), p. 62.
11. "U.S. and Italy Agree on Red Brigades Policy," *New York Times,* December 30, 1981.

CHAPTER 20: RETRIBUTION — EASIER SAID THAN DONE

1. Robin Wright, *Sacred Rage* (New York: Simon & Schuster, 1985), p. 69.

2. Radio Address to the Nation, *Papers of the Presidents of the United States, Ronald Reagan, 1983–1986* (Washington, D.C.: U.S. Government Printing Office), pp. 576–577.
3. Ibid., p. 1097.
4. Ihsan A. Hijazi, "Disruption of Peace Parley Is Termed Terrorists' Goal," *New York Times,* October 24, 1983.
5. Interview with *Wall Street Journal* reporters as reported in *Wall Street Journal,* February 3, 1984.
6. David C. Martin and John Walcott, *Best Laid Plans* (New York, Harper & Row, 1988), p. 138.
7. Report of the DOD Commission on Beirut International Airport Terrorist Act, October 23, 1983, December 20, 1983, Foreword, Part IIA, Para 3.
8. Ibid., Conclusions and Recommendations, Part Three, Para. A(2)(a), p. 136.
9. Chapter 23, *Candide.*
10. Report of the DOD Commission, Conclusions and Recommendations, Part Nine, Para. D(1)(a), p. 141.
11. Remarks and a Question and Answer Session with Reporters on the Pentagon Report on the Security of United States Marines in Lebanon, December 27, 1983, *Papers of the Presidents of the United States, Ronald Reagan, 1983–1986,* p. 1748.
12. David Ignatius, "U.S. Readies Anti-Terrorism Policy," *Wall Street Journal,* March 12, 1984.
13. Bernard Gwertzman, "Redeployment Set," *New York Times,* February 8, 1984.

CHAPTER 21:
HOSTAGES AGAIN — INTELLIGENCE "FAILURE" AGAIN

1. David Hoffman, "Reagan Ties Beirut Attack to Curb on Intelligence," *Washington Post,* September 27, 1984.
2. "On Reagan's Last Day, He Thinks of Hostages," *San Francisco Chronicle,* Chronicle Wire Services, January 21, 1989: "President Reagan said yesterday that he was frustrated over his inability to free Americans held hostage in Lebanon and conceded, a day before leaving office, 'We don't know where they are.' "
3. David C. Martin and John Walcott, *Best Laid Plans* (New York: Harper & Row, 1988), p. 158.

4. Department of State Bulletin, July 1988, p. 8.
5. Hoffman, "Reagan Ties Beirut Attack . . ."
6. David Hoffman, "Reagan Telephones Carter on Beirut Remarks," *Washington Post,* September 29, 1984.

CHAPTER 22: STILL NO RETRIBUTION

1. Christopher Dawson, *The Judgment of Nations* (London: Sheed & Ward, 1943), p. 8.
2. Executive Session of Commission on Organization of Government for the Conduct of Foreign Policy (Murphy Commission), U.S. Capitol, 1975.
3. David C. Martin and John Walcott, *Best Laid Plans* (New York: Harper & Row, 1988), p. 159; and Bob Woodward and Charles R. Babcock, "Antiterrorist Plan Rescinded After Unauthorized Bombing," *Washington Post,* May 12, 1985.
4. Excerpts from Shultz's Address on International Terrorism, *New York Times,* December 2, 1984.
5. Terrence Smith, "When Terror Threatens What U.S. Has Learned," *New York Times,* December 2, 1984.
6. Bernard Gwertzman, "Tougher Policy Against Terror Is Seen Gaining," *New York Times,* October 28, 1984.
7. "Terrorism and the Modern World," Current Policy, No. 629, U.S. Department of State, Bureau of Public Affairs, Washington, D.C., October 25, 1984.
8. "Terrorism, the Challenge to the Democracies," Current Policy, No. 589, U.S. Department of State, Bureau of Public Affairs, Washington, D.C., June 24, 1984. (Italics added.)
9. For example, see Robert Bau, "Britain Moves Toward Release of 'Birmingham Six,' Bomb Suspects," *Washington Post,* February 26, 1991.
10. Abraham D. Sofaer, "Terrorism and the Law," *Foreign Affairs,* Vol. 64, No. 5, Summer 1986.
11. Robin Wright, *Sacred Rage* (New York: Simon & Schuster, 1985), pp. 95–96.
12. "Terrorism, the Challenge to the Democracies."
13. Definition developed in CIA, 1980.

CHAPTER 23: THE FADLALLAH FOLLY

1. Robert C. Toth, "CIA Denies Role in Beirut Blast, but Questions Remain," *Los Angeles Times,* May 26, 1985.

2. "Soviet Espionage: 'A Big Effort — And It Pays Off Big'," *U.S. News and World Report*, June 17, 1985.
3. Ibid.
4. U.S. House of Representatives, 99th Congress, 1st Session, Resolution of Inquiry Concerning Terrorist Bombings in Beirut, Lebanon, June 12, 1985. Referred to the House Calendar and ordered to be printed.
5. Bob Woodward, *Veil: The Secret Wars of the CIA* (New York: Simon & Schuster, 1987), p. 396.
6. David C. Martin and John Walcott, *Best Laid Plans* (New York: Harper & Row, 1988), p. 157.
7. "Soviet Espionage: 'A Big Effort — And It Pays Off Big'."
8. "U.S. Willingness to Use Force Against Terrorists," *Washington Post*, March 26, 1985.
9. For example, "Repeal Order 12333, Legalize 007," by David Newman and Bruce Bueno de Mesquita, *New York Times*, January 26, 1989.
10. Alleged Assassination Plots Involving Foreign Leaders — An Interim Report of the Select Committee to Study Governmental Operations with Respect to Intelligence Activities, United States Senate (Washington, D.C.: U.S. Government Printing Office, 1975).

CHAPTER 24: A MEDIA HIJACKING

1. In a speech in Chicago Heights, Illinois, on June 28, 1985, during the time the crew and passengers of hijacked airliner TWA 847 were being held captive in Beirut. *Public Papers of the Presidents of the United States, Ronald Reagan, 1985* (Washington, D.C.: U.S. Government Printing Office), p. 832.
2. John Dillin, "News Media Coverage of Hostage Story Raises Glaring Questions," *Christian Science Monitor*, July 2, 1985.
3. Bernard Gwertzman, "Futile Rage, Patient Effort Mark a Week of Terror," *New York Times*, June 23, 1985.
4. Ibid.
5. In an interview with the author on September 20, 1985, in San Francisco, California.
6. Transcript of *This Week with David Brinkley*, ABC, June 23, 1985, p. 1d.
7. News Conference of June 18, 1985, *Public Papers of the Presidents of the United States, Ronald Reagan, 1983–1986*, p. 784.

8. Ihsan A. Hijazi, "U.S. Raid Would Doom Hostages, T.W.A. Pilot Warns in Interview," *New York Times*, June 20, 1985.
9. "Hostages, at Beirut News Session, Beseech U.S. Not to Try a Rescue," *New York Times*, June 21, 1985.
10. Remarks delivered by Fred W. Friendly to the House Subcommittee on Europe and the Middle East of the Committee on Foreign Affairs, Washington, D.C., July 30, 1985, p. 2.
11. Karen DeYoung, "U.S. Considering Talks on Hijacking Coverage," *Washington Post*, July 18, 1985.
12. Remarks of the Reverend William Sloane Coffin, "The Iran Hostage Crisis — A Chronology of Daily Developments," Report prepared for the Committee on Foreign Affairs, U.S. House of Representatives (Washington, D.C.: U.S. Government Printing Office, 1981), p. 69.
13. DeYoung, "U.S. Considering Talks . . ."
14. Tyler Marshall, "Meese Suggests Media Code for Government News Coverage During Actions by Terrorists," *Los Angeles Times*, July 18, 1985.
15. "No Voice for Terrorists," *New York Times*, June 24, 1990.
16. Fred W. Friendly to the House Subcommittee on Europe and the Middle East.

CHAPTER 25: STILL NO RESCUES

1. R. W. Apple, Jr., "This Time Reagan Let Actions Do His Talking," *New York Times*, October 13, 1985.
2. Bernard Gwertzman, "State Department Angry at Speedy Accord with Gunmen," *New York Times*, October 10, 1985.
3. David C. Martin and John Walcott, *Best Laid Plans* (New York: Harper & Row, 1988), p. 238.

CHAPTER 26: WE WILL MAKE DEALS

1. In a speech to the American Bar Association as plans to have Israel sell arms to Iran and secure the return of hostages were being developed. "Excerpts from the President's Address Accusing Nations of 'Acts of War,' " *New York Times*, July 9, 1985.
2. Preliminary Inquiry into the Sale of Arms to Iran and Possible Diversion of Funds to the Nicaraguan Resistance, Report of the Select Committee on Intelligence, United States Senate, February

2, 1987 (Washington, D.C.: U.S. Government Printing Office, 1987), p. 3.

3. Report of the President's Special Review Board, February 26, 1987, New Executive Office Building, Room 5221, Washington, D.C., p. III–11.

4. Iran-Contra Affair, Report of the Congressional Committees Investigating the Iran-Contra Affair, S. Rept. No. 100–216 and H. Rept. No. 100–433, Washington, D.C., 1987, p. 229.

5. Ibid., p. 13.

6. "Secret Military Assistance to Iran and the Contras — A Chronology of Events and Individuals," National Security Archive, Washington, D.C., p. 314.

7. Haynes Johnson, "Future of Reagan Presidency in Doubt," *Washington Post*, March 1, 1987.

8. Barbara W. Tuchman, "Perdicaris Alive or Raisuli Dead," *American Heritage*, August 1959, pp. 98–100.

9. Bernard Weinraub, "Reagan's Struggle to Avoid Becoming a Hostage," *New York Times*, June 30, 1985.

10. This finding was published in open sources in the course of the Iran-Contra hearings. See "Secret Military Assistance to Iran and the Contras," exhibit following p. 381. (Italics added.)

11. Report of the President's Special Review Board, p. B-102.

12. "Public Report of the Vice President's Task Force on Combatting Terrorism," Superintendent of Documents (Washington, D.C.: U.S. Government Printing Office, 1986), p. 7.

CHAPTER 27: AN UNEXPECTED IMPACT OF
"SWIFT AND EFFECTIVE RETRIBUTION"

1. Don Oberdorfer, "The Three Scenarios of Confrontation," *Washington Post*, April 20, 1986.

2. Michael R. Beschloss, "The Man Who Kept the Secret," review of *Casey,* by Joseph E. Persico, *New York Times*, October 7, 1990.

3. Bernard Gwertzman, "U.S. Expels Libyans and Closes Mission, Charging Terrorism," *New York Times*, May 7, 1981.

4. Bernard Gwertzman, "U.S. Puts Pressure on Allies to Join Libyan Sanctions," *New York Times*, January 3, 1986.

5. Interview with European Journalists on Libya, January 10, 1986, *Papers of the Presidents of the United States, Ronald Reagan, 1983–1986*, p. 34.

6. David C. Martin and John Walcott, *Best Laid Plans* (New York: Harper & Row, 1988), pp. 277–284.
7. Ibid., p. 284.
8. Ibid., p. 301.
9. Barry Sussman, "76% of Americans Polled Back Bombing of Libya," *Washington Post,* April 30, 1986.
10. Transcript of Address by Reagan on Libya, *New York Times,* April 15, 1986.
11. Jack Anderson and Dale Van Atta, "Reagan Raid Failed Intended Aims," *Washington Post,* August 10, 1990.
12. Vaughn Davis Bornet, *The Presidency of Lyndon B. Johnson* (Lawrence: University of Kansas Press, 1983), pp. 211–212.
13. "There May Be Trouble Over Asia Next November," *New York Times,* February 11, 1968.
14. Loren Jenkins, "Europeans Criticize U.S. Stand on Terror," *Washington Post,* April 20, 1986.
15. Oberdorfer, "The Three Scenarios . . ."
16. Christoph Bertram, "We Europeans Better Get Our Act Together," *Washington Post,* April 26, 1986.

CHAPTER 28: NO SILVER BULLETS BUT ROOM FOR HOPE

1. Irving Louis Horowitz, "The Routinization of Terrorism and Its Unanticipated Consequences," *Terrorism, Legitimacy and Power* by Martha Crenshaw (Middletown, Conn.: Wesleyan University Press, 1983), p. 42.
2. Report of the President's Commission on Aviation Security and Terrorism, May 15, 1990, Washington, D.C., pp. 115 and 125.
3. Ibid., p. 69.
4. See, for example, Bruce Fein, "How Can We Win a War Against Terrorists?," *Washington Times,* May 16, 1989; Kenneth de-Graffenreid, "Our Policy Doesn't Deter Terrorists," *Washington Post,* August 6, 1989; Robert F. Turner, "Killing Saddam: Would It Be a Crime?," *Washington Post,* October 7, 1990; and Daniel Schorr, "Hypocrisy About Assassination," *Washington Post,* February 3, 1991.
5. Remarks of Brian Keenan on *The MacNeil/Lehrer NewsHour,* Thursday, August 30, 1990, transcript of Show #3849, p. 10.
6. Peter J. Boyer, "Arab's Interview Stirs News Debate," *New York Times,* May 7, 1986.

7. David C. Martin and John Walcott, *Best Laid Plans* (New York: Harper & Row, 1988), p. 206.

8. Report of the President's Commission on Aviation Security and Terrorism, pp. 28–29.

9. David C. Martin and John Walcott, "How to Survive the Coming Terrorism," *Washington Post,* June 16, 1988.

10. Article 4, 32 U.S.T. 1485, 1491, T.I.A.S., No. 9785.

11. Horowitz, "Routinization of Terror," p. 42.

INDEX